GRAND PRIX

RAINER W. SCHLEGELMILCH

GRAND PRIX

FASCINATION FORMULA 1

KÖNEMANN

© 1993 Könemann Verlagsgesellschaft mbH
    Bonner Straße 126 · D-50968 Köln

Photography & concept: Rainer W. Schlegelmilch
Text: Hartmut Lehbrink

Design: Detlev Schaper, Hannover · Rainer W. Schlegelmilch, Frankfurt
Cover design: Peter Feierabend, Berlin
(Colour separation: Repro Service Werner Pees, Essen)
Editing: Daniela Kumor, Köln
Translations: Hartmut Lehbrink, Schalkenbach (English) ·
Patricia Blotenberg (French) · Maria Ordoñez-Rey, Kiel (Spanish)

Typesetting: RZ-Werbeagentur, Hannover
Typeface: Futura light, light oblique, extra bold · Linotype-Hell AG, Eschborn
Colour separation: Columbia Offset, Singapore
Printing & binding: Neue Stalling, Oldenburg

Printed in Germany
ISBN 3 - 89508 - 006 - 3

ÜBER DIESES BUCH

Als mich Bernard Cahier 1966 in Zandvoort bat, nach dem Training ins Goodyear-Motorhome zu kommen, wußte ich nicht, daß ich Mitbegründer einer Vereinigung für Journalisten und Fotografen werden sollte, der International Racing Press Association, kurz IRPA genannt. Fortan galt über 20 Jahre deren rote Armbinde als Zeichen für Professionalität, für Kompetenz, und jeder trug sie voller Stolz am Arm oder am Gürtel.

Doch die Zeit blieb nicht stehen, und wie die Entwicklung in Design und Technik der Formel 1 gewaltige Schritte nach vorn tat, so mußte persönlichkeitsbezogenes Vereinsdenken dem modernen Konzept effizienter Medienpolitik weichen. Sendezeiten weltweit im Fernsehen, Auflagenhöhen der Fach- und der Tagespresse, Veröffentlichungen national wie international sind die Kriterien, die den Wert des heutigen Medienmenschen ausmachen. Kreativität und Kunst sind Fremdwörter geworden, der Augenblickswert eines Fotos ist heute wichtiger als seine Ästhetik, seine Stimulanz für die Fantasie des Betrachters. Doch manche Aufnahmen zeigen ihren Wert erst nach Jahren, wenn ihre inhaltliche und gestalterische Intention immer noch beeindruckt. Jeder engagierte Fotograf träumt daher von seinem eigenen Buch, und auch ich sehe die beste Möglichkeit darin, meine Motorsportfotografie über ein Vierteljahrhundert in einem Bildband zu präsentieren, konzipiert und gestaltet nach meinen eigenen Vorstellungen.

Gewiß hat der Historiker oft andere Maßstäbe für die Bewertung eines Fahrers, Wagens oder Teams als ich, der ich ganz bewußt subjektiv meine persönlichen Ansichten und Sympathien zum Ausdruck bringen möchte, und zwar ohne den Anspruch auf Vollständigkeit. Gleichwohl habe ich mich bemüht, eine wirklichkeitsnahe Dokumentation zu schaffen. Die Bilder dienen dabei nicht zur Ausschmückung des geschriebenen Worts, sondern sind Aussage an sich, während die einführenden Texte das bessere Verständnis der fotografischen Inhalte ermöglichen sollen. Mein Buch soll aber auch Zeugnis sein der Entwicklung und des heutigen Standes im technologisch höchstentwickelten Sport, der Formel 1. Zugleich stellt es eine Hommage dar an seine Fahrer und alle, die diesen Sport durch ihre persönliche Leistung oder aber durch ihre Begeisterung ermöglichen.

„Grand Prix – Faszination Formel 1" ist nicht zuletzt ein Beleg meiner fotografischen Arbeit, um die Unterstützung zu rechtfertigen, die mir Veranstalter, Organisatoren und Teams zuteil werden lassen.

Rainer W. Schlegelmilch

ABOUT THIS BOOK

In 1966 at Zandvoort, Bernard Cahier suggested I stop in at the Goodyear Motorhome after practice. I little guessed I was about to become the co-founder of an association of journalists and photographers: the International Racing Press Association (IRPA). For over 20 years, IRPA's red armband was the badge of professional expertise, and members wore it on their arms or belts with pride.

Time, of course, did not stand still. Formula One design and technology leapt ahead, and in turn the thinking that lies behind associations centred upon personalities was superseded by modern concepts of efficient media relations. TV air time worldwide, the circulation figures of the trade and daily press, and other national and international publications, are now the criteria that determine the value of media personalities. Creativity and art are not words in the active vocabulary. Nowadays, a photograph is taken for the passing moment, and its importance lies in that rather than in its aesthetic qualities or its effect on people's imaginations. Even so, there are shots whose value only becomes apparent years later, when the impact of the content and approach prove undiminished. Small wonder that every true professional dreams of his own book of photos – myself included. A book of photos, laid out in accordance with my own ideas, is the best way of showcasing 25 years of work in motorsport photography.

No doubt the historians will have criteria for assessing drivers, teams, and cars that differ from mine. I aim to express my personal views and preferences subjectively, and make no claim to be comprehensive. Nevertheless, I have tried to put together a documentary account of how things really were. The pictures are not only there to illustrate the text, but constitute statements in themselves, while the commentaries in turn make it easier to grasp what is going on in the photos. The book also records the evolution and current state of Formula One, technologically the most highly developed sport in the world. And it is a homage to the drivers, and all the people whose dedication and enthusiasm make motorsport possible.

"Grand Prix – Fascination Formula 1" is a record of photographic work made possible by the many organizers and teams who have supported me over the years. To all of them, my thanks.

Rainer W. Schlegelmilch

A PROPOS DE CE LIVRE

Le jour où Bernard Cahier m'a prié de monter dans le motorhome Goodyear après des essais à Zandvoort en 1966, j'ignorais que j'allais devenir co-fondateur d'une association pour journalistes et photographes, l'International Racing Press Association, abrégée en IRPA. Dès lors, son bracelet rouge fut un signe de professionnalisme et de compétence pendant plus de vingt ans: tout le monde le portait, tout fier, au bras ou à la ceinture.

Mais le temps ne s'est pas arrêté et de même que l'évolution du design et de la technique en Formule 1 a fait des pas de géant, la façon de penser de l'association fixée sur des personnes a dû céder la place au concept moderne d'efficacité dans la politique des médias. Les temps d'émission à la télévision, au niveau mondial, l'ampleur des tirages de la presse spécialisée et quotidienne, les publications nationales et internationales représentent les critères qui font la valeur de l'homme actuel des médias. La créativité et l'art sont devenus des mots étrangers, la valeur instantanée d'une photo est plus importante aujourd'hui que son esthétique, sa stimulation de l'imagination de celui qui la regarde. Seulement, certains clichés dévoilent leur valeur quelques années plus tard seulement, quand leur intention en matière de contenu et de forme impressionne toujours. Par conséquent, tout photographe engagé rêve de son propre livre et j'y vois, moi aussi, la meilleure possibilité de présenter ma photographie du sport automobile sur plus d'un quart de siècle en un volume conçu et arrangé d'après mes propres aspirations.

Certes, l'historien a une autre échelle des valeurs que moi en ce qui concerne un pilote, une voiture ou une équipe, moi qui, très consciemment, veux exprimer subjectivement mes sympathies et mes avis personnels, et ce, sans prétendre à l'exhaustivité. Néanmoins, je me suis efforcé de créer une documentation proche de la réalité. Les photos ne servent pas de décoration au mot écrit mais parlent d'elles-mêmes, tandis que les textes d'introduction sont là pour rendre possible une meilleure compréhension des contenus photographiques. Mais mon livre doit être aussi le témoignage de l'évolution et de l'état actuel du sport le plus hautement développé technologiquement, celui de la Formule 1. Et, en même temps, il représente un hommage à ses pilotes et à tous ceux qui rendent ce sport possible grâce à leur engagement personnel et leur enthousiasme.

«Grand Prix – Fascination Formule 1» est, il ne faut pas l'oublier, un document de mon travail photographique qui justifie le soutien que les organisateurs et les équipes m'ont apporté.

Rainer W. Schlegelmilch

SOBRE ESTE LIBRO

Cuando en 1966 Bernard Cahier me pidió en Zandvoort que fuera al Goodyear-Motorhome después del entrenamiento, ignoraba aún que yo fuera a convertirme en miembro fundador de una asociación de periodistas y fotógrafos, la International Racing Press Association (IRPA). Durante los veinte años siguientes la pulsera roja característica de la sociedad era un símbolo de profesionalismo, de competencia, y sus miembros la llevaban orgullosos en el brazo o en el cinturón.

Pero el tiempo siguió su curso y, del mismo modo que el diseño y la técnica de la Fórmula 1 avanzaba hacia el futuro a pasos gigantes, la ideología centrada en personalidades que practicaba la asociación tuvo que ceder el paso a la concepción moderna de una eficiente política de medios de comunicación. Tiempo de programación a nivel mundial en televisión, volumen de edición de la prensa diaria y especializada, publicaciones nacionales e internacionales, estos son los criterios que determinan el valor de un periodista de hoy. Creatividad y arte se han vuelto palabras ajenas, el valor instantáneo de una fotografía es hoy más importante que su estética, su estimulación en la fantasía del observador. Sin embargo hay fotos cuyo valor no se hace patente hasta pasados los años, cuando su intención estética y de contenido todavía impresiona. Por eso, todo fotógrafo comprometido sueña presentar mis fotografías del deporte del motor, que abarcan un cuarto de siglo, en un libro de fotografías concebido y diseñado según mi propio criterio.

No cabe duda que el historiador aplica una escala de valores diferente a la mía a la hora de tasar a un conductor, un coche o un equipo, pues yo procuro expresar mis puntos de vista y simpatías con subjetividad consciente, y ello sin pretender la perfección. Al mismo tiempo, siempre me he esforzado por lograr una documentaión cercana a la realidad. Las fotos no están al servicio del embellecimiento de la palabra escrita, sino que son mensajes por sí mismas, mientras que los textos introductorios tienen la función de facilitar la comprensión de los contenidos fotográficos. Pero mi libro ha de ser también testimonio de la evolución y del estado actual del deporte tecnológicamente más desarrollado, la Fórmula 1. Constituye igualmente un homenaje a sus corredores y a todos aquellos que mediante su aportación personal o su entusiasmo hacen posible este deporte.

No en vano «Grand Prix – Fascinación Fórmula 1» es un testimonio de mi trabajo fotográfico para justificar el apoyo que organizadores y equipos me prestan.

Rainer W. Schlegelmilch

DIE AUTOREN

Rainer W. Schlegelmilch sah sein erstes Rennen 1962, als er bei den 1000 Kilometern auf dem Nürburgring eine Serie von Porträts für sein Abschlußexamen an der Bayerischen Staatslehranstalt für Photographie in München machte. Achtzehn Monate später eröffnete er sein Studio für Fotodesign in Frankfurt, aber der Rennsport blieb stets ein bedeutsamer Teilbereich seines Schaffens.

Von Anfang an fotografierte Schlegelmilch für renommierte Publikationen wie *auto motor und sport, Powerslide, ADAC Motorwelt, Sports Car Graphic, Car & Driver* sowie *Road & Track*, zunächst ausschließlich in Schwarzweiß.

Ab 1969 widmete er sich der Farbfotografie, und seine Bilder erschienen auch in Kalendern und Büchern und auf Postern. Große Firmen wie *Philip Morris, Mobil, Shell, Champion* und viele andere verwenden seine typischen Zoom Shots als visuelle Kaufanreize für ihre Produkte.

Schlegelmilch ist einer der Gründer der International Racing Press Association sowie Mitglied der Guild of Motoring Writers und des Sportpresseclubs Wiesbaden. Seit 1974 konzentriert er sich auf die Weltmeisterschaftsläufe der Formel 1 und besitzt mit rund 150.000 Diapositiven und 15.000 Schwarzweißbildern eines der größten Archive in der Grand Prix-Szene. Das vorliegende Buch stellt die Erfüllung einer langgehegten Ambition dar, an der Schlegelmilch, abgesehen von Unterbrechungen, acht Jahre lang gearbeitet hat.

Hartmut Lehbrink infizierte sich schon früh mit dem Motorsport-Virus. Das war 1950, und das Rennen hieß *Rund um den Kellersee* in seiner schleswig-holsteinischen Heimat Malente.

In den fünfziger Jahren suchte er die Nähe seiner Idole Dr. Farina, Ascari, Castellotti und Fangio in Spa und am Nürburgring und schreckte dabei auch vor Anreisen mit dem Fahrrad über 200 Kilometer und den Übernachtungen in kalten Scheunen und Dachzimmern nicht zurück.

Ein emotionaler Einschnitt war für ihn der Tod seines Freundes Paul Hawkins am Pfingstmontag 1969 bei einem Sportwagenrennen in Oulton Park, ohne ihn indessen in Zukunft von den Rennstrecken fernhalten zu können.

Lehbrink studierte englische und deutsche Philologie in Genf, Münster und Bonn und schreibt seit 1970 für die Publikationen *auto motor und sport, ADAC Motorwelt* und *Welt am Sonntag*. Er ist darüber hinaus Verfasser zweier Bücher, *Seriensportwagen von 1945 bis 1980* und *Chronologie des Automobils bis 1970*.

Aus 20 Jahren Zusammenarbeit mit Rainer Schlegelmilch gingen eine große Zahl von Zeitschriftenartikeln sowie eine Reihe von Formel 1-Bildbänden hervor.

THE AUTHORS

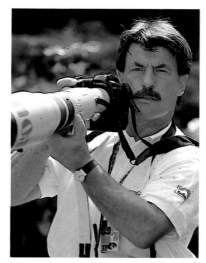

Rainer W. Schlegelmilch saw his first motor race in 1962 at the Nürburgring when he shot a series of portraits during the 1,000 Kilometre Race for his final examination at the School of Photography in Munich. Eighteen months later he started his own studio of photo design at Frankfurt, Germany, motor racing photography remaining a very important part of his activities.

As a freelancer he worked for renowned magazines such as *auto motor und sport, Powerslide, ADAC Motorwelt, Sports Car Graphic, Car & Driver* and *Road & Track*, first in black and white only.

From 1969 on Schlegelmilch has concentrated on colour photography, his pictures of the motor racing scene appearing in calendars and books, and on posters. Big companies like *Philip Morris, Mobil, Shell,* and *Champion* have used his typical zoom shots as visual eye catchers for their products.

He was one of the founding members of the International Racing Press Association, also being a member of the Guild of Motoring Writers and the Sportpresseclub Wiesbaden. Since 1974 he has focused his work on Formula One world championship events gathering one of the largest archives in Grand Prix photography with about 150,000 colour slides as well as 15,000 black and white photos. This book is the realisation of a long-cherished ambition, on which Schlegelmilch has worked on and off for the past eight years.

Hartmut Lehbrink fell a prey to the motor racing bug as early as 1950. The race at his native Malente in Schleswig-Holstein was called *Rund um den Kellersee*.

Throughout the fifties he did not mind 140-mile trips by bike and chilly nights in barns and attics to see his idols Dr. Farina, Ascari, Castellotti, and Fangio in action at Nürburgring and Spa.

Lehbrink was thoroughly shaken by the death of his friend Paul Hawkins in a sports car race at Oulton Park on Whit Monday 1969 although it did not affect his love of the sport.

He studied German and English philology at Geneva, Münster, and Bonn and has worked for the German publications *auto motor und sport, ADAC Motorwelt,* and *Welt am Sonntag* since 1970, also writing two books, *World Sports Cars* and *Chronology of the Motor Car until 1970*.

From a twenty-year cooperation with Rainer Schlegelmilch emerged a great many magazine articles as well as a couple of Formula One books of pictures.

LES AUTEURS

Rainer W. Schlegelmilch a vu sa première course automobile en 1962 aux 1000 kilomètres du Nürburgring quand il a fait une série de portra its pour son examen final à l'école de photographie bavaroise de Munich. Dix-huit mois plus tard, il ouvre son propre studio de design photo à Francfort, mais les photos de course automobile représentent toujours une partie très importante de ses activités.

Depuis le début, il a travaillé comme photographe indépendant pour des magazines renommés comme *auto motor und sport*, *Powerslide*, *ADAC Motorwelt*, *Sports Car Graphic*, *Car & Driver* et *Road and Track*, au début en noir et blanc seulement.

A Partir de 1969, Schlegelmilch se consacre à la photo couleur et ses photos de courses automobiles apparaissent aussi dans des calendriers et des livres ainsi que sur des posters. De grandes compagnies, telles *Philip Morris*, *Mobil*, *Shell* et *Champion* et bien d'autres, utilisent ses clichés au zoom typique comme accrocheur visuel pour leurs produits.

Il est l'un des membres fondateurs de l'association de presse de course internationale (International Racing Press Association) ainsi que membre du Guild of Motoring Writers et du Sportpresseclub de Wiesbaden. Depuis 1974, il concentre son travail sur le championnat international de Formule I, recueillant ainsi l'une des plus grandes archives de photos de Grand Prix avec environ 150.000 diapositives ainsi que 15.000 photos en noir et blanc. Ce livre est la réalisation d'une ambition longuement nourrie à laquelle Schlegelmilch a travaillé occasionnellement tout au long des huit dernières années.

Hartmut Lehbrink a été très tôt contaminé par le virus du sport automobile. C'était en 1950 et la course s'appelait *Rund um den Kellersee* dans sa ville natale du Schleswig-Holstein, Malente.

Dans les années 50, il chercha à s'approcher de ses idoles Dr. Farina, Ascari, Castellotti et Fangio à Spa et sur le Nürburgring et, pour ce faire, il n'avait pas peur de faire plus de 200 kilomètres à bicyclette et de passer la nuit dans des granges froides ou dans des mansardes.

Pour lui, la mort de son ami Paul Hawkins le lundi de la Pentecôte 1969, dans une course automobile à Oulton Park, a été un tournant émotionnel qui n'a pourtant pas pu l'éloigner par la suite des circuits.

Lehbrink a étudié la philologie anglaise et allemande à Genève, Münster et Bonn et il écrit depuis 1970 pour les revues *auto motor und sport*, *ADAC Motorwelt* et *Welt am Sonntag*. En plus, il est l'auteur de deux livres *Voitures de sport. Séries construites entre 1945 et 1980* et *Chronologie de l'automobile jusqu'en 1970*.

20 ans de travail avec Rainer Schlegelmilch se sont concrétisés dans un grand nombre d'articles ainsi qu'une série de volumes de photos sur la Formule I.

LOS AUTORES

Rainer W. Schlegelmilch asistió a su primera carrera automovilística en 1962 en el Nürburgring, donde sacó una serie de retratos mientras se corrían los 1000 kilómetros para su examen final en la Escuela de fotografía de Munich. Dieciocho meses más tarde abrió su propio estudio fotográfico en Francfort, Alemania, siendo la fotografía de carreras automovilísticas una importante parte de su actividad.

Trabajó como independiente para revistas de renombre como *auto motor und sport*, *Powerslide*, *ADAC Motorwelt*, *Sports Car Graphic*, *Car and Driver* y *Road & Track*. Al principio fotografiaba exclusivamente en blanco y negro, pero a partir de 1969 comienza a concentrarse en la fotografía a color, publicando sus fotos de la escena automovilística en calendarios, libros y posters. Grandes compañías como *Philip Morris*, *Mobil*, *Shell* y *Champion* han utilizado sus típicas fotos con zoom como cebo visual de sus productos.

Fue uno de los miembros fundadores de la International Racing Press Association, siendo también miembro del Guild of Motoring Writers y del Sportpresseclub Wiesbaden. Desde 1974 viene enfocando su trabajo en los Campeonatos Mundiales de Fórmula 1 y está en poder de uno de los más grandes archivos de fotografías de Grand Prix —unas 150000 diapositivas en color y 15000 fotos en blanco y negro—. Este libro, en el que Schlegelmilch ha estado trabajando durante ocho años, constituye para él la realización de una ambición largamente abrigada.

Hartmut Lehbrink se contagió ya muy temprano con el virus del deporte del motor. Sucedió en 1950, durante la carrera llamada *Rund um den Kellersee* que se realizaba en su nativa Malente (en Schleswig-Holstein). En los años cincuenta se acercó a sus ídolos Dr. Farina, Ascari, Castellotti y Fangio en Spa y en el Nürburgring, recorriendo más de 200 kilómetros en bicicleta y pasando las noches en fríos cobertizos o buhardillas.

La muerte de su amigo Paul Hawkins el domingo de Pentecostés de 1969 en una carrera automovilística en Oulton Park le causó un profundo trauma, aunque por esto no se alejó de las pistas de carreras. Lehbrink estudió Filología inglesa y alemana en Ginebra, Münster y Bonn, y desde 1970 escribe para las publicaciones alemanas *auto motor und sport*, *ADAC Motorwelt* y *Welt am Sonntag*. Es además autor de dos libros: *Coches deportivos. Series años 1945-1980* y *Cronología del automóvil hasta 1970*.

Los veinte años de colaboración con Rainer Schlegelmilch han dado por fruto un gran número de artículos de revistas, así como una serie de libros de fotografías de Fórmula 1

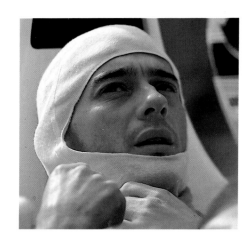

An der Schwelle zum 21. Jahrhundert sieht sich die Formel 1 Bedrohungen von vielen Seiten ausgesetzt und ist gezwungen, sich schneller als je zuvor zu wandeln. Der Streit zwischen der FISA und einigen Top Teams über das Verbot elektronischer Hilfen für den Piloten ist nur ein Aspekt der endlosen Jagd nach höheren Zuschauerzahlen und Einschaltquoten und damit letztlich nach mehr Geld.

Auch die allgemeine Rezession hat ihre Auswirkungen auf die Formel 1. Weiterhin besteht die Notwendigkeit, bestimmte Dinge zu ändern, damit Millionen von Fans überall in der Welt eine bessere Show geboten wird. So erleben wir eine Zeit des Übergangs in unserem Sport. Aber die Zeichen stehen keineswegs nur ungünstig. Immer schon war die Formel 1 Veränderungen unterworfen, und stets gelang es ihr, ihren Platz an der Spitze des Motorsports zu halten. Ich bezweifle nicht, daß es so bleiben wird.

Der deutsche Fotograf Rainer Schlegelmilch folgt dem Formel 1-Zirkus seit über 25 Jahren und kann das bezeugen. Wenn der Leser – oder besser gesagt, der Betrachter – sich den vorliegenden sorgsam zusammengestellten Auszug aus seiner Arbeit anschaut, wird er etwas von der erregenden Kraft und Aggression eines Formel 1-Rennwagens spüren.

Ich hoffe aufrichtig, daß Rainers Engagement, das in seiner Liebe zum Rennsport wurzelt, mehr ist als nur ein Tribut an die Sache, die einen erheblichen Teil meines Lebens ausgefüllt hat, bezeugt es doch auch eindringlich die unerschöpfliche Fähigkeit der Formel 1, sich selbst zu erneuern.

Ayrton Senna

As Formula One approaches the 21st century, the sport is threatened from many sides and is being forced to change more rapidly than at any other time before. The dispute between FISA and some of the top teams over the banning or not of electronic driver aid systems is the result of a never-ending quest for attendances, television viewing figures, and, by extension, finances.

The world recession has had its effects on the matter, too. Undoubtedly there is a need to modify things in order to provide a better show for the millions of Formula One supporters all over the world. It is a changing time for Formula One. But it is not, by any means, all gloom. There have always been a lot of changes in the sport but it has invariably managed to be the pinnacle of motor racing. I have no doubt that it will continue that way.

The German photographer, Rainer Schlegelmilch, has been following the Formula One circus for over 25 years and he is a witness to that. In this carefully gathered compilation of his work through that period, the reader – or should I say viewer? – will be able to feel for themselves some of the thrilling power and aggression of the Formula One car.

I sincerely hope that Rainer's dedication, due to his love of motor racing, will not only be a tribute to the sport I have dedicated most of my life to, but also be a definite proof of the endless capacity of Formula One to renew itself.

Ayrton Senna

Au seuil du XXIe siècle, la Formule I se trouve exposée à des menaces venant de toutes parts et est forcée de changer plus rapidement que jamais. La dispute entre la FISA et quelques équipes supérieures à propos de l'interdiction d'auxiliaires électroniques pour les pilotes n'est qu'un aspect de la chasse sans fin aux spectateurs aux résultats de l'audimat et donc, à davantage d'argent.

De plus, la récession générale a des effets sur la Formule I et il est nécessaire de changer des choses bien précises afin de montrer à des millions de fans partout dans le monde un meilleur spectacle. C'est ainsi que l'on vit un temps de transition dans notre sport. Mais les signes ne sont pas seulement défavorables. De tous temps, la Formule 1 a été soumise à des changements et elle a toujours réussi à tenir sa place à la pointe du sport automobile. Je ne doute pas que cela reste ainsi.

Le photographe allemand Rainer Schlegelmilch suit le cirque de la formule I depuis plus de 25 ans et peut en témoigner. Si le lecteur ou plutôt l'observateur regarde l'extrait de son travail présent, agencé avec soin, il ressentira l'agressivité et la force excitante d'une voiture de course de Formule I.

J'espère sincèrement que l'engagement de Rainer qui est enraciné dans son amour pour le sport automobile est plus qu'un tribut à ce qui a rempli une partie importante de ma vie et que cela témoigne bien aussi profondément de la capacité infatigable de la Formule I à se renouveler d'elle-même.

Ayrton Senna

En el umbral del siglo XXI la Fórmula 1 se encuentra expuesta a múltiples peligros y se ve obligada a transformarse con más rapidez que nunca. La controversia entre la FISA y algunos de los *top teams* sobre la prohibición de ayudas electrónicas para los pilotos es sólo un aspecto de la interminable persecución buscando un aumento del número de espectadores y del índice de audiencia y, en último término, de más dinero.

La recesión general también ha hecho sentir sus efectos sobre la Fórmula 1. Además, es imprescindible determinados cambios para poder ofrecer un mejor *show* a los millones de aficionados de todo el mundo. Vivimos pues una época de transición en nuestro deporte. Pero sería injusto afirmar que todo es negativo. La Fórmula 1 siempre ha estado sujeta a cambios y siempre ha logrado conservar su puesto a la cabecera del deporte del motor y no me cabe duda que seguirá siendo así.

Más de 25 años lleva ya el fotógrafo alemán Rainer Schlegelmilch siguiendo de cerca el circo de la Fórmula 1 y lo puede atestiguar. Cuando el lector o, —mejor dicho, el espectador— observe la presente selección de su trabajo reunida cuidadosamente, experimentará la excitante energía y la agresión de un coche de carreras Fórmula 1.

Espero sinceramente que el compromiso de Rainer, arraigado en el amor a las carreras de automóviles, sea algo más que un tributo al deporte que ha llenado una importante parte de mi vida, pues su trabajo documenta enfáticamente la inagotable capacidad de la Fórmula 1 de renovarse a sí misma.

Ayrton Senna

VORWORT

25 Jahre im Gefolge der Grand Prix – wird da nicht das Abenteuer, alljährlich penibel vorbereitet und in 16 Erlebnisraten aufgefächert, zum Trott, an dem sich jede noch so heillos scheinende Begeisterung abnutzt? Ist es gar an der Zeit, Schluß zu machen und sich neu zu orientieren im Leben? Man wird ja wohl noch fragen dürfen, sogar sich selbst… Aber dann steigt aus den tieferen Schichten des Unterbewußtseins dieses „Nein!" bei jedem, den die Sucht des Nüchternen nach der Droge Rennsport gepackt hat. Und „Undenkbar!" kommt es aus derselben Quelle, wenn die Frage in gewissen Augenblicken gestellt wird. Am Vorplatz des Casinos von Monte Carlo zum Beispiel, wenn Alain Prost zur Pole Position unterwegs ist. Oder an der unheimlichen Links-Rechts-Links-Kombination Eau Rouge in Spa, wenn Michael Schumacher bei Regen ganz offensichtlich die Gesetze der Physik und auch der Psychologie außer Kraft setzt. Früher ließ man sie gar nicht erst aufkommen, 1980 etwa am Österreichring, wenn Jean-Pierre Jabouille im Renault Turbo die gigantische Haarnadel mit dem unverfänglichen Namen Boschkurve durchpfeilte. Oder 1976 in Zandvoort an der Tarzankurve, vielleicht der aufregendsten von allen. Dort – so steht es in den ungeschriebenen Gesetzen der Formel 1 – fährt man nicht nebeneinander. Aber James Hunt, McLaren und John Watson, Penske, taten just dies Runde für Runde. Oder 1970 an der alten Rennstrecke von Spa, als Pedro Rodriguez mit seinem BRM in dem ewigen Rechtsbogen Burnenville den menschlichen Selbsterhaltungstrieb verhöhnte.

Man schimpft und mokiert sich, gewiß: über den aufgeblähten Kommerz und den Basar der Egos in Monaco, über den Morgentau zwischen Buckingham und dem Haupteingang zum britischen Nationalheiligtum Silverstone, über die üble Laune des Superstars und die allgemeine Abkühlung des Betriebsklimas in der Formel 1. Aber dann schaut man in das Gesicht eines Gilles Villeneuve, in dem sich Wille und Sensibilität zusammenfinden. Oder ein Mechaniker läßt in der Box eine Ferrari-Maschine warmlaufen, die böse klingt und aggressiv und einfach schön – das absolute Geräusch. Oder die Spannung baut sich auf in der Stunde vor dem Start, die immer gleiche Choreographie der tausend Handgriffe und dennoch immer neu und immer erregend. Oder Jean Alesi kämpft mit seinem Ferrari in dem S hinter der Zielgeraden von Magny-Cours um Grenzwerte jenseits von schnell. Dann weiß man, daß man von der Sache nicht loskommt, daß das Phänomen Grand Prix zum Grundnahrungsmittel für die Seele geworden ist, unentbehrlich wie Wasser und Brot.

Zugegeben: Alle diese Impressionen sind subjektiv wie das ganze Buch, das vor Ihnen liegt und trotz der Fülle seiner Bilder keinen Anspruch auf enzyklopädische Vollständigkeit erhebt. Anders als ein Nachschlagewerk, für das die Dinge erst einmal statistisch zur Ader gelassen werden müssen, soll es Blickwinkel und Eindrücke vermitteln von diesem Sport, der einen entweder entschieden abstößt oder magisch anrührt, immer aber herausfordert.

PREFACE

25 years in the wake of the Grand Prix circus – does that not mellow the most effusive enthusiasm, time even to call it quits and do something reasonable after all? But then rises that peremptory "no" from the deeper layers of your subconscious. And "unthinkable" is the message from the same source if somebody asks you that question in certain moments. Witnessing Alain Prost's pole lap at Casino Square in Monaco for instance. Or watching Michael Schumacher in the rain tampering with the laws of physics as well as psychology in the daunting S ominously called Eau Rouge at Spa. After 25 years your memory abounds with such instants of intense thrill: seeing Jean-Pierre Jabouille negotiating that enormous Zeltweg hairpin harmlessly named Boschkurve with his Renault Turbo in 1980. Or viewing the late James Hunt, McLaren, and John Watson, Penske, going side by side through the notorious Zandvoort Tarzan Corner in 1976, although an unwritten motor racing law says you must never do that there, with countless bent cars and egos bearing witness to it. Or at the majestic old Spa circuit, observing Pedro Rodriguez poking fun at his instinct of self-preservation all through the seemingly endless downhill righthander of Burnenville only to furiously slam on the brakes of his BRM for the Malmedy chicane installed in 1970 to slow down the cars .

Of course you grumble and sneer at the vanity fair of Monaco, the inevitable traffic jam between Buckingham and the main entrance to the Silverstone circuit, the superstar's ill humour and the ever worsening climate that has been haunting Formula One in recent years. But then you look in the face of Gilles Villeneuve with its moving mixture of will and sensitiveness. Or a lonesome Ferrari twelve cylinder is being warmed up in one of the pits producing the ultimate sound a racing engine can produce. Or tension is building up during the last hour before the start, always complying with the same choreography and always exciting, though. Or Jean Alesi is fighting with his Ferrari in his quest for the last hundredth of a second through Parabolica at Monza, accompanied by the noisy acclamations of the tifosi. Then you realize you have become a hopeless addict and cannot do without racing, that it has become a must like any basic food.

Of course all these impressions are subjective like the whole book lying in front of you, which, for all the lavish multitude of its pictures, does not claim to be a comprehensive encyclopedia. It is meant to convey to its readers the authors' angle and attitude towards a sport that either provokes or fascinates you but is always a challenge.

PREFACE

25 ans de Grand Prix. Est-ce que l'aventure, préparée dans les moindres détails tous les ans, et répartie en 16 épisodes, ne devient pas un train-train dans lequel s'émousse tout enthousiame aussi fervent qu'il soit? N'est-ce pas le moment d'en finir et de donner une nouvelle orientation à la vie? On a quand même bien encore le droit de le demander et même de se le demander… Mais, il y a alors ce «Non» qui remonte du fin fond du subconscient chez tous ceux que saisit cette passion de la drogue «course automobile»! Et il y a cet «inconcevable» qui surgit de la même source quand la question est posée à certains moments: devant le casino de Monte Carlo, par exemple, quand Alain Prost est en train de se mettre en Pole Position. Ou dans l'inquiétante combinaison Eau Rouge gauche-droite-gauche à Spa quand, sous la pluie, Michael Schumacher abroge les lois de la physique ainsi que celles de la psychologie. Autrefois, on n'y pensait même pas: quand, en 1980, par exemple, Jean-Pierre Jabouille, sur le circuit d'Autriche, passait comme une flèche dans une Renault turbo dans l'épingle à cheveux gigantesque qui porte le nom innocent de virage Bosch. Ou, en 1976, à Zandvoort, au virage de Tarzan, peut-être le plus palpitant de tous. Là-bas, dans les lois coutumières de la Formule 1, on ne roule pas les uns à côté des autres. Mais James Hunt, McLaren et John Watson, Penske n'ont pas arrêté de le faire tour après tour. Ou en 1970, sur l'ancien circuit de Spa, quand Pedro Rodriguez se moquait bien de l'instinct de conservation avec sa BRM dans l'éternel virage à droite de Burnenville.

On jure et on se moque bien sûr: du commerce exagéré et du bazar des egos à Monaco, des embouteillages matinaux entre Buckingham et l'entrée principale de Silverstone, lieu sacro-saint britannique, de la méchante humeur de la superstar et du rafraîchissement général du climat dans l'entreprise de la Formule 1. Mais c'est alors que l'on regarde le visage d'un Gilles Villeneuve dans lequel sont réunis volonté et sensibilité, ou encore un mécanicien qui fait chauffer dans un box le moteur d'une Ferrari qui a un son à la fois méchant et agressif, et tout simplement beau – le bruit génial par excellence. Ou encore, la tension monte peu à peu une heure avant le départ, la chorégraphie, toujours la même, des mille dernières mises au point et c'est pourtant toujours aussi nouveau et excitant. Ou Jean Alesi qui lutte pour arriver à des résultats au-delà du rapide avec sa Ferrari dans le S derrière la dernière ligne droite du Magny-Cours. C'est alors que l'on sait que l'on ne peut pas s'en défaire, que le phénomène du Grand Prix est devenu un aliment spirituel fondamental, indispensable comme l'eau et le pain.

Avouons-le: Toutes ces impressions sont subjectives, tout comme le livre que vous avez devant vous et qui, malgré ses nombreuses photos n'a pas la prétention de posséder une intégralité encyclopédique. A la différence d'un ouvrage de référence dans lequel on a dû commencer par choisir les sujets, ce livre-ci veut transmettre différentes façons de voir et des impressions de ce sport qui repousse ou envoûte mais qui, de toutes façons, est toujours un défi.

PRÓLOGO

25 años en el séquito del Grand Prix: ¿No acaba convirtiéndose la aventura —preparada con esmero año tras año y desplegada en 16 episodios para ser experimentados a plazos— en trajín capaz de acabar con el entusiasmo más incurable? ¿No va siendo hora de poner punto final y reorientarse en la vida? Preguntar se podrá preguntar, digo yo, incluso a sí mismo… Pero enseguida brota de las capas más profundas del subconsciente ese «¡No!» en los ávidos adictos a la droga de las carreras automovilísticas, «¡Imposible!», responderían en determinados momentos. En la entrada del casino de Monte Carlo, por ejemplo, cuando Alain Prost se dirige a la *pole position*. O en la inquietante combinación izquierda-derecha-izquierda del Eau Rouge en Spa, cuando Michael Schumacher, rodando sobre mojado, pone con toda evidencia las leyes de la física y de la psicología en tela de juicio. En otros tiempos no se les daba ninguna oportunidad a los principios de la física, como cuando en 1980, en el Österreichring, Jean-Pierre Jabouille al mando de su Renault turbo se lanzaba como una flecha a través de la curva cerrada con el inofensivo nombre de curva Bosch. O en 1976 en Zandvoort en la curva de Tarzán, quizá la más sensacional de todas. Allí —como consta en las normas no escritas de la Fórmula 1— no se rueda al lado de otro bólido. Pero James Hunt, Mclaren y John Watson, Penske, lo hacían vuelta tras vuelta. O en 1970 en el viejo circuito de Spa, cuando Pedro Rodríguez, a bordo de su BRM, se mofaba del instinto de conservación humano en la eterna curva hacia la derecha llamada Burnenville.

Por supuesto, uno se cabrea y se burla: del ostentoso comercio y de la feria de vanidades de Mónaco, de la congestión del tráfico mañanero entre Buckingham y la entrada principal al santuario británico Silverstone, de la mala leche de las superstars y el enfriamiento general del ambiente en el negocio de la Fórmula 1. Pero luego miras el rostro de un Gilles Villeneuve, en el que se congratulan decisión y sensibilidad. O un mecánico deja que una máquina Ferrari se caliente en el *box*, y el motor ruge malvado y agresivo y sencillamente hermoso —el sonido por excelencia—. O la tensión se va acumulando en la hora antes de la salida, la misma coreografía de siempre con sus mil maniobras y, sin embargo, siempre nueva y siempre excitante. O Jean Alesi lucha con su Ferrari en la Sprevia a la recta final de Magny-Cours, valores límite más allá de la rapidez. Entonces es cuando eres consciente de que no puedes dejarlo, de que el fenómeno del Grand Prix se ha convertido en alimento básico de tu alma, tan imprescindible como el agua y el pan.

Concedido: todas estas impresiones son tan subjetivas como lo es el presente libro, que, a pesar de la plétora de fotografías, carece de pretensiones enciclopédicas. Más que una obra de consulta, para la que hay que hacer primero una sangría a las cosas con el objeto de volverlas estáticas, nuestro libro deberá ofrecer puntos de vista e impresiones de este deporte que repele a unos y conmueve mágicamente a otros, y desafía a todos.

GRAND PRIX 1969-1993

Mit dem Notstand kam das große Geld: Noch zum Grand Prix von Südafrika 1968, Jim Clarks letztem, traten die Lotus im traditionellen English Racing Green an. Bereits in Monaco erschienen sie in der rot-weißgoldenen Livree des externen Geldgebers Gold Leaf. Lotus-Chef Colin Chapman, Revolutionär von Beruf, hatte den stillen Umsturz angezettelt, die Machtübernahme branchenferner Konzerne im Rennsport. Und die Legislative CSI segnete ab, was vielen als Verrat an der reinen Lehre erschien.

Seitdem sind Große Preise Werbespots mit Überlänge, nur daß die einzelnen Sponsor-Botschaften miteinander verwoben und verknotet sind zu einer Polyphonie des Bitte-kauf-mich. Da streiten sich, vom Fernsehen weltweit erst recht in Szene gesetzt, im Kampf um Märkte, Meter und Sekunden Marlboro und Camel, Boss und Benetton, aber auch Hitachi gegen Footwork, Warsteiner gegen Parmalat und Denim gegen ICI. Modernes Marketing kennt nur den totalen Krieg und den totalen Sieg: Da wurde 1972 aus dem Lotus 72 der schwarzgoldene John Player Special, und Emerson und Wilson Fittipaldis Fittipaldi wurde 1975 als Copersucar ebenfalls in nomineller Identität mit einem Produkt geboren. Der Toleman von 1981 mendelte sich gar in sanften Metamorphosen zum Benetton von heute herüber, einst wie jetzt nichts weiter als firmeneigene Rollkommandos an der Grand Prix-Front. Selbst bis dato sorgsam gehegte nationale Profile verwischen sich, wenn der altehrwürdige englische Große Preis zum Woolmarket Grand Prix wird und der nicht minder in Ehren ergraute französische zum Rhône-Poulenc Grand Prix. Aber auch persönliche: Da warb Nichtraucher Jacky Ickx pausbackig für Kent-Zigaretten, da wand sich John Surtees, der sich vor lauter Geldnot dem Kondom-Giganten Durex verschrieben hatte, vor Verlegenheit, wenn Fans ihn um Warenproben ersuchten. Mit dem Gold-Regen von außen, aber auch unter der zielstrebigen Regie von Formel 1-Impresario Bernie Ecclestone, wandelte sich das Erscheinungsbild der Rennstrecken von Grund auf.

Neben einem Fahrerlager von 1968 nimmt sich ein heutiges aus wie ein Villenvorort von Lugano gegenüber einem Pfadfinderbiwak. Wo Öl und Dreck und die Unbilden der Witterung den Mechanikern das Leben sauer machten und durch blauäugigen Idealismus kompensiert werden mußten, herrschen heute die aseptische Sauberkeit und das wohltemperierte Ambiente einer Entbindungsstation. McLaren-Boß Ron Dennis brüstet sich damit, sich nie die Hände schmutzig zu machen – wie ein friderizianischer Offizier. In der zweiten und dritten Reihe aber parken die Wagenburgen, zusammengefahren aus Transportern und Motorhomes, Luxusyachten auf Rädern, splitternacktes Overstatement, die Zurschaustellung von Macht und Überfluß. Fahrer, Teamchefs und Konstrukteure, alle Superstars im Rennzirkus von heute, sind unnahbarer und unzugänglicher geworden im eigentlichen Sinne der Wörter in diesen tiefgekühlten Eremitagen. Und wenn der Bittsteller sich endlich Audienz verschafft hat, kommt er sich vor wie der fremde Cowboy im Western, der den Saloon voller einheimischer Raufbolde betritt, wie der englische Grand Prix-Journalist Nigel Roebuck einmal treffend formuliert hat.

Dafür erwarten den Berichterstatter entschieden verbesserte Arbeitsbedingungen: gläserne, vollklimatisierte Säle über den Boxen, wo er den Rennverlauf ständig mit Daten verpflegt live und am individuellen Bildschirm verfolgen darf. Gab es früher schon einmal ein Gerangel um ein einsames Telefon, ist man nun kommod vernetzt mit dem Rest der Welt.

Unter dem bunten Sponsor-Gewand indessen hat sich das darwinistische Pilot-Projekt Formel 1 wieder einmal nur den veränderten Gegebenheiten angepaßt, lauert der Kampfsport Grand Prix pur wie eh und je. Magische Momente bezeugen das, jeder einzelne ebenbürtig Juan Manuel Fangios berühmter Siegesfahrt auf dem Nürburgring 1957. Immer gut dafür: das Fürstentum Monaco, historischer Boden und Anachronismus zugleich, und zwar einer von schon atemberaubender Unangemessenheit. 1970 zum Beispiel, als Jochen Rindt nach einer elektrisierenden Jagd auf die Spitze den ausgebufften Alt-Professional Jack Brabham in der allerletzten Kurve in die Leitplanke zwang. Oder 1981: Da prügelte Gilles Villeneuve seinen störrischen Ferrari 126CK so lange durch die dreistöckigen Metallschluchten im Schatten des Grimaldi-Palastes, bis die Anzeigetafel am Hafen mit riesigen Ziffern unter dem infernalischen Gebrüll der tifosi die Nummer 27 als Sieger herausschrie. Auf keinem Fußballplatz der Erde wurde je die Metapher vom Hexenkessel mehr Ereignis als hier. Oder am 3. Juni 1984, einem schwarzgrauen, eiskalten Regentag. Rennleiter Jacky Ickx entschied kraft souveräner Willkür, daß das Rennen kurz vor Halbzeit abgebrochen werde. Alain Prost lag mit dem McLaren-Porsche in Führung. Hinter ihm jedoch empfahlen sich zwei talentierte junge Männer der Aufmerksamkeit: Ayrton Senna mit dem klobigen Toleman, dessen Hart-Maschine erst in den höchsten Drehzahlen ihre volle Leistung herausrückte, und Stefan Bellof am Lenkrad des Tyrrell, der allerdings für die unwirtlichen Bedingungen jenes Tages wie geschaffen war.

Bevor viele Rennstrecken durch Schikanen entmannt wurden, gerieten Grand Prix häufig zu Windschattenschlachten, den Zuschauern zur Freude, zum Leidwesen all derer, die eine Rundenzähltabelle zu führen hatten. Die dramatischste von allen: Monza 1971, als sich Peter Gethin, Ronnie Peterson, François Cevert, Mike Hailwood und Howden Ganley innerhalb einer Sekunde über die Ziellinie rauften. Gethin erzählte später einmal, er habe bei dem letzten desperaten Spurt aus der Parabolica mit 12.500 Umdrehungen weit über den Verhältnissen seines BRM-Triebwerks gelebt. Auch Clay Regazzoni hatte in diesem Jahrhundert-Rennen geführt, Ronnie Peterson, Jackie Stewart, François Cevert, Mike Hailwood, Jo Siffert und Chris Amon.

Am 1. Juli 1979 wurde in Dijon-Prenois gleich zweifach Grand Prix-Geschichte geschrieben. Jean-Pierre Jabouille verbuchte vor einem vaterländisch gestimmten Publikum den ersten Erfolg für einen Renault Turbo, einen Heimsieg zumal. Beim Kampf um den zweiten Platz jedoch gingen sein Teamgefährte René Arnoux und Ferrari-Pilot Villeneuve miteinander um wie Fünftkläßler bei einer Schulhofkeilerei. Wieder und wieder berührten sich die beiden Wagen in der Schlußphase des Rennens, und lachend wie zwei Pennäler schüttelten sich die Kontrahenten anschließend die Hände nach ihrer Stippvisite im Graubereich zwischen Sein und Nichtsein.

Ein Feuerwerk von nur reichlich einer Minute: Keke Rosbergs Pole-Runde in Silverstone 1985. Aber spätestens, als sein Williams-Honda in der Schikane vor Woodcote bei einsetzendem Nieselregen über die Curbs flog, spürten alle, daß hier ein Mann an und jenseits der Grenze des Vertretbaren unterwegs war. Mit dem Kriegernamen „The Rocket Man" ehrten ihn englische Gazetten am nächsten Tag.

Ausgleichende Gerechtigkeit und dazu das Phänomen Ayrton Senna: In Spa 1992 fuchste der junge Stürmer und Dränger Michael Schumacher im Ardennenregen den mit allen Wassern gewaschenen dreifachen Champion beim Reifenpoker aus und gewann seinen ersten Grand Prix, den achtzehnten in seiner kurzen Karriere. In Donington 1993 aber schlug der Brasilianer zurück mit jener Grausamkeit, zu der nur er fähig ist, schlug sie alle bei ganz ähnlichen Bedingungen mit geradezu absurd anmutender Leichtigkeit in einem weiteren Kapitel der Senna-Legende.

Grand Prix – das ist ein Teil der Faszination, die von ihnen ausgeht – bedeuten aber auch latent drohende Gefahr. Der Unfall ist programmiert, allerdings bleibt die Hoffnung, daß er glimpflich ausgeht. Wie in Jarama 1970: Da verkrallten sich der Ferrari von Jacky Ickx und der BRM von Jackie Oliver in der zweiten Runde ineinander. Ein feuriges Inferno waberte empor, aber beide Piloten entkamen, nur zart angesengt.

Oder Silverstone 1973: Nach der ersten Runde sah der Start- und Zielbereich aus wie nach einem Flugzeugabsturz. Gebeutelt von einer furiosen Profilneurose hatte der wüste junge Südafrikaner Jody Scheckter eine Kettenreaktion des Schreckens ausgelöst. Acht Fahrer rappelten sich konsterniert aus dem Millionen-Schrott ihrer Autos empor. Nur Andrea de Adamich wurde relativ leicht verletzt vom Wrack seines Brabham festgehalten. Während in dem Italiener der Entschluß reifte, seinen schwarzen Sturzhelm an den Nagel zu hängen, beschloß der deutsche Debütant Jochen Mass weiterzumachen, obwohl sich ihm sein neues Gewerbe als reichlich unattraktiv vorgestellt hatte.

Zum Aufbruch in einen bodendeckenden Trümmerhaufen gerieten auch die beiden ersten Starts zum Großen Preis von Österreich 1987 in Zeltweg. Verletzt wurde keiner, Grand Prix-Makler Bernie Ecclestone indessen hatte einen höchst willkommenen Vorwand, das ungeliebte Rennen in Zukunft aus dem Terminkalender zu streichen.

Wurden diese und andere Stunts gewissermaßen im Formationsflug bewältigt, gab es auch spektakuläre solistische Einlagen. Besonders tat sich 1980 der Ire Derek Daly mit Maschinen des Fabrikats Tyrrell hervor. In Monaco erhob er sich dreißig Meter vor dem Nadelöhr Sainte Dévote zu einer Exkursion zu Häupten seiner Konkurrenten, die der Schikane auf konventionellen Wegen zueilten, und landete dann auf dem Wagen seines buchstäblich bestürzten Teamgefährten Jarier, zum Frust seines Chefs Ken Tyrrell und zur Freude des Sponsors Candy, denn die Sequenz wurde rund um die Welt im Fernsehen wieder und wieder vorgeführt, mit ihr der Produktname.

In Zandvoort folgte Dalys zweiter Streich, als er am Ende der Zielgeraden ungespitzt in die Reifenwälle der Tarzan-Kurve hämmerte, wieder ohne sich sonderlich weh zu tun. Und weil das so schön war, lieferte René Arnoux zwei Jahre später an der gleichen Stelle mit seinem Renault die Doublette dieses Abgangs, ironischerweise direkt unter dem frohen Lächeln des Michelin-Männchens auf einer riesigen Reklametafel.

Aber es gab auch andere Augenblicke, schlimme, die nicht einmündeten in Aufatmen und Erleichterung. Dann fiel das Schweigen in die Fahrerlager ein, die Trauer um den unwiederbringlichen Verlust, die sonst verhohlene Frage nach dem Sinn des Ganzen. Als Jochen Rindt 1970 in Zandvoort aufs Siegerpodest stieg, kräuselte sich am Horizont noch der Qualm vom Flammentod seines Freundes Piers Courage. Und die untröstlichen Williams-Mechaniker warfen just mit dumpfem Knall die Hecktür des leeren Transporters zu, in dem Courages De Tomaso nach England gebracht werden sollte, eine Szene von niederdrückender Symbolik.

Wie aus einem Nachtmar auch: die Höllenfahrt des jungen Walisers Tom Pryce in Kyalami 1977. Ein Streckenposten rannte über die Strecke, wurde bei Tempo 280 vom Vorderrad des Rennwagens gepackt. Seine Löschflasche, zehn Kilogramm schwer, schlug wie eine Bombe im Cockpit des Shadow ein, und kopflos in des Wortes furchtbarster Bedeutung raste Pryce noch die Zielgerade hinunter, bis der Wagen in Crowthorne Corner zerschellte. Beispiele nur... Eines der bewegendsten: als am 8. Mai 1982 in Zolder die Schreckenskunde die Runde machte, Gilles Villeneuve sei tot. Auf der Hatz nach der Pole Position war der Frankokanadier, den Enzo Ferrari den Prinzen der Zerstörung nannte, auf das langsam dahinrollende Auto von Jochen Mass geprallt. Villeneuve hatte keine Chance, einer, der keine Feinde hatte und den alle liebten. Noch sieben Jahre später stand in Monza auf der Piste geschrieben: Gilles, du lebst – in uns.

Millionen sahen die Szene, von dem sterilen Medium Fernsehen kalt-analytisch in Bewegungsabläufe gehackt. Denn auch das hat sich geändert in diesen 25 Jahren: die Weltmeisterschaft wurde geschrumpft und erweitert zur TV-Serie, Happening in Raten vor einem Milliarden-Publikum, gelegentlich zum Nutzen des Sports, viel öfter aber zu seinem Schaden.

GRAND PRIX 1969-1993

At the South African Grand Prix of 1968, Jim Clark's last, the Lotuses were still in their conventional English racing green. At Monaco, however, they showed up in the red, white and gold livery of the cigarette brand Gold Leaf. That indefatigable innovator, Lotus boss Colin Chapman, had done it again, hatching another silent revolution when he invited a sponsor from outside the sport into Formula One as well as getting the go-ahead from CSI, the then racing legislature.

Ever since Grand Prix have been overlength ads uniting commercial messages into a dissonant polyphony, further encouraged by the presence of television in the continual struggle for markets, metres, and seconds. It is Marlboro versus Camel, Boss versus Benetton, but also Hitachi pitted against Footwork and Denim against ICI. Modern marketing knows total war and total victory only. In 1972 the Lotus 72 changed into the black and gold John Player Special, and Emerson and Wilson Fittipaldi's Fittipaldi, né in 1975 as Copersucar, hence was also nominally identical with a Brazilian product at first. In 1986 the Toleman of 1981 turned into today's Benetton then as now carrying its very owners' colours and logos at the Grand Prix front. Even time-honoured national profiles are reduced to insignificance when the British Grand Prix becomes the Woolmarket Grand Prix or its French counterpart the Rhône Poulenc Grand Prix. But so do personal profiles, with non-smoker Jacky Ickx praising the superior quality of Kent cigarettes or John Surtees, whose cars used to be painted in the attractive gold of the condom giant Durex, writhing with embarrassment when people asked him for samples. With all that money, helped on by Bernie Ecclestone's sophisticated management of the Grand Prix circus, today's circuits look totally different from yesterday's.

While mechanics and other Grand Prix personnel used to be exposed to mud and oil and the vicissitudes of the weather, modern pit and paddock complexes remind you of the aseptic cleanliness prevailing in a maternity ward. Typically, McLaren boss Ron Dennis prides himself upon never having dirty fingernails. In the second and third rows, however, you will find the Grand Prix laager, all those transporters and motorhomes, luxury yachts on wheels ostentatiously displaying power and abundance. The racing stars of today have virtually become inaccessible in their splendid isolation. And if you did manage to have the ear of one of the high and mighty you sometimes cannot help feeling like the strange cowboy entering a saloon full of local ruffians, as the English racing reporter, Nigel Roebuck, once put it.

On the other hand journalists enjoy much improved working conditions sometimes quite remote from the actual circuit, glassy air-conditioned halls full of electronic equipment comfortably linking them to the rest of the world and meticulously keeping them informed about what is happening on the track.

But under the motley garbs of the sponsors the Darwinist pilot project Formula One has once again adjusted to changing circumstances, competitive as ever. This is testified by magic moments, every single one on par with Juan Manuel Fangio's famous Nürburgring drive in 1957. Always a good soil for these: Monaco, historical ground as well as an anachronism of breathtaking dimensions. In 1970 for example, when Jochen Rindt had seasoned campaigner Jack Brabham slide into the armco of the very last corner after an electrifying hunt for the lead. Or in 1981, when Gilles Villeneuve manhandled his clumsy Ferrari 126CK through the narrow streets of the principality until the big screen at the harbour as well as his numerous fans roared that number 27 was the winner. Or on June 3rd, 1984, a ghastly day when the race was discontinued shortly before half-time because of torrential rains hammering down onto the Grimaldis' little realm. Alain Prost was leading with his TAG McLaren Porsche, but behind him two talented young men made a splash indeed: Ayrton Senna on the difficult-to-drive Toleman and Stefan Bellof, whose little Tyrrell admittedly was much better suited to those extraordinary circumstances.

Before the introduction of chicanes a lot of Grand Prix invariably turned into pitched slipstreaming battles, much to the joy of the spectators and much to the chagrin of all those who had to keep a lapchart. Certainly the most spectacular one was the Italian in 1971 when Pete Gethin, Ronnie Peterson, François Cevert, Mike Hailwood and Howden Ganley all rushed over the line within one second after the lead had changed innumerable times.

And in 1979 two quite different chapters of Grand Prix history were written at Dijon-Prenois when Jean-Pierre Jabouille scored the first turbo win for Renault under the partisan eyes of a patriotic crowd while behind him his team mate René Arnoux and Ferrari driver Gilles Villeneuve were banging wheels as if they were engaged in a schoolyard brawl. And like schoolboys, laughing, they shook hands after the race shrugging off their excursion into the no-man's land between being and not being.

A fireworks of little more than one minute: Keke Rosberg's Silverstone pole lap in 1985. It was beginning to drizzle and when his Williams Honda came flying over the curbs of the Woodcote chicane at the latest everybody was aware that the Flying Finn was doing the impossible. "The Rocket Man" an English paper called him the next day.

Equally thrilling was the way shooting star Michael Schumacher outfoxed old hand Ayrton Senna on a very wet Spa circuit in 1992 taking advantage of the tyre gamble to win his first Grand Prix. But then the shrewd Brazilian turned the tables on the young German and everybody else in 1993 just outdriving and outwitting them in rain-soaked Donington to complete yet another chapter of the Senna legend.

Grand Prix, that goes without saying, are a dangerous sport. Doubtless, that accounts for some of the fascination emanating from them. Accidents are part and parcel of the system, as it were. Most of them go off well, such as the spectacular collision of Jacky Ickx' Ferrari and Jackie Oliver's BRM at Jarama in 1970 resulting in a fiery inferno, from which both drivers escaped only slightly singed.

Or in 1973 when the Silverstone start and finish area looked as if a jumbo jet had gone down. Ridden by fierce ambition young Jody Scheckter had overdone it with his McLaren after the first lap causing the track to be littered with the debris of eight cars after a chain reaction of horror. But only Andrea de Adamich suffered minor injuries, the bespectacled Italian spontaneously deciding to hang up his black helmet for good whereas Grand Prix novice Jochen Mass only found his new job somewhat exciting.

The first two starts to the 1987 Austrian Grand Prix also led to mayhem worth millions of pounds providing racing's top impresario Bernie Ecclestone with a welcome pretext to have the race cancelled from the Grand Prix schedule altogether. All these stunts were carried out in formation flight, so to say.

But of course there was also the odd impressive solo act. A particularly busy performer was Irishman Derek Daly in 1980, writing off his respective Tyrrells in great style. At Monaco he rose 30 yards before Sainte Devote over the heads of his comrades who rushed towards that chicane in more orthodox ways only to crash down onto his bewildered team mate Jean-Pierre Jarier's car. Team Boss Ken Tyrrell did not appreciate that in contrast to sponsor Candy as the accident was shown worldwide again and again on TV and so was the brand name.

At Zandvoort Daly thundered into the tyre walls at Tarzan, again without doing any harm to himself, the exact replica of which could be admired two years later when René Arnoux landed up in precisely the same spot with his Renault, right under the happy smile of the Michelin man on a large hoarding.

But there were also those terrible moments when all of a sudden sad silence prevailed in pit and paddock. Then somebody had gone off never to return and racing showed its darkest face. When Jochen Rindt climbed on to the rostrum after his Zandvoort win in 1970 there still was that ominous black and silver cloud curling on the horizon indicating the holocaust in which his friend Piers Courage had died. The disconsolate Williams mechanics, however, with a hollow thud, banged the boot door of the empty transporter which was to have taken Courage's De Tomaso back to England, the symbolism of the scene almost unbearable.

Another nightmare: young Welshman Tom Pryce's death during the 1977 South African Grand Prix. As his car was approaching at 175 mph, an inexperienced marshal ran over the track and was hit by the Shadow's front wheel. The man was killed instantaneously. But his heavy fire extinguisher bottle flew into the cockpit smashing the head of the driver who, lifeless already, carried on for another half mile before the car was eventually destroyed in Crowthorne Corner almost collecting some other competitors. And nobody who was present will ever forget May 8th, 1982 when, at Zolder, the unbelievable news made the round that Gilles Villeneuve had killed himself hitting the slow car of Jochen Mass while being out for pole position. The little Franco-Canadian, whom Enzo Ferrari called "The Prince of Destruction", was indeed universally loved, and seven years later there was still written on a piece of tarmac in Monza "Gilles, you live – in us".

Time and again the moment of his death was shown on TV, hacked into slow-motion fragments by that cold and analytical medium. This, too, has changed in those 25 years: Grand Prix racing has become a TV soap opera delivered in 16 or so instalments every year, to the detriment rather than the benefit of the sport.

GRAND PRIX 1969-1993

C'est dans un état d'urgence que vint la grande fortune. C'est au Grand Prix d'Afrique du Sud en 1968, le dernier de Jim Clark, que les Lotus se présentèrent dans l'English Racing Green traditionnel. A Monaco déjà, elles étaient apparues en livrée rouge-blanc-jaune du donneur d'argent externe Gold Leaf. Colin Chapman, chef de Lotus et révolutionnaire professionnel avait tramé la chute tranquille: une prise de pouvoir sur le sport automobile de konzerns n'ayant rien à voir avec cette branche . Et la CSI législative a donné sa bénédiction considérée par beaucoup comme une trahison au pur esprit.

Depuis, les Grands Prix sont des spots publicitaires de longueur excessive et les différents messages des sponsors sont tissés et rattachés les uns aux autres dans une polyphonie de «S'il te plaît achète-moi». Et c'est là que se disputent – et la télévision s'est bien chargée de mettre tout cela en scène mondialement – les luttes pour accéder à des marchés, à des mètres et à des secondes: Marlboro et Camel, Boss et Benetton, mais aussi Hitachi contre Footwork, Warsteiner contre Parmalat et Denim contre ICI. Le marketing moderne ne connaît que la guerre totale et la victoire totale: c'est ainsi que la Lotus 72 a fait naître la John Player Special noir et jaune. Fittipaldi est né aussi en 1975 sous l'apparence de Copersucar mais aussi sous son identité nominale accompagnée d'un produit. La Toleman de 1981 s'est même métamorphosée doucement en Benetton actuelle, autrefois comme aujourd'hui, rien de plus que des patrouilles appartenant à la firme et qui se trouvaient sur le front des Grands Prix. Même les profils nationaux entretenus avec soin jusqu'à aujourd'hui s'effacent quand le vénérable Grand Prix anglais devient le Grand Prix Wollmarket et que le non moins digne Grand Prix français, vieilli dans les honneurs, devient le Grand Prix Rhône-Poulenc. Mais il y en a aussi de personnels: là, c'est Jacky Ickx, non-fumeur joufflu qui fait de la publicité pour les cigarettes Kent, là, c'est John Surtees qui, dans la misère, a dû s'apparenter au géant des préservatifs Durex et qui se trouvait toujours très gêné quand des fans lui demandaient des échantillons de cette marchandise. C'est avec la pluie d'or extérieure mais aussi sous la direction de Bernie Ecclestone, l'imprésario qui sait ce qu'il veut, que l'image du circuit s'est fondamentalement modifiée.

Comparer un paddock de 1968 à celui d'aujourd'hui, c'est comparer une banlieue de villas à Lugano à un bivouac de scouts. Là où l'huile et la saleté ainsi que les aléas du temps rendaient amère la vie des mécaniciens et devaient être compensés par un idéalisme naïf, règne aujourd'hui la propreté aseptisée et l'ambiance bien tempérée d'une maternité. Le boss de chez McLaren, Ron Dennis, se vante de ne jamais se salir les mains, comme un officier de Frédéric II. Mais dans la deuxième et troisième rangée, il y a des multitudes de voitures qui sont garées: des camions et des maisons à moteur, des yachts de luxe sur roues, l'exagération à nu, un show du pouvoir et du superflu. Les pilotes, les chefs d'équipe et les constructeurs, toutes les superstars du cirque automobile d'aujourd'hui sont devenus de plus en plus inaccessibles et inabordables au sens propre des mots, dans ces ermitages surgelés. Et quand le solliciteur a enfin obtenu une audience,

il a la même impression que le cowboy étranger dans un wester, qui arrive dans un saloon rempli de batailleurs locaux, comme l'a formulé très justement une fois le journaliste anglais du Grand Prix Nigel Roebuck.

En contrepartie, des conditions de travail considérablement améliorées attendent les reporters: des salles vitrées, complètement climatisées au-dessus des boxes où il est constamment nourri de données et où il peut suivre le déroulement de la course, en direct, sur un écran individuel. Si, autrefois, il arrivait qu'on se bouscule pour prendre le seul téléphone existant, maintenant on est relié commodément au reste du monde.

En attendant, sous le vêtement multicolore du sponsor, le projet pilote darwinien de la Formule 1 n'a fait que s'adapter une nouvelle fois aux événements, la lutte pour le Grand Prix pur est toujours aux aguets. Il y a des moments magiques qui en témoignent, comme le célèbre parcours de la victoire de Juan Manuel Fangio sur le Nürburgring en 1957. Incontournable la principauté de Monaco, à la fois sol historique et anachronisme, une de celles qui vous coupe déjà bien le souffle. En 1970, par exemple, quand Jochen Rindt a forcé ce vieux professionnel de Jack Brabham, qui a plus d'un tour dans son sac, dans le tout dernier virage, à aller dans le parapet après une chasse électrisante au sommet. Ou en 1981. Là, c'est Gilles Villeneuve qui a malmené sa Ferrari 126CK, intraitable entre les parois de métal à trois étages qui bordent la route à l'ombre du palais des Grimaldi, tant et si bien que le tableau indicateur du port avec ces chiffres immenses a dû hurler que le numéro 27 était vainqueur dans les crix infernaux des tifosi. Sur aucun terrain de football la métaphore du chaudron des sorcières n'a été aussi forte qu'ici. Ou le 3 juin 1984, un jour de pluie gris noir et glacial. Le directeur de la course Jacky Ickx décida souverainement d'interrompre la course peu avant la mitemps. Alain Prost menait avec la Porsche McLaren. Mais derrière lui pourtant, l'attention avait été attirée par deux jeunes hommes talentueux: Ayrton Senna avec la Toleman grossière dont le moteur Hart était le plus performant quand il arrivait à atteindre les plus grandes vitesses et Stefan Bellof au volant de Tyrrell qui était fait de toutes façons pour les conditions déplorables de ce jour-là.

Avant que de nombreux circuits n'aient été fermés par des chicanes, les Grands Prix étaient souvent devenus des luttes dans lesquelles on s'abritait derrière les plus rapides, à la joie des spectateurs mais au détriment de tous ceux qui avaient à gérer un tableau du nombre des tours. La plus dramatique de toutes: Monza en 1971, quand Peter Gethin, Ronnie Peterson, François Cevert, Mike Hailwood et Howden Ganley se sont battus durement et jusqu'au bout et même une seconde après la ligne d'arrivée. Gethin a raconté plus tard qu'il avait poussé sa BRM dans le dernier sprint désespéré à 12.500 tours. Clay Regazzoni avait été vainqueur, lui aussi dans cette course du siècle, Peterson, Jackie Stewart, Cevert, Hailwood, Jo Siffert et Chris Amon.

Le 1er juillet 1979, le Grand Prix de Dijon-Prenois est entré deux fois dans l'histoire. Jean-Pierre Jabouille encaissa le premier succès devant un public patriotique avec une Renault turbo; en plus, c'était une victoire dans son pays natal. Dans la lutte pour la deuxième place pourtant, son coéquipier René Arnoux et le pilote de la Ferrari Villeneuve se sont comportés comme des écoliers dans une bagarre de cour d'école. Les deux voitures n'avaient de cesse de se toucher dans la phase finale de la course et c'est en riant comme deux écoliers que les deux adversaires se sont serré la main après leur visite-éclair aux portes de la mort.

Un feu d'artifice d'une longue minute: le tour en première position de Keke Rosberg à Silverstone en 1985. Mais c'est au plus tard quand sa Honda Williams vola par-dessus la bordure dans la dispute devant Woodcote, dans une bruine qui commençait à tomber, que tout le monde sentit qu'il y avait là un homme à la limite du soutenable. C'est avec le nom guerrier de «Rocket man» que des gazettes anglaises lui ont fait honneur le lendemain.

Justice compensatoire et supplémentaire: le phénomène Ayrton Senna: à Spa en 1992, le jeune Michael Schumacher impétueux fit râler le triple champion qui a plus d'un tour dans son sac. Sous la pluie des Ardennes, dans un poker de pneus, il gagne ainsi son premier Grand Prix, le dix-huitième de sa courte carrière. Mais en 1993, à Donington, le Brésilien se vengea avec une cruauté dont il est le seul capable et il les a tous battus dans des conditions analogues et avec une facilité proprement incroyable dans un chapitre supplémentaire de la légende de Senna.

Les Grands Prix, une partie de fascination en émane, mais aussi un danger latent. L'accident est programmé comme élément du système, mais bien sûr, il reste l'espoir de s'en tirer à bon compte. Comme à Jarama en 1970: La Ferrari de Jacky Ickx s'est encastrée dans la BRM de Jackie Oliver au deuxième tour. Un enfer de feu s'embrasa mais les deux pilotes s'en sortirent indemnes, juste un peu roussis.

Ou Silverstone en 1973: après le premier tour, les zones d'arrivée et de départ donnaient l'impression qu'un avion s'y était écrasé. Le jeune Sudafricain sauvage Jody Scheckter avait déclenché une réaction en chaîne de l'horreur. Huit pilotes consternés ont réussi à s'extirper de la ferraille de leurs voitures qui avaient valu des millions. Seul Andrea de Adamich fut légèrement blessé parce qu'il avait été pris dans la carcasse de sa Brabham. Tandis que dans l'Italien mûrissait la décision de remettre au clou son casque noir, le débutant allemand Jochen Mass décidait de poursuivre, bien que sa nouvelle activité se soit montrée très peu attrayante.

Les deux premiers départs du Grand Prix d'Autriche 1987 à Zeltweg ont été eux aussi un fiasco. Personne ne fut blessé, mais l'agent d'affaires Bernie Ecclestone avait trouvé là un excellent prétexte pour l'avenir: rayer de l'agenda la course qu'il n'aimait pas. Si on parvenait à maîtriser ces exercices périlleux, en vol de formation pour ainsi dire, il y avait aussi des apports spectaculaires de solistes. Et c'est particulièrement l'Irlandais Derek Daly qui s'est mis en va-

leur en 1980 avec des modèles de Tyrrell. A Monaco, trente mètres avant le resserrement de Sainte Dévote, il a fait une excursion en volant au-dessus des têtes de ses concurrents qui avançaient rapidement en empruntant les chemins conventionnels et a atterri ensuite sur la voiture de Jarier, son coéquipier littéralement renversé, à la grande frustration de son chef Ken Tyrrell mais à la joie du sponsor Candy, car cette séquence n'a pas cessé de passer à la télévision dans le monde entier, et le nom du produit bien sûr.

A Zandvoort a suivi la seconde plaisanterie de Daly, quand au bout de la dernière ligne droite, il s'est mis soudain à marteler les remparts de pneus du virage Tarzan sans se faire particulièrement mal. Et cela avait été si beau que René Arnoux a remonté le même spectacle deux ans plus tard au même endroit, avec sa Renault. Ironie du sort: directement sous le bonhomme Michelin d'un immense panneau publicitaire.

Mais il y eut aussi de graves moments qui n'ont pas fini par des soupirs de soulagement. Alors, le silence se répandait dans le paddock, le deuil sur la perte irréversible, la question d'ordinaire dissimulée: cela a-t-il vraiment un sens? Quand en 1970, à Zandvoort, Jochen Rindt est monté sur le podium des vainqueurs, il y avait encore à l'horizon la fumée de l'accident de son ami Piers Courage, mort dans les flammes. Et les mécaniciens inconsolables de Williams venaient de refermer dans un déclic assourdi le hayon du camion vide dans lequel la De Tomaso de Courage aurait due être emportée en Angleterre, scène d'un symbolisme accablant.

Sortie tout droit d'un cauchemar elle aussi: la descente aux enfers du jeune Gallois Tom Pryce à Kyalami en 1977. Un contrôleur du circuit traversa le parcours, et fut saisi à 280 km/h par la roue avant de la voiture de course. Son extincteur de 10 kilos explosa comme une bombe dans le cockpit de la Shadow et Pryce, décapité, est descendu dans la dernière ligne droite comme un bolide et la voiture a volé en éclats dans le Crowthorne Corner. Des exemples … L'un des plus émouvants: quand le 8 mai 1982 à Zolder la nouvelle horrible est tombée, celle de la mort de Gilles Villeneuve. Dans la chasse à courre pour la Pole Position, le Franco-Canadien qu'Enzo Ferrari nommait le prince de la destruction, avait heurté la voiture de Jochen Mass qui s'éloignait en roulant doucement. Villeneuve n'avait aucune chance de l'éviter, c'était l'un de ceux qui n'avait pas d'ennemis et que tous aimaient. Sept ans plus tard, on pouvait encore lire à Monza sur la piste: Gilles, tu vis – en nous.

Des millions de spectateurs virent la scène, hachée en séquences de mouvements analytiques par le medium stérile qu'est la télévision. Car cela aussi a changé au cours des 25 dernières années. Le championnat international a perdu en substance et on en a fait une série de télévision, un happening à épisodes pour des millions de personnes, pour servir le sport à l'occasion, mais bien plus souvent pour lui nuire.

GRAND PRIX 1969-1993

Con el estado de necesidad llegó también la gran fortuna: todavía al Grand Prix de Sudáfrica de 1968, el último de Jim Clark, acudieron los Lotus pintados con en el tradicional *racing green* británico. Pero ya en Mónaco hicieron su aparición con la librea roja-blanca-dorada del patrocinador externo Gold Leaf. El jefe de la Lotus, Colin Chapman, de profesión revolucionario, había urdido el silencioso golpe de estado, la toma del poder en el deporte automovilístico por consorcios ajenos al ramo. Y la legislativa CSI bendijo lo que muchos consideraban una traición del modelo puro.

Desde entonces, los Grand Prix son anuncios publicitarios de gran duración, sólo que los distintos mensajes de los patrocinadores se hallan entretejidos y entrelazados unos con otros hasta formar una polifonía del cómprame-por-favor. Y así, marcas que se han abierto camino en la escena mundial gracias a la televisión, se pelean por los mercados, los metros y los segundos: Marlboro contra Camel, Boss contra Benetton, pero también Hitachi contra Footwork, Warsteiner contra Parmalat y Denim contra ICI. El marketing moderno sólo conoce la guerra total y la victoria total: en 1972 el Lotus 72 se transformó en John Player Special negro-dorado, y el Fittipaldi de Emerson y Wilson Fittipaldi renació en 1975 como Copersucar, en identidad nominal con un producto. El Toleman de 1981 se convirtió, tras una blanda metamorfosis, en el Benetton de hoy, y tanto ahora como entonces no es otra cosa que un destacamento sobre ruedas de una firma en el frente del Grand Prix. Incluso perfiles nacionales cuidadosamente protegidos hasta la fecha se borran cuando el viejo y honorable Gran Premio inglés se convierte en el Grand Prix de Woolmarket y el no menos canoso en honores Premio francés se convierte en el Grand Prix de Rhône-Poulenc. Y en el terreno personal: el no fumador Jacky Ickx anunciaba mofletudo cigarrillos Kent, y John Surtees, que, de pura necesidad económica, había vendido su alma al gigante del condón Durex, se moría de vergüenza cada vez que un(a) fan le pedía una muestra del artículo. Con la lluvia de oro externa, pero también gracias a la perseverante dirección del empresario Bernie Ecclestone en la Fórmula 1, la imagen de los circuitos sufrió una metamorfosis total.

En comparación con un *paddock* de 1968, uno actual parece un barrio de villas en las afueras de Lugano frente a un campamento de boy scouts. Donde el aceite y la suciedad amargaban la vida a los mecánicos, que compensaban su situación con un idealismo ciego, domina hoy la limpieza aséptica y el ambiente bien templado de una sala de partos. El *boss* de McLaren, Ron Dennis, se ufana de no haberse ensuciado nunca las manos —ni que fuera un oficial de Federico el Grande—. Pero en segunda o tercera fila aparcaban las barreras de carros, una convulsión de coches de transporte y *motorhomes*, yates de lujo sobre ruedas, exceso superfluo en pelotas, demostración de poder y derroche. Corredores, patrones de equipo y constructores, todos ellos *superstars* del circo automovilístico de hoy, se han vuelto más inaccesibles e impenetrables —en el sentido más literal de las palabras— en estos santuarios congelados.

Y cuando el solicitante ha conseguido por fin audiencia, se siente como un *cowboy* forastero en el oeste entrando en el *saloon* lleno de bravucones lugareños, como acertadamente formulara una vez el periodista inglés de Grand Prix Nigel Roebuck.

Como contrapartida, el informante dispone de condiciones de trabajo decisivamente mejores: salas de cristal aclimatizadas sobre las cabinas, desde donde puede seguir el transcurso de la carrera en directo y con constante aprovisionamiento de datos, o en la pantalla individual. Donde antes se batía una multitud por el único teléfono, hoy está uno cómodamente comunicado con el resto del mundo.

Entretanto, bajo el vistoso manto de los patrocinadores, el darwiniano proyecto piloto Fórmula 1 sólo se ha adaptado a las nuevas circunstancias, pero la lucha deportiva por el Grand Prix sigue al acecho con la pureza de siempre. Hay momentos mágicos que lo confirman, momentos de la alcurnia de la famosa carrera victoriosa realizada por Juan Manuel Fangio en el Nürburgring en 1957. Un terreno fecundo para momentos mágicos: el principado de Mónaco, suelo histórico y anacrónico al mismo tiempo, dominado por una inoportunidad emocionante. En 1970, por ejemplo, cuando Jochen Rindt, tras una electrizante persecución por la primera línea, forzaba al viejo y astuto profesional Jack Brabham al guardarraíl en la última curva. O en 1981: Gilles Villeneuve castigando a su pertinaz Ferrari 126CK a lo largo de las cañadas de metal de tres pisos a la sombra del Palacio Grimaldi hasta que el marcador del puerto proclamó con cifras enormes, entre los infernales rugidos de los tifosi, el número 27 como vencedor. En ningún estadio de fútbol del mundo se podría aplicar la metáfora de estar metido en un atolladero con tanta propiedad como aquí. O el 3 de junio de 1984, un día gris, helado y lluvioso. El encargado de la carrera, Jacky Ickx, decidió con arbitrariedad soberana interrumpir la carrera poco antes del medio tiempo. Alain Prost iba a la cabeza con su Porsche McLaren. Tras él, dos hombres jóvenes con talento se habían ganado la atención del público: Ayrton Senna, con el macizo Toleman cuyo motor Hart no rendía al máximo hasta encontrarse en el más alto número de revoluciones, y Stefan Bellof al volante del Tyrrell, un bólido hecho a la medida de las inhóspitas condiciones climáticas del día.

Antes de que muchos circuitos hubieran sido castrados con chicanas, los Grand Prix se convertían a menudo en batallas a sotavento, para alegría de los espectadores y tormento de los encargados de un marcador de las vueltas. La más dramática de todas: Monza 1971, cuando Peter Gethin, Ronnie Peterson, François Cevert, Mike Hailwood y Howden Ganley se pelearon durante un segundo por la línea de llegada. Gethin contaría más tarde que en el desesperado esfuerzo final para salir de la Parabólica, con el motor a 12500 revoluciones, conducía muy por encima de las posibilidades de su BRM. También Clay Regazzoni había llevado la delantera en esta carrera del siglo, y Peterson, Jackie Stewart, Cevert, Hailwood, Jo Siffert y Chris Amon. El 1 de julio de 1979 se ha escrito historia del Grand Prix por partida doble en Dijon-Prenois. Jean-Pierre Jabouille asentó, ante un público patriota, el primer éxito de un Renault turbo, que fue además un éxito en casa. Pero en la lucha por el segundo puesto, su compañero de equipo René Arnoux y el piloto del Ferrari Villeneuve se comportaron como chiquillos en una trifulca de recreo escolar. Una y otra vez se rozaban los dos coches en la fase final de la carrera y finalmente los dos contrincantes se dieron la mano con una sonrisa como dos colegiales después de su visita relámpago a la zona gris entre el ser y no ser.

Fuegos artificiales de sólo un minuto largísimo: la vuelta *pole* de Keke Rosberg en Silverstone en 1985. Pero cuando su Honda Williams, en la chicane previa a Woodcote, voló sobre el bordillo bajo la fina lluvia que empezaba a caer, todos eran conscientes de que el hombre estaba sobrepasando los límites de lo justificable. Con el nombre de guerra «The Rocket Man» le rindieron honores las gacetas inglesas al día siguiente.

Justicia compensatoria y además el fenómeno Ayrton Senna: en 1992, en Spa, el brioso Michael Schumacher se metió en el bolsillo al experimentado campeón triple en un póker de neumáticos y ganó su primer Grand Prix, el dieciocho en que participaba en su corta carrera. Pero en 1993, en Donington, el brasileño devolvió el golpe con una brutalidad de la que sólo él era capaz, venció a todos en condiciones muy similares con una elegante soltura que casi resultaba absurda, firmando con ello un nuevo capítulo de la leyenda Senna.

Los Grand Prix son parte de la fascinación que irradian los pilotos, pero, al mismo tiempo, significan una amenaza latente. El accidente está programado como parte del sistema, si bien en la esperanza de que resulte indulgente. Como en 1970 en el Jarama: el Ferrari de Jacky Ickx y el BRM de Jackie Oliver colisionaron en la segunda vuelta. Un infierno de llamas lamió los aires, pero ambos pilotos salieron con vida, sólo ligeramente chamuscados.

O en 1973 en Silverstone: después de la primera vuelta parecía como si se hubiera caído un avión en la parrilla de salida y la meta. Cernido por una furiosa neurosis de perfilarse, el joven y salvaje sudafricano, Jody Scheckter, había provocado una reacción de pánico en cadena. Ocho corredores emergieron consternados de la chatarra de coches por valor de millones. Sólo Andrea de Adamich sufrió heridas, relativamente leves, al quedar aprisionado por la ruina de su Brabham. Mientras que el italiano maduraba la idea de tirar la toalla, el debutante alemán Jochen Mass decidió continuar, aunque su nueva profesión se le había presentado con bien poco atractivo.

También en el Gran Premio de Austria de 1987 acabaron las dos primeras *stars* en un montón de chatarra en el Zeltweg. Ninguno resultó herido, pero el agente de Grand Prix Bernie Ecclestone recibió en bandeja la más que deseada disculpa para, en el futuro, borrar de su agenda las nada apetecidas carreras.

Si este tipo de ejercicios acrobáticos se superaban, por así decirlo, en vuelo de formación, había también espectaculares aportaciones solistas. En esta especialidad descolló en 1980 el

irlandés Derek Daly con máquinas del fabricante Tyrrell. En Mónaco se elevó treinta metros por los aires ante la entrada al ojo de aguja Sainte Dévote, realizando una excursión por encima de las cabezas de sus concurrentes —que aceleraban por la chicana de la manera convencional— y aterrizando finalmente encima de su aterrado compañero de equipo Jarier, para frustración de su jefe, Ken Tyrrell, y alegría del patrocinador, Candy, cuyo reclamo dio la vuelta al mundo en compañía de la secuencia emitida hasta la saciedad en televisión.

En Zandvoort realizó Daly su siguiente jugarreta: esta vez se incrustó de lleno en el bastión de neumáticos de la curva de Tarzán tras la recta final y nuevamente sin hacerse demasiado daño. Y como había quedado tan bonita, René Arnoux ofreció, dos años más tarde en el mismo lugar, la repetición de la jugada con su Renault, que, irónicamente, fue a parar a los pies de un sonriente hombre Michelín que hacía propaganda en una enorme valla.

Pero había también instantes de menos fortuna, que no acababan precisamente en suspiros de alivio. En esos casos se cernía el silencio sobre el *paddock*, el duelo por la pérdida irrecuperable, la pregunta normalmente encubierta por el sentido de las carreras. Cuando Jochen Rindt subía al podio del vencedor en Zandvoort en 1970 sobre el horizonte todavía ondeaba el humo de la muerte en llamas de su amigo Piers Courage. Y los inconsolables mecánicos de la Williams cerraban en ese momento con un ruido sordo la puerta trasera del coche de transporte vacío que debería llevar a Courage. De Tomaso a Inglaterra, una escena de oprimente simbolismo.

De pesadilla: la carrera infernal del joven galés Tom Pryce en Kyalami en 1977. Un hombre del servicio de seguridad que corría por el circuito fue atrapado por la rueda delantera del coche de carrera a la velocidad de 280. Su extintor de incendios de diez kilos de peso azotó como una bomba el *cockpit* del Shadow y Pryce se lanzó sin cabeza, en el sentido más espantoso de la palabra, por la recta de llegada hasta que el coche se estrelló en la Crowthorne Corner. Ejemplos nada más… Uno de los más conmovedores: cuando el 8 de mayo de 1982 rondaba la horrorosa noticia de que Gilles Villeneuve había muerto. En la estampida por la *pole position*, el francocanadiense, al que Enzo Ferrari denomiba el príncipe de la destrucción, chocó contra el coche de Jochen Mass que se acercaba lentamente. No cabía la menor esperanza para Villeneuve, uno de los que no tenían enemigos y al que todos apreciaban. Todavía siete años después se podía leer en el circuito de Monza: Gilles, tu vives —en nosotros—.

Fueron millones los que contemplaron la escena, transmitida por el estéril medio televisivo en forma fría, analítica, desguazada en secuencias de movimiento. Pues éste es también uno de los aspectos que han cambiado en estos últimos 25 años: el Campeonato Mundial se redujo, y se amplió a serie televisiva, acontecimiento a plazos ante millones de espectadores, algunas veces para bien del deporte, la mayoría de ellas para su perjuicio.

Start / Start at / Départ de / Salida en
Silverstone (GB)

1. Reihe / front row of the grid /
1ère rangée / 1ª fila:

Jochen Rindt (A), Gold Leaf Lotus Ford
Jackie Stewart (GB), Matra Elf Ford
Denis Hulme (NZ), McLaren Ford

1

2, 3

4

5

6

1 - 3 Start / Start / Départ / Salida

Jacky Ickx (B), Brabham Ford
vor / ahead of / devant / adelante de
Jackie Stewart (GB), Matra Ford

Nürburgring (D)

4 Bruce McLaren (NZ)
McLaren Ford
Nürburgring (D)

5 Jochen Rindt (A)
Gold Leaf Lotus Ford
Nürburgring (D)

6 Piers Courage (GB)
Brabham Ford
Nürburgring (D)

7   Joseph Siffert (CH)
    Lotus Ford
    Nürburgring (D)

8   Graham Hill (GB)
    Gold Leaf Lotus Ford
    Nürburgring (D)

9   Weltmeister / World Champion
    Champion du monde / Campeón mundial

    Jackie Stewart (GB)
    Matra Elf Ford
    Nürburgring (D)

10 Hohe Flügel beim Training in Monaco

    High spoilers during practice in Monaco

    Ailerons arrières pendant les essais de
    Monaco

    Alerones altos durante el fogueo en
    Mónaco

11 Graham Hill (GB), Gold Leaf Lotus Ford

    fünffacher Sieger und »ungekrönter König
    von Monaco« auf seiner Ehrenrunde /
    five-time winner and uncrowned »King of
    Monaco«, during his lap of honour /
    cinq fois vainqueur et «roi de Monaco»
    sans couronne, pendant son tour
    d'honneur /
    cinco veces triunfador y »rey de Mónaco«
    sin investidura, en su ronda de honor

Vorherige Seite / Previous page /
Page précédente / Página anterior:

Jacky Ickx (B)
Ferrari
Clermont - Ferrand (F) 1970

2

1, 2 *Start / Start / Départ / Salida*   Jackie Stewart (GB), March Elf Ford
Spa - Francorchamps (B):   Jochen Rindt (A), Gold Leaf Lotus Ford
                                                Chris Amon (NZ), STP March Ford

1

2

3

1 Derek Bell (GB), Brabham Ford,

chauffiert / acting as chauffeur to / sert de chauffeur à / conduce a

Jackie Stewart (GB)

Spa - Francorchamps (B)

2 Jackie Stewart (GB), Elf Tyrrell Ford,

siegt im Jarama (E) nach einem schweren Unfall zwischen Jacky Ickx (B), Ferrari, und Jackie Oliver (GB), Yardley - BRM.

wins at Jarama (E) after a serious accident between Jacky Ickx (B), Ferrari, and Jackie Oliver (GB), Yardley - BRM.

gagne à Jarama (E), après un grave accident entre Jacky Ickx, Ferrari, et Jackie Oliver (GB), Yardley - BRM.

triunfa en Jarama (E) después de un grave accidente entre Jacky Ickx, Ferrari, y Jackie Oliver (GB), Yardley - BRM.

3 Pedro Rodríguez (MEX), Yardley - BRM

Sieger in / winner at / vainqueur à / triunfador en

Spa - Francorchamps (B)

4 Österreichring, Zeltweg (A)

5 Jack Brabham (AUS)
Brabham Ford BT 33
Monaco

6 Jacky Ickx (B)
Ferrari 312 B
Monaco

7 Pedro Rodríguez (MEX)
BRM P 135
Monaco

8 Jackie Stewart (GB)
March Ford 701
Monaco

1

3, 4

Vorherige Seite / Previous page /
Page précédente / Página anterior:

Weltmeister / World Champion /
Champion du monde / Campeón mundial
1970

Jochen Rindt (A)
Gold Leaf Lotus Ford
Clermont - Ferrand (F)

1   Start in / Start at / Départ de / Salida en
    Monza (I)

    4:   Clay Regazzoni (CH), Ferrari
    9:   Peter Gethin (GB), Yardley BRM
    3:   Jacky Ickx (B), Ferrari
    20: Joseph Siffert (CH), Yardley BRM
    12: Chris Amon (NZ), Matra Simca
    2:   François Cevert (F), Elf Tyrrell Ford

2   Joseph Siffert (CH), Yardley - BRM
    Ronnie Peterson (S), March Ford
    Mike Hailwood (GB), Surtees Ford
    François Cevert (F), Elf Tyrrell Ford

    Monza (I)

3   Start in / Start in / Départ de / Salida en
    Zeltweg (A)

34

4 Jacky Ickx (B), Ferrari
Emerson Fittipaldi (BR), Gold Leaf Lotus Ford
Ronnie Peterson (S), March Ford

Silverstone (GB)

5 *Weltmeister / World Champion /
Champion du monde / Campeón mundial*

Jackie Stewart (GB)
Elf Tyrrell Ford
Silverstone (GB)

1 François Cevert (F), Elf Tyrrell Ford
   Jo Siffert (CH), Yardley BRM

   Montjuich, Barcelona (E)

2 Rolf Stommelen (D), Surtees Ford
   Henri Pescarolo (F), March Politoys Ford

   Paul Ricard (F)

3 Clay Regazzoni (CH)
   Ferrari
   Zandvoort (NL)

4 Henri Pescarolo (F)
   March Politoys Ford
   Silverstone (GB)

5 Jacky Ickx (B)
   Ferrari
   Silverstone (GB)

6 Reine Wisell (S)
   Gold Leaf Lotus (Turbine)
   Silverstone (GB)

7 Emerson Fittipaldi (BR)
   Gold Leaf Lotus Ford
   Silverstone (GB)

8

9

10

11, 12

13, 14

8 Clay Regazzoni (CH)
Ferrari
Montjuich, Barcelona (E)

9 Graham Hill (GB)
Brabham Ford
Montjuich, Barcelona (E)

10 Ronnie Peterson (S)
STP March Ford
Nürburgring (D)

11 John Surtees (GB)
Surtees Ford
Silverstone (GB)

12 Denis Hulme (NZ)
McLaren Ford
Silverstone (GB)

13 Chris Amon (NZ)
Matra Simca
Silverstone (GB)

14 Graham Hill (GB)
Brabham Ford
Silverstone (GB)

1

Vorherige Seite / Previous page /
Page précédente / Página anterior:

Peter Gethin (GB)
McLaren Ford
Monaco 1971

1   François Cevert (F)
    Elf Tyrrell Ford
    Brands Hatch (GB)

2   Clay Regazzoni (CH)
Ferrari
Nürburgring (D)

GRAND PRIX

1

2

3

4, 5

6, 7

1 Ronnie Peterson (S)
STP March Ford
Nürburgring (D)

2 Rolf Stommelen (D)
Eifelland Ford, Colani - Design
Jarama, (E)

3 Niki Lauda (A)
STP March Ford
Monaco

4 *Sieger in Monaco:*
Winner in Monaco:
Vainqueur à Monaco:
Triunfador en Mónaco:

Jean - Pierre Beltoise (F)
Marlboro BRM

5 Denis Hulme (NZ)
Yardley McLaren Ford
Monaco

6 Clay Regazzoni (CH)
Ferrari
Monaco

7 Chris Amon (NZ)
Matra Simca
Monaco

8

9

8   *Start in / Start at / Départ de / Salida en*
    Monza (I)

    Chris Amon (NZ), Matra Simca
    Jacky Ickx (B), Ferrari

9   Jackie Stewart (GB)
    Elf Tyrrell Ford
    Brands Hatch (GB)

1

1   Start in / Start at / Départ de / Salida en
    Zolder (B)

Vorherige Seite / Previous page /
Page précédente / Página anterior:

Weltmeister / World Champion /
Champion du monde / Campeón mundial
1972

Emerson Fittipaldi (BR)
JPS Lotus Ford
Brands Hatch (GB), 1972

2 Ronnie Peterson (S)
JPS Lotus Ford
Österreichring, Zeltweg (A)

GRAND PRIX

1, 2 Jackie Stewart (GB), Elf Tyrrell Ford

überholt / overtaking / double /
sobrepasando a
Ronnie Peterson (S), JPS Lotus Ford

Anderstorp (S)

3, 4 *Start / Start / Départ / Salida*
Silverstone (GB)

Unfall von Jody Scheckter (ZA)
Jody Scheckter's accident (ZA)
accident de Jody Scheckter (ZA)
accidente de Jody Scheckter (ZA)

Yardley - McLaren Ford

5 Emerson Fittipaldi (BR)
JPS Lotus Ford
Österreich, Zeltweg (A)

6 Carlos Pace (BR)
Surtees TS 13A
Monaco

7 James Hunt (GB)
Hesketh March 731
Monaco

8 Graham Hill (GB)
Shadow DN 1
Monaco

9 Jackie Stewart (GB)
Tyrrell Ford 006
Monaco

10 Howden Ganley (NZ)
ISO Rivolta Ford
Monaco

14

15

11 Jean - Pierre Beltoise (F)
BRM P 160 E
Monaco

12 Arturo Merzario (I)
Ferrari 312 B3
Monaco

13 Chris Amon (NZ)
Martini Tecno PA 123
Monaco

14 François Cevert (F)
Elf Tyrrell Ford 006
Zolder (B)

15 *Weltmeister / World Champion /*
Champion du monde / Campeón mundial
1973

Jackie Stewart (GB), Elf Tyrrell Ford

vor / ahead of / devant / delante de
Emerson Fittipaldi (BR), JPS Lotus Ford

Österreichring, Zeltweg (A)

1

1 *Weltmeister / World Champion /*
   Champion du monde / Campeón mundial
   1974

Emerson Fittipaldi (BR)
Marlboro Texaco McLaren Ford
Monaco

2

2 Start in / Start in / Départ de / Salida en Monaco

Denis Hulme (NZ),
Marlboro Texaco McLaren Ford

*kämpft gegen / battling with / lutte contre /
en disputa con*

Jean - Pierre Beltoise (F), BRM Motul

Dahinter / Behind them / Derrière /
Detrás de ellos viene:

Emerson Fittipaldi (BR),
Marlboro Texaco McLaren Ford

1 Jody Scheckter (ZA)
   Elf Tyrrell Ford 007
   Anderstorp (S)

2 Graham Hill (GB)
   Embassy Lola Ford
   Monaco

3 Patrick Depailler (F)
   Elf Tyrrell Ford 007
   Monaco

4 Hans Stuck (D)
   March 741
   Monaco

5

6

5 Clay Regazzoni (CH)   6 Clay Regazzoni (CH)
   Ferrari 312 B3   Ferrari 312 B3
   Nürburgring (D)   Monaco

1, 2

3, 4

5

6, 7

8, 9

1	Vittorio Brambilla (I) March Ford 751 Nürburgring (D)	3	Jody Scheckter (ZA) Elf Tyrrell Ford 007 Nürburgring (D)

1 Vittorio Brambilla (I)
March Ford 751
Nürburgring (D)

2 John Watson (GB)
JPS Lotus Ford 72 D
Nürburgring (D)

3 Jody Scheckter (ZA)
Elf Tyrrell Ford 007
Nürburgring (D)

4 Mario Andretti (USA)
Parnelli Ford VPJ 4
Nürburgring (D)

5 Vittorio Brambilla (I)
March Ford 751
Nürburgring (D)

6 Carlos Reutemann (ARG)
Brabham Ford BT 44 B
Nürburgring (D)

7 James Hunt (GB)
Hesketh Ford 308
Nürburgring (D)

8 Patrick Depailler (F)
Elf Tyrrell Ford 007
Nürburgring (D)

9 Hans Stuck (D)
March Ford 751
Nürburgring (D)

10 Start in / Start at / Départ de / Salida en
    Anderstorp (S)

11 Sekunden danach!

    Seconds later!

    Quelques secondes après.

    ¡Segundos después!

1 Ronnie Peterson (S)
JPS Lotus Ford
Zandvoort (NL)

2 Niki Lauda (A)
Ferrari 312 T
Anderstorp (S)

3 Tom Pryce (GB)
UOP Shadow Ford
Anderstorp (S)

4 Jochen Mass (D)
Texaco Marlboro McLaren Ford
Montjuich (E)

5 *Weltmeister / World Champion /*
Champion du monde / Campeón mundial
1975

Niki Lauda (A)
Ferrari 312 T
Monaco

GRAND PRIX

1   *Start in / Start at / Départ de / Salida en*
Brands Hatch (GB)

Mario Andretti (USA), JPS Lotus Ford

*bleibt stehen / remains on the grid / reste
sur place / se queda detenido*

2   *Weltmeister / World Champion /
    Champion du monde / Campeón mundial
    1976*

    James Hunt (GB)
    Texaco Marlboro McLaren Ford
    Jarama (E)

3   Niki Lauda (A)
    Ferrari
    Monaco

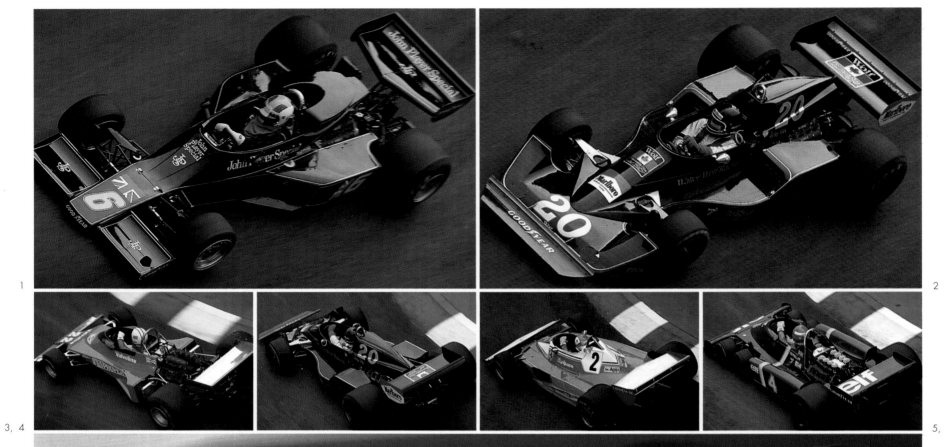

1 Gunnar Nilsson (S)
   JPS Lotus Ford

2 Jacky Ickx (B)
   Williams Ford

3 Chris Amon (NZ)
   Ensign Ford

4 Jacky Ickx (B)
   Wolf Williams Ford

5 Clay Regazzoni (CH)
   Ferrari

6 Patrick Depailler (F)
   Elf Tyrrell Ford P 34

7 Patrick Depailler (F)
   Elf Tyrrell Ford P 34

8   Arturo Merzario (I)
March Ford

9   Harald Ertl (D)
Hesketh Ford

10   Jochen Mass (D)
Texaco Marlboro McLaren Ford

11   Clay Regazzoni (CH)
Ferrari

12   Tom Pryce (GB)
UOP Shadow Ford

13   Vittorio Brambilla (I), March Ford
Carlos Reutemann (ARG),
Martini Brabham Alfa

14   »Do it in the streets«

15   Michel Leclère (F)
Wolf Williams Ford

1 Start / Start / Départ / Salida

Carlos Reutemann (ARG), Ferrari
Jody Scheckter (ZA), Wolf Ford
Mario Andretti (USA), JPS Lotus Ford

2 *Unfall / Accident / Accident / Accidente*

James Hunt (GB), Marlboro McLaren Ford
Carlos Reutemann (ARG), Ferrari

3 Carlos Reutemann (ARG)
Ferrari

1 Ronnie Peterson (S)
   Elf FNCB Tyrrell Ford P 34
   Dijon - Prenois (F)

2 Emerson Fittipaldi (BR)
   Copersucar Ford
   Long Beach (USA)

3 James Hunt (GB)
   Marlboro McLaren Ford
   Long Beach (USA)

4

5

4   James Hunt (GB)
    Marlboro McLaren Ford
    Monaco

5   Gunnar Nilsson (S)
    JPS Lotus Ford
    Jarama (E)

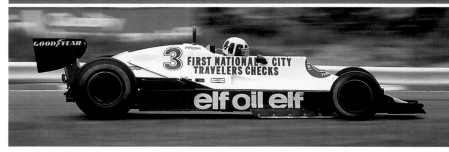

Vorherige Seite / Previous page /
Page précédente / Página anterior:

Weltmeister / World Champion /
Champion du monde / Campeón mundial

Niki Lauda (A)
Ferrari 312 T3
Long Beach (USA) 1977

1 Jean - Pierre Jabouille (F)
Renault Turbo
Hockenheim (D)

2 Jacques Laffite (F)
Ligier Matra
Brands Hatch (GB)

3 Gilles Villeneuve (CDN)
Ferrari
Hockenheim (D)

4 Jody Scheckter (ZA)
Wolf Ford
Brands Hatch (GB)

5 Alan Jones (AUS)
Williams Ford
Brands Hatch (GB)

6 Rolf Stommelen (D)
Arrows Ford
Hockenheim (D)

7 Hans Stuck (D)
Tabatip Shadow Ford
Hockenheim (D)

8 Didier Pironi (F)
Elf Tyrrell Ford
Brands Hatch (GB)

9 Brett Lunger (USA)
Chesterfield McLaren Ford
Brands Hatch (GB)

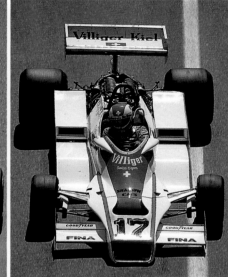

10, 11

12, 13

14

15

16, 17

18

10 Mario Andretti (USA) JPS Lotus Ford	13 Jochen Mass (D) ATS Ford	16 Didier Pironi (F) Tyrrell Ford
11 Carlos Reutemann (ARG) Ferrari	14 Patrick Tambay (F) Marlboro McLaren Ford	17 Jody Scheckter (ZA) Wolf Ford
12 Clay Regazzoni (CH) Tabatip Shadow Ford	15 Jean - Pierre Jabouille (F) Renault Turbo	18 Niki Lauda (A) Parmalat Brabham Alfa Romeo

1 *Start in / Start in / Départ de / Salida en*
Hockenheim (D)

*Weltmeister / World Champion /
Champion du monde / Campeón mundial
1978*

Mario Andretti (USA), JPS Lotus Ford

Ronnie Peterson (S), JPS Lotus Ford

2   Niki Lauda (A)
Brabham Parmalat Alfa Romeo
Jarama (E)

Vorherige Seite / Previous page /
Page précédente / Página anterior:

Weltmeister / World Champion /
Champion du monde / Campeón mundial
1978

Mario Andretti (USA)
JPS Lotus Ford
Monaco 1978

1, 2   *Weltmeister / World Champion*
Champion du monde / Campeón mundial
1979

Jody Scheckter (ZA)
Ferrari
Monaco

3   Gilles Villeneuve (CDN)
Ferrari
Österreichring (A)

4   Gilles Villeneuve (CDN)
Ferrari
Monaco

1   Nelson Piquet (BR)
    Brabham Parmalat Alfa Romeo

2   Jochen Mass (D)
    Warsteiner Arrows Ford

3   Mario Andretti (USA)
    Martini Lotus Ford

4   Riccardo Patrese (I)
    Warsteiner Arrows Ford
    Hockenheim (D)

5   Jacques Laffite (F)
    Ligier Gitanes Ford

6   Alan Jones (AUS)
    Saudia Williams Ford

7   René Arnoux (F)
    Jean - Pierre Jabouille (F)
    Renault Turbo

1, 2

3

Vorherige Seite / Previous Page /
Page précédente / Página anterior:

John Watson (GB)
Marlboro McLaren Ford
Monaco 1979

1   Jean - Pierre Jabouille (F)
    Renault Turbo
    Monaco

2   Carlos Reutemann (ARG)
    Saudia Williams Ford
    Long Beach (USA)

3   Jochen Mass (D)
    Warsteiner Arrows Ford
    Paul Ricard (F)

4   Patrick Depailler (F)
Marlboro Alfa Romeo
Monaco

1 *Weltmeister / World Champion / Champion du monde / Campeón mundial 1980*

Alan Jones (AUS)
Saudia Leyland Williams Ford
Monaco

2 Gilles Villeneuve (CDN)
Ferrari
Österreichring (A)

3 Alain Prost (F)
Marlboro McLaren Ford
Österreichring (A)

4 Jacques Laffite (F)
Ligier Gitanes Ford
Brands Hatch (GB)

5 Elio de Angelis (I)
Essex Lotus Ford
Paul Ricard (F)

6 Nelson Piquet (BR)
Brabham Parmalat Ford
Monaco

7

8

7 *Start in / Start at / Départ de / Salida en*
  Long Beach (USA)

8 Jody Scheckter (ZA)
  Ferrari
  Long Beach (USA)

1

1   *Weltmeister / World Champion /*
    Champion du monde / Campeón mundial
    1981

Nelson Piquet (BR)
Brabham Parmalat Ford
Long Beach (USA)

2 Gilles Villeneuve (CDN)
Ferrari Turbo
Long Beach (USA)

3 Nigel Mansell (GB)
Essex JPS Lotus Ford
Monaco

4 Mario Andretti (USA)
Marlboro Alfa Romeo
Long Beach (USA)

1 Keke Rosberg (SF), Fittipaldi Ford
   Andrea de Cesaris (I), Marlboro McLaren Fc
   Nelson Piquet (BR), Brabham Parmalat Ford

   Rascasse, Monaco

2 *Start / Start / Départ / Salida*
   Long Beach (USA)

3 Elio de Angelis (I)
Essex JPS Lotus Ford
Österreichring (A)

4 Alain Prost (F)
Renault Turbo
Österreichring (A)

5 Carlos Reutemann (ARG)
Williams Saudia TAG Ford
Österreichring (A)

6 Mario Andretti (USA)
Marlboro Alfa Romeo
Monaco

7 Jacques Laffite (F)
Talbot Ligier Gitanes Matra
Monaco

1 - 5 *Start und Unfall in Brands Hatch (GB)*
zwischen

René Arnoux (F), Renault Turbo, und
Riccardo Patrese (I),
Brabham Parmalat BMW Turbo

Start at Brands Hatch (GB) and accident
between

René Arnoux (F), Renault Turbo, and
Riccardo Patrese (I),
Brabham Parmalat BMW Turbo

Départ de Brands Hatch (GB) et accident
entre

René Arnoux (F), Renault Turbo, et
Riccardo Patrese (I),
Brabham Parmalat BMW Turbo

Salida en Brands Hatch (GB) y accidente
entre

René Arnoux (F), Renault Turbo, y
Riccardo Patrese (I),
Brabham Parmalat BMW Turbo

6

7

6 *Weltmeister / World Champion /*
   Champion du monde / Campeón mundial
   1982

   Keke Rosberg (SF)
   Williams Saudia TAG Ford
   Österreichring (A)

7 *Start in / Start at / Départ de / Salida en*
   Zolder (B)

   Keke Rosberg (SF),
   Williams Saudia TAG Ford
   zwischen / between / entre / entre

   René Arnoux (F)
   und / and / et / y
   Alain Prost (F), Renault Turbo

1 - 3 René Arnoux (F)
Renault Turbo
Zandvoort (NL)

4 Didier Pironi (F)
Ferrari Turbo
Monaco

5 Gilles Villeneuve (CDN)
Ferrari Turbo
Long Beach (USA)

6 Bruno Giacomelli (I)
Marlboro Alfa Romeo
Long Beach (USA)

7 Mario Andretti (USA)
Williams Saudia TAG Ford
Long Beach (USA)

8 Andrea de Cesaris (I)
Marlboro Alfa Romeo
Monaco

9 *Start / Start / Départ / Salida*
Österreichring (A)

Nelson Piquet (BR),
Brabham Parmalat BMW Turbo

Alain Prost (F), Renault Turbo

10 John Watson (GB)
Marlboro McLaren Ford
Monaco

1   *Weltmeister / World Champion /*
    Champion du monde / Campeón mundial

    Nelson Piquet (BR)
    Brabham Parmalat BMW Turbo
    Hockenheim (D)

2   Marc Surer (CH)
    Arrows Ford
    Hockenheim (D)

3   Stefan Johansson (S)
    Spirit Honda Turbo
    Hockenheim (D)

4   Derek Warwick (GB)
    Toleman Hart Turbo
    Hockenheim (D)

5 *Start in / Start at / Départ de / Salida en*
Silverstone (GB)

René Arnoux (F), Ferrari (28)
Alain Prost (F), Renault Elf (15)
Eddie Cheever (USA), Renault Elf (16)
Patrick Tambay (F), Ferrari (27)
Elio de Angelis (I), JPS Lotus (4)

6 Elio de Angelis (I)
JPS Lotus Renault Turbo
Hockenheim (D)

1   Alain Prost (F)
Renault Elf Turbo
Paul Ricard (F)

2   Niki Lauda (A)
Marlboro McLaren Ford
Paul Ricard (F)

3   Eddie Cheever (USA)
Renault Elf Turbo
Monaco

4   Andrea de Cesaris (I)
Marlboro Alfa Romeo
Monaco

5   René Arnaux (F)
Ferrari Turbo
Monaco

6   Keke Rosberg (SF)
Saudia Williams Ford
Monaco

7   R. Boesel (BR), Ligier Gitanes Ford
Eddie Cheever (USA), Renault Elf Turbo
Monaco

8

9

10

1, 12

13, 14

8 René Arnoux (F)
Ferrari Turbo
Monaco

9 Patrick Tambay (F)
Ferrari Turbo
Paul Ricard (F)

10 Nigel Mansell (GB)
JPS Lotus Ford
Long Beach (USA)

11 Manfred Winkelhock (D)
ATS BMW Turbo
Monaco

12 John Watson (GB)
Marlboro McLaren Ford
Monaco

13 Jean - Pierre Jarier (F)
Ligier Gitanes Ford
Monaco

14 Jacques Laffite (F)
Saudia Williams Ford
Monaco

1   Ayrton Senna (BR)
Toleman Hart Turbo
Monaco

2 *Weltmeister / World Champion /*
Champion du monde / Campeón mundial
1984

Niki Lauda (A)
Marlboro McLaren TAG Porsche Turbo
Monaco

3 Niki Lauda (A)
Marlboro McLaren TAG Porsche Turbo
Imola (RSM)

1, 2

3, 4

5

6, 7

8, 9

1 Nelson Piquet (BR)
 Brabham Parmalat BMW Turbo
 Dijon - Prenois (F)

2 Ayrton Senna (BR)
 Toleman Hart Turbo
 Dijon - Prenois (F)

3 Thierry Boutsen (B)
 Arrows BMW Turbo
 Dijon - Prenois (F)

4 Eddie Cheever (USA)
 Benetton Alfa Romeo Turbo
 Dijon - Prenois (F)

5 Unfall in / accident at / accident de
 accidente en
 Brands Hatch (GB)

6 Alain Prost (F)
 Marlboro McLaren TAG Porsche Turbo
 Zeltweg (A)

7 Jacques Laffite (F)
 Saudia Williams Honda Turbo
 Monaco

8 Elio de Angelis (I)
JPS Lotus Renault Turbo
Monaco

9 Manfred Winkelhock (D)
ATS BMW Turbo
Imola (RSM)

10 Stefan Bellof (D)
Tyrrell 012 Ford
Monaco

11 *Start in / Start at / Départ de / Salida en*
Estoril (P)

Stefan Johansson (S)
Ferrari Turbo
Monaco

1

2

3

4

5

1   Nigel Mansell (GB)
    Williams Honda Turbo
    Imola (RSM)

2   Nelson Piquet (BR)
    Brabham Olivetti BMW Turbo
    Le Castellet (F)

3   Start / Start / Départ / Salida en
    Spa - Francorchamps (B)

4, 5   Niki Lauda (A),
       Marlboro McLaren TAG Porsche Turbo

       überholt / overtaking / double /
       sobrepasando a

       Marc Surer (CH),
       Brabham Olivetti BMW Turbo

       Zandvoort (NL)

6

7

8

9

6 *Weltmeister / World Champion /*
   Champion du monde / Campeón mundial
   1985

   Alain Prost (F)
   Marlboro McLaren TAG Porsche Turbo
   Monaco

7 Elio de Angelis (I)
   JPS Lotus Renault Turbo
   Monaco

8 Jonathan Palmer (GB)
   Zakspeed Turbo
   Monaco

9 Michele Alboreto (I)
   Ferrari Turbo
   Monaco

1

2, 3

1 *Weltmeister / World Champion/*
   Champion du monde / Campeón mundial
   1986

   Alain Prost (F)
   Marlboro McLaren TAG Porsche Turbo
   Monaco

2 Ayrton Senna (BR)
   JPS Lotus Renault Turbo
   Monaco

3 Patrick Tambay (F)
   Lola Ford Turbo
   Le Castellet (F)

4 Die »neue« Schikane am Hafen von Monaco

The »new« chicane at the harbour in Monaco

La »nouvelle« courbe dans le port de Monaco

La »nueva« curva en el puerto de Mónaco

1   Stefan Johansson (S)
    Ferrari Turbo
    Monaco

2   Gerhard Berger (A)
    Benetton BMW Turbo
    Brands Hatch (GB)

3   Keke Rosberg (SF)
    Marlboro McLaren TAG Porsche Turbo
    Monaco

4   Jonathan Palmer (GB)
    Zakspeed Turbo
    Hockenheim (D)

5, 6 Nigel Mansell (GB)
    Canon Williams Honda Turbo
    Monaco

7   Canon Williams Honda Turbo
    Zeltweg (A)

8 *Start in / Start in / Départ de / Salida en*
Hockenheim (D):

Unfall zwischen / accident between /
accident entre / accidente entre

Stefan Johansson (S), Ferrari Turbo
und / and / et / y
Theo Fabi (I), Benetton BMW Turbo

9 *Unfall beim Start in / Accident during the*
start at / accident au départ de /
accidente a la salida de
Brands Hatch (GB)

10 *Schnellster aus dem Fahrzeug / The*
quickest one out of his vehicle / Le premier
à sortir de son véhicule / El primero en
salir de su vehículo

Jonathan Palmer (GB)
Zakspeed Turbo
Brands Hatch (GB)

Vorherige Seite / Previous Page /
Page précédente / Página anterior:

Stefan Johansson (S)
Marlboro McLaren Tag Porsche Turbo
Imola (RSM) 1987

1   Stefan Johansson (S)
    Marlboro McLaren TAG Porsche Turbo
    Hockenheim (D)

2   Michele Alboreto (I)
    Ferrari Turbo
    Spa - Francorchamps (B)

3 *Funkenregen !*
   Flying sparks !
   Pluie d'étincelles !
   Chisporroteo !

Andrea de Cesaris (I),
Brabham BMW Turbo
Stefan Johansson (S),
Marlboro McLaren TAG Porsche Turbo

Zeltweg (A)

1-7 Start am Österreichring (A), letztes Formel 1- Rennen in Zeltweg (A)

Start at the Österreichring (A). Last Formula 1 race in Zeltweg (A)

Départ de Österreichring (A). Dernière course de Formule 1 à Zeltweg (A)

Salida en Österreichring (A). Ultima carrera de fórmula 1 en Zeltweg (A)

8

9

10

1, 12

13, 14

8   Stefan Johansson (S)
    Marlboro McLaren TAG Porsche Turbo
    Imola (RSM)

9   Thierry Boutsen (B)
    Benetton Ford Turbo
    Monaco

10 *Die Funken fliegen auch in Jerez (E)*
    The sparks fly at Jerez (E), too!
    Les étincelles volent aussi à Jerez (E)
    Las chispas también vuelan en Jerez (E)

    Andrea de Cesaris (I)
    Brabham BMW Turbo

11 Gerhard Berger (A)
    Ferrari Turbo
    Monaco

12 Thierry Boutsen (B)
    Benetton Ford Turbo
    Monaco

13 Nigel Mansell (GB)
    Williams Honda Turbo
    Hungaroring (H)

14 *Weltmeister / World Champion /*
    Champion du monde / Campeón mundial
    1987

    Nelson Piquet (BR)
    Williams Honda Turbo
    Monaco

1

2, 3

Vorherige Seite / Previous page /
Page précédente / Página anterior:

Thierry Boutsen (B)
Benetton Ford
Monza (I) 1988

1   Nigel Mansell (GB)
    Williams Judd
    Monaco

2   Andrea de Cesaris (I)
    Rial Ford
    Monaco

3   Mauricio Gugelmin (BR)
    March Judd
    Estoril (P)

4   *Weltmeister / World Champion /*
    Champion du monde / Campeón mundial
    1988
    Ayrton Senna (BR),
    Marlboro McLaren Honda Turbo

    Gerhard Berger (A), Ferrari Turbo

    Silverstone (GB)

GRAND PRIX

1 Alessandro Nannini (I)
   Benetton Ford
   Monaco

2 *Start zum GP England*
   Start of the British Grand Prix
   Départ du Grand Prix d'Angleterre
   Salida del Gran Premio de Inglaterra

   Silverstone (GB)

3 Riccardo Patrese (I)
   Williams Judd
   Monaco

4 Nelson Piquet (BR)
   Lotus Honda Turbo
   Monaco

5 Andrea de Cesaris (I), Rial Ford

   dreht sich vor / spins in front of / fait un tour
   sur lui - même devant / girando frente a

   Alain Prost (F)
   Marlboro McLaren Honda Turbo

   Monaco

6 Philippe Alliot (F)
   Lola Ford
   Monaco

7 Thierry Boutsen (B)
   Benetton Ford
   Spa - Francorchamps (B)

8 Bernd Schneider (D)
   Zakspeed Turbo
   Spa - Francorchamps (B)

9 Gerhard Berger (A)
   Ferrari Turbo
   Rascasse, Monaco

10 Alessandro Nannini (I)
   Benetton Ford
   Rascasse, Monaco

GRAND PRIX

1 Thierry Boutsen (B)
  Williams Renault
  Monaco

2 Satoru Nakajima (J)
  Lotus Judd
  Monaco

3 Johnny Herbert (GB)
  Benetton Ford
  Monaco

4 Bernd Schneider (D)
  Zakspeed Yamaha
  Monaco

5 Bertrand Gachot (F)
  Onyx Ford
  Monaco

6 Philippe Alliot (F)
  Lola Lamborghini
  Monaco

7 Christian Danner (D)
  Rial Ford
  Monaco

8 *Start in / Start at / Départ de / Salida en*
  Spa - Francorchamps (B)

9

10

11

14

15

16

2, 13

9 *Weltmeister / World Champion*
Champion du monde / Campeón mundial
1989

Alain Prost (F)
Marlboro McLaren Honda
Hungaroring (H)

10 Nigel Mansell (GB)
Ferrari
Paul Ricard (F)

11 Pierluigi Martini (I)
Minardi Ford
Paul Ricard (F)

12 René Arnoux (F)
Ligier Ford
Paul Ricard (F)

13 Ayrton Senna (BR)
Marlboro McLaren Honda
Paul Ricard (F)

14 Eddie Cheever (USA)
Arrows Ford
Paul Ricard (F)

15 Jonathan Palmer (GB)
Tyrrell Ford
Paul Ricard (F)

16 Stefano Modena (I)
Brabham Judd
Paul Ricard (F)

1

2

1 - 7 Unfall beim Start in Paul Ricard (F): Der
Fahrer Mauricio Gugelmin (BR),
March Judd, bleibt unverletzt und startet
eine 1/2 Stunde später mit seinem
Zweitwagen.

Accident at the start at Paul Ricard (F). Driver Mauricio Gugelmin (BR), March Judd, is unhurt in the accident and is able to start half an hour later with his spare vehicle

Accident au départ de Paul Ricard (F). Le pilote Mauricio Gugelmin (BR), March Judd, reste sain et sauf et démarre une demie-heure plus tard avec sa deuxième voiture

Accidente durante la salida en Paul Ricard (F). El piloto Mauricio Gugelmin (BR), March Judd, queda ileso y sale media hora más tarde en su segundo coche

1

2

1 Alex Caffi (I)
Arrows Ford
Warm - up

Monza (I)

2 Ferrari
Spa - Francorchamps (B)

3

4

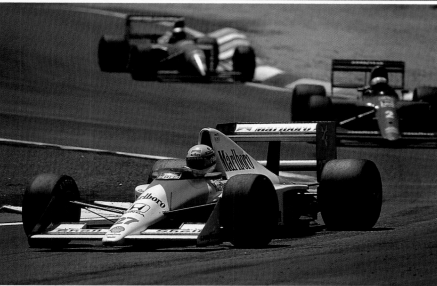

5

3 Gerhard Berger (A)
Marlboro McLaren Honda

beim Abschlußtraining in Monza (I)
during final qualifying practice at Monza (I)
pendant le derniers essais de Monza (I)
durante el fogueo final en Mónza (I)

4 Riccardo Patrese (I)
Williams Renault
Hungaroring (H)

5 Ayrton Senna (BR),
Marlboro McLaren Honda
vor / ahead of / devant / adelante de

Nigel Mansell (GB), Ferrari
und / and / et / y de
Alessandro Nannini (I), Benetton Ford

Paul Ricard (F)

GRAND PRIX

1, 2

3, 4

5

6

7

1   Alessandro Nannini (I)
    Benetton Ford
    Hockenheim (D)

2   Nigel Mansell (GB)
    Ferrari
    Hockenheim (D)

3   Thierry Boutsen (B)
    Williams Renault
    Hockenheim (D)

4   Ayrton Senna (BR)
    Marlboro McLaren Honda
    Hockenheim (D)

5   *Weltmeister / World Champion /
    Champion du monde / Campeón mundial
    1990*

    Ayrton Senna
    Marlboro McLaren Honda
    Jerez (E)

6, 7   *Trainingsunfall
       Accident during practice
       Accident pendant les essais
       Accidente durante el fogueo*

       Martin Donnelly (GB)
       Lotus Lamborghini
       Jerez (E)

8 Thierry Boutsen (B)
Williams Renault
Interlagos (BR)

9 *Riccardo Patrese (I), Williams Renault
überholt innen
Nelson Piquet (BR), Benetton Ford*

Riccardo Patrese (I), Williams Renault,
overtaking Nelson Piquet (BR), Benetton Ford,
on the inside

*Riccardo Patrese (I), Williams Renault,
double Nelson Piquet (BR), Benetton Ford,
par l'intérieur*

*Riccardo Patrese (I), Williams Renault,
sobrepasando por el lado interior a
Nelson Piquet (BR), Benetton Ford*

Monza (I)

10 Alain Prost (F)
Ferrari
Silverstone (GB)

11 Nigel Mansell (GB)
Ferrari
*Pit stop / Arrêt au stand /
Paranda en la jaula*
Spa - Francorchamps (B)

12 Nigel Mansell (GB)
Ferrari
Montreal (CDN)

13 Jean Alesi (F)
Tyrrell Ford
Paul Ricard (F)

GRAND PRIX

Vorherige Seite / Previous page /
Page précédente / Página anterior:

Alain Prost (F)
Ferrari
Paul Ricard (F) 1990

1 Gerhard Berger (A)
   Marlboro McLaren Honda
   Interlagos (BR)

2 Jean Alesi (F)
   Ferrari
   Imola (RSM)

3 Martin Brundle (GB)
   Brabham Yamaha
   Monza (I)

4 - 9 Start in / Start in / Départ de / Salida en
       Imola (RSM)

10

10 Riccardo Patrese (I), Williams Renault

vor / ahead of / devant / delante de
Ayrton Senna (BR), Marlboro McLaren Honda

GRAND PRIX

1 *Ferrari - Mechaniker / Ferrari mechanic /
   Mécanicien de Ferrari / Mecánico de
   Ferrari*
   Phoenix (USA)

2 Alain Prost (F)
   Ferrari
   Hungaroring (H)

3 Mauricio Gugelmin (BR)
   Leyton House March Ilmor
   Estoril (P)

4 Mika Häkkinen (SF)
   Lotus Judd
   Monaco

5 Alex Caffi (I)
   Footwork Porsche
   Monaco

6 Roberto Moreno (BR)
   Benetton Ford
   Monaco

7 JJ. Lehto (SF)
   Dallara Judd
   Monaco

8

9

10

11

12

8, 9 Weltmeister / World Champion /
Champion du monde / Campeón mundial
1991

Ayrton Senna (BR)
Marlboro McLaren Honda
Monaco

10 Der Sieger / The winner /
Vainqueur / Triunfador
Nigel Mansell (GB), Williams Renault

chauffiert / acting as chauffeur to /
sert de chauffeur à / conduciendo a
Ayrton Senna (BR),
Marlboro McLaren Honda

Silverstone (GB)

11 Nigel Mansell (GB), Williams Renault
Ayrton Senna (BR),
Marlboro McLaren Honda

Barcelona (E)

12 Ayrton Senna (BR)
Marlboro McLaren Honda
Monza (I)

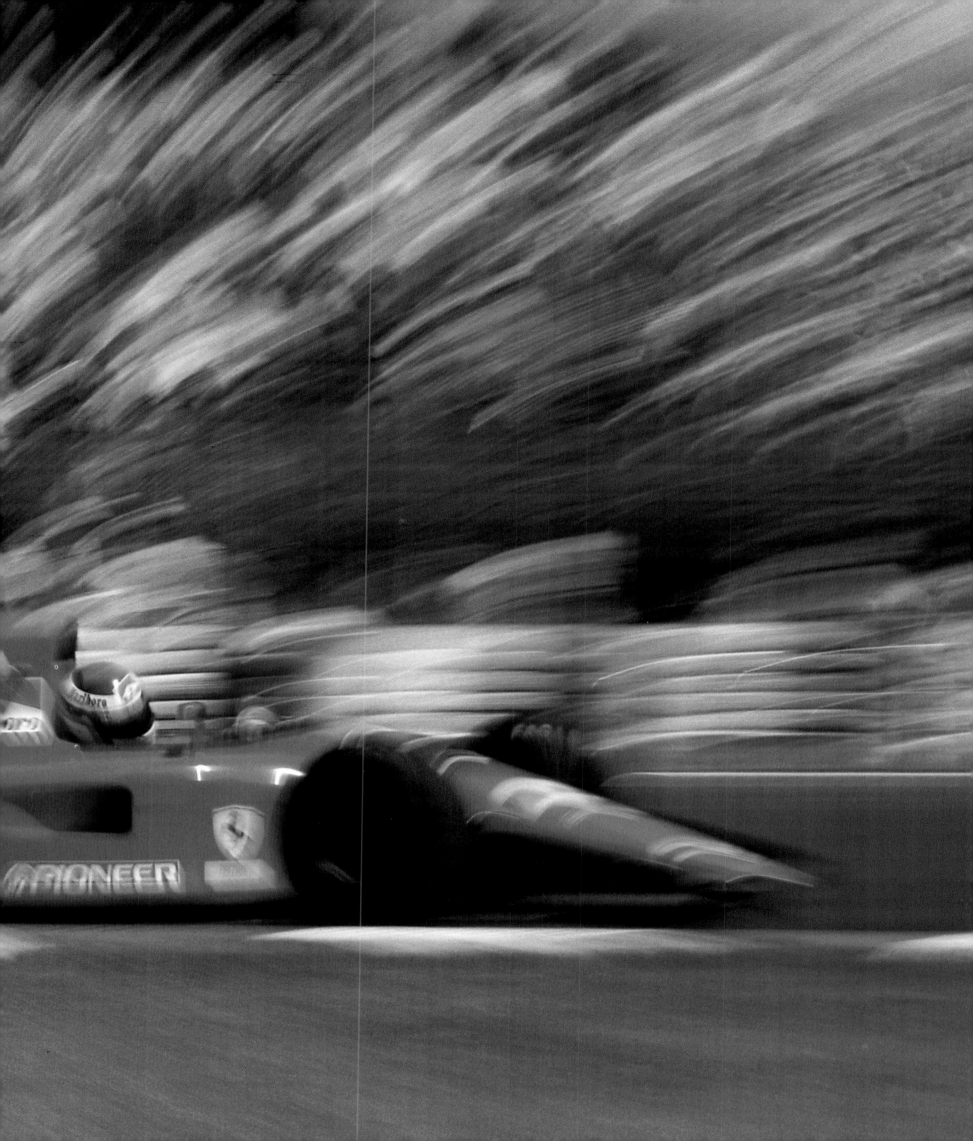

Vorherige Seite / Previous page /
Page précédente / Página anterior:

Jean Alesi (F)
Ferrari
Montreal (CDN) 1991

1 Michael Schumacher (D), Benetton Ford
rammt / ramming / accroche /
embistiendo a

Jean Alesi (F), Ferrari
in der Loews - Kurve / on the Loews corner /
dans la courbe Loews / en la curva Loews

Monaco

2 *Unfall nach dem zweiten Start*
Accident after the restart
Accident après le deuxième départ
Accidente después de la segunda salida

Michael Schumacher (D)
Benetton Ford
Magny - Cours (F)

3 Michael Schumacher (D)
Benetton Ford
Hungaroring (H)

4 *2. Platz / 2nd place /*
2ème place / 2º lugar

Michael Schumacher (D)
Benetton Ford
Barcelona (E)

5

5 Ayrton Senna (BR)
Marlboro McLaren Honda
Parabolica

Monza (I)

1

2

3, 4

5, 6

1 *Start / Start / Départ / Salida*
   Hungaroring (H)

2 Gerhard Berger (A)
   Marlboro McLaren Honda
   Magny - Cours (F)

3 Stefano Modena (I)
   Jordan Yamaha
   Monaco

4 Mika Häkkinen (SF)
   Lotus Ford
   Monaco

5 Ukyo Katayama (J)
   Larrousse - Venturi Lamborghini
   Monaco

6 Gianni Morbidelli (I)
   Minardi Lamborghini
   Monaco

7 *Unfall im Training*
   Accident during practice
   Accident pendant les essais
   Accidente durante el fogueo

   Martin Brundle (GB), Benetton Ford
   Stefano Modena (I), Jordan Yamaha

   Zolder (B)

8 Ayrton Senna (BR), Marlboro McLaren Honda

   Sieger vor / wins ahead of /
   vainqueur devant / triunfador, seguido de
   Nigel Mansell (GB), Williams Renault

   Monaco

9 Jean Alesi (F), Ferrari

   vor / ahead of / devant /delante de
   Ivan Capelli (I), Ferrari

   Barcelona (E)

1

2

3, 4

5, 6

Vorherige Seite / Previous page / Page précédente / Página anterior:

Weltmeister / World Champion / Champion du monde / Campeón mundial 1992

Nigel Mansell (GB)
Williams Renault
Estoril (P) 1992

1 Michael Andretti (USA),
   Marlboro Mclaren Ford
   Alain Prost (F), Williams Renault

   Barcelona (E)

2 Ayrton Senna (BR)
   Marlboro McLaren Ford
   Monaco

3 Michael Andretti (USA)
   Marlboro McLaren Ford
   Montreal (CDN)

4, 5 Andretti und Senna setzen ihre Wagen im Zeittraining nacheinander genau an der gleichen Stelle in die Boxenmauer!

During qualifying practice, Andretti and Senna, one after the other, run their cars into precisely the same section of pit wall!

Pendant les essais chronométrés, Andretti et Senna ont successivement effleurés avec leur voiture le mur du stand exactement au même endroit.

Andretti y Senna topan con sus vehículos consecutivamente contra el mismo sitio del muro de jaulas durante la toma de tiempo.

Imola (RSM)

6 *Sieger von Monaco / Monaco winner / Vainqueur de Monaco / Triunfador de Mónaco*

   Ayrton Senna (BR)
   Marlboro McLaren Ford

7 Alain Prost (F)
Williams Renault
Montreal (CDN)

8 *Start / Start / Départ / Salida*
Montreal (CDN)

9 Damon Hill (GB)
Williams Renault
Barcelona (E)

1   Martin Brundle (GB)
Ligier Renault
Monaco

2   JJ. Lehto (SF)
Sauber Ilmor
Monaco

3   Johnny Herbert (GB)
Lotus Ford
Monaco

4   Fabrizio Barbazza (I)
Minardi Ford
Monaco

5   Karl Wendlinger (A)
Sauber Ilmor
Montreal (CDN)

6   Mark Blundell (GB)
Ligier Renault
Barcelona (E)

7   Michele Alboreto (I)
Luca Badoer (I)
BMS Lola Ferrari

Interlagos (BR)

8 Gerhard Berger (A)
Ferrari
Montreal (CDN)

9 Jean Alesi (F)
Ferrari
Monaco

10 Riccardo Patrese (I)
Benetton Ford
Interlagos (BR)

11 Michael Schumacher (D)
Benetton Ford
Montreal (CDN)

DIE FAHRER 1993-1969

„Die Grand Prix-Piloten von heute müssen jung und hungrig sein", sagte Jim Clark einmal 1963, „die farbigen Charaktere von gestern passen nicht mehr in unser wissenschaftliches Zeitalter." Was sich aus späterer Sicht liest wie eine Kampfansage an die nörgelnden Befürworter der guten alten Zeit, gilt indessen sogar für die Generationen nach seinem mysteriösen Tod in Hockenheim am 7. April 1968 nur bedingt: Selbst Rennfahrer bilden einen repräsentativen Querschnitt durch die menschliche Gesellschaft, ein Panoptikum von Typen mit dem kleinsten gemeinschaftlichen Vielfachen, schneller Auto fahren zu können als andere.

Da finden sich der Brillante und der eher Unbedarfte, wie der Italiener Elio de Angelis, der nach Aussehen, Virtuosität und Manieren auch einen guten Pianisten abgegeben hätte, und sein Landsmann Vittorio Brambilla, den sie den Monza-Gorilla nannten, ausgestattet vor allem mit schmutzigen Fingernägeln sowie dem Talent zu schier unbändiger Freude. Als er als Sieger des Regenrennens in Zeltweg 1975 in unbedachtem Triumph die Arme hochriß, prallte sein March gleich einem Billardball gegen die Leitplanken.

Da gibt es Männer von der brillenhaften Intellektualität des einstigen Ferrari-Piloten und heutigen Journalisten Andrea de Adamich im gleichen Rennen wie den verwegenen Jochen Rindt, dem nur noch Holzbein und schwarze Dayan-Augenklappe fehlten zur völligen Identität mit dem Klischee vom Freibeuter. Selbst das Vorrollen zum Start geriet ihm zum populistischen Auftritt, wenn er schon mal die eine oder andere Pirouette einstreute aus lauter Vergnügen an seinem Handwerk.

Da sind der Komplexe und der Trieb- und Überzeugungstäter: der zehnfache Motorrad-Champion Mike Hailwood, für den der Rennsport immer nur die wichtigste Nebensache der Welt war, und Gilles Villeneuve, der mit dem Wohnmobil anreiste, damit ihm Drum, Dran und Rummel erspart blieben und er sich auf das eine konzentrieren konnte, für das er lebte und starb: Rennen zu fahren. Wenn Hailwood in Chris Barbers Jazzband die Gitarre oder die Klarinette spielte oder zusammen mit Barber und Pat Halcox „Down by the riverside" sang, zeigte er damit andere, viel harmlosere Möglichkeiten seiner Existenz auf. Alles war kompliziert, die Welt im Grunde unbegreiflich und undeutbar, und so weinte er einmal während eines Interviews einfach deshalb, weil das Leben so ist, wie es ist.

Für Villeneuve hingegen, der ausschaute wie ein trotziger Junge, dem sie seinen Roller weggenommen und ein viel gefährlicheres Spielzeug in die Hand gedrückt hatten und der immer schneller fuhr, als es ging, war sein Ferrari alleiniges Medium der Selbstdarstellung. Die Massen spürten das und honorierten es ihm: Sobald der schüchterne kleine Frankokanadier auch nur zu einer Trainingsrunde aufbrach, ging ein Stöhnen um die Piste, in Monza ein Aufschrei.

Die charismatische Persönlichkeit vom Schlage eines Nelson Piquet, der in den Formel 1-Zirkus einen Hauch von glutäugiger Exotik und katzenhafter Geschmeidigkeit einbrachte, versehen mit allen Segnungen üppigen Wohllebens wie Mädchen, Yacht und Lear Jet, ist ebenso ein Teil der Szene wie der redliche Handwerker, Thierry Boutsen etwa oder Derek Warwick, die unbeirrbar ihr Bestes geben.

Da ist Spiel-Raum für den Verspielten à la Hans-Joachim Stuck, jenen Paganini des practical joke, der den bayerischen Jodler auch im Cockpit eines Brabham Alfa möglich und salonfähig machte, den schlitzohrigen Schelm René Arnoux und das Kasperle Arturo Merzario, dürr wie ein Stück Draht und zäh wie ein uraltes Steak. Männer wie das langmähnige Pop-Idol James Hunt, der auch sonst nie etwas anbrennen ließ, der virile Tessiner Clay Regazzoni oder der schöne Pariser Juwelierssohn François Cevert lieferten die verschiedensten Interpretationen zum Thema Playboy ab. Auf Ceverts zeitweilige Lebensgefährtin Brigitte Bardot wartete man in den Fahrerlagern indessen stets vergebens.

Da ist der begnadete Selbstdarsteller Nigel Mansell, stark und wehleidig bis hinunter an die Grenze zur Schmierenkomödie, der die Emotionen der Menge aufzurühren vermag wie niemand sonst, wie auch das Mysterium Carlos Reutemann, später Gouverneur der Provinz Santa Fé in seinem Heimatland Argentinien. Da schlachtet der weltläufige Jackie Stewart, unter dessen sensiblen Händen aber auch wirklich alles zum Pfund Sterling gerät, unermüdlich den Ruhm der frühen Jahre mit levantinischem Geschäftssinn aus, während Mimen-Sohn Paul Belmondo dem Moloch Formel 1 Dollar-Millionen in den Rachen wirft für das dubiose Vergnügen, auf einigen wenigen Grand Prix die dicken Hinterräder der anderen von hinten betrachten zu dürfen.

Da ist die kuriose Laufbahn des Nikolaus Lauda, der sich massiv dagegen sperrt, in irgendeine Schublade gestopft zu werden. Nur ein Partikel aus einer Karriere voller Widersprüche: daß er sechs Wochen nach seinem Feuerunfall am Nürburgring 1976, bereits totgesagt von der Boulevardpresse, in Monza wieder im Rennwagen saß, zum Mythos geworden, aber auch gebrandmarkt fürs Leben. Weitere sechs Wochen später verschleuderte er seine zweite Weltmeisterschaft an James Hunt, als am Mont Fuji auf regennasser Piste kreatürliche Angst sich regte und Lauda nach der zweiten Runde ausstieg.

Da waren die Alten, gereift in den wilden Sechzigern, Denkmäler, die sich im Grunde zu Beginn des neuen Jahrzehnts überlebt hatten. Jack Brabham fand den Absprung 1970 ins Private und ins Management seiner Söhne gerade rechtzeitig. Der stille Australier wurde er genannt, weil er die Zähne nicht auseinander bekam. Aber bei seiner Verabschiedung erhob er sich plötzlich und hielt eine 45minütige witzige Rede, zum Leidwesen derer, die einen einstündigen Film über sein Leben gedreht und 45 Sekunden für seine letzten Worte ausgespart hatten.

Oder der sarkastische Londoner Graham Hill, Botschafter seines Sports, der sich, am Ende seiner Laufbahn zum Statisten geworden, den Spottnamen Tantchen Hill gefallen lassen mußte. Ironie des Schicksals: Im November 1975, neun Monate, nachdem er sich widerstrebend zum Rücktritt durchgerungen hatte, stürzte Hill mit dem Flugzeug ab, ebenso wie 1982 der deutsche Grand Prix-Frührentner Harald Ertl und 1977 der Brasilianer Carlos Pace, der noch viel vorgehabt hatte in seinem Metier.

Oder der einsame Kämpfer John Surtees, in seiner Jugend für alle Big John, später jedoch der Graue Wolf. Was er 1969 begann und 1978 frustriert an den Nagel hängte, hätte er am besten ganz gelassen, nämlich unter die Rennwagenkonstrukteure zu gehen. Vier schnellste Runden waren der kümmerliche Lohn, und noch Jahre später zankte sich der Weltmeister von 1964 gerichtlich mit Sponsoren herum, die nie gezahlt hatten.

Da waren die Damen, die in der Nachfolge der Italienerin Maria Teresa de Filippis zum Ansturm auf die letzte Bastion des männlichen Chauvinismus sich anschickten und enttäuscht wieder davon abließen: die rundliche Lella Lombardi, die wilde Divina Galica, die ehrgeizige Desiré Wilson, die hübsche Giovanna Amati.

Und da ist eine neue Generation von Trägern großer Namen, in dem schwierigen Versuch begriffen, aus dem langen Schlagschatten ihrer Väter herauszutreten: Damon Hill, Michael Andretti, Christian Fittipaldi. Denn die Passion für den Rennsport wird mit dem Erbgut überliefert, manchmal schwächer, manchmal stärker. Begabung und Ambition, Charakterstärke und Furchtlosigkeit gehören dazu. Treffen die Exponenten aufeinander, dann entstehen Spannungen und Konfrontation, ausgefochten mit dem brisantesten aller Sportgeräte, wenn es auch in den letzten Jahren immer robuster geworden ist.

Auch darin zeigten sich Profil und Persönlichkeit: wie der heißblütige Brite Nigel Mansell und der kalte Brasilianer Ayrton Senna 1987 in Spa in feindseliger Eintracht die Strecke verließen, weil beide zur gleichen Zeit die gleiche Linie beansprucht hatten. Oder wie das Handgemenge zwischen Sennas McLaren und Alain Prosts Ferrari beim Grand Prix von Japan 1990 die Weltmeisterschaft zugunsten des halsstarrigen Südamerikaners entschied.

Überhaupt dieser Senna: eine Sphinx, launisch wie eine Eisprinzessin, vielleicht oder sogar sehr wahrscheinlich der Größte von allen spätestens dann, wenn er bei Regen die allerletzten Grenzen des Machbaren aufzeigt. Schon bevor er auf der Pressekonferenz nach jedem Grand Prix mit sanfter Stimme schlüssig den Beweis führt, daß er eigentlich gar nicht hätte gewinnen dürfen, wird sein Umgang mit Rennwagen zur Provokation und zur impertinenten Beweisführung für die Binsenwahrheit, der Bessere sei des Guten Feind.

Rivalität konnte aber auch stiller verlaufen, unter der Oberfläche und dennoch genauso verletzend für den Leidtragenden. Zwar gewann Jackie Stewart den Großen Preis von Deutschland 1973 im überlegenen Tyrrell-Tandem gegen seinen Stallgefährten François Cevert. Aber noch am gleichen Abend vertraute er Teamchef Ken Tyrrell an, der Franzose hätte ihn schlagen können, wenn er nur gewollt hätte. Ein paar Wochen später eskortierte er ihn zur letzten Ruhe, denn Cevert war in Watkins Glen bei einem brutalen Trainingsunfall ums Leben gekommen.

Das Berufsrisiko des Formel 1-Piloten, der potentielle Preis für Glanz, Glamour und Glorie dieses Sports, war hoch in jenen Jahren und droht heute wie damals. Auch Jo Schlesser und Gerhard Mitter mußten ihn zahlen, Piers Courage und Jochen Rindt, Jo Siffert, Roger Williamson, Peter Revson, Helmut Koinigg, Mark Donohue, Tom Pryce, Ronnie Peterson, Patrick Depailler, Gilles Villeneuve, Ricardo Paletti und Elio de Angelis, jung und hungrig auch sie alle im Sinne Jim Clarks. Und farbig — jeder auf seine Art.

THE DRIVERS 1993-1969

"The Grand Prix pilots of today must be young and hungry. Yesterday's colourful characters no longer fit into our scientific age", that is what Jim Clark had to say as early as 1963. But this dictum does not even necessarily go for the driver generations after his mysterious death at Hockenheim on April 7th, 1968. Racing may be a very special microcosm, but its protagonists are a cross-section through human society, with the common denominator that they can drive faster than everybody else and that there is a magnetism and a vitality about them arising from their flirtation with death.

There are the brilliant and the many-sided as well as the dyed-in-the-wool racers, such as the Italian Elio de Angelis, who was also an expert piano player with film star looks, as well as his compatriot Vittorio Brambilla dubbed the "Monza Gorilla", whose oily hands left no doubt regarding his engineering obsession. He was also capable of exuberant joy: When he raised his arms in wild triumph after winning the 1975 Austrian Grand Prix in appalling weather conditions, his March banged into the armco like a billiard ball.

There were men of the scholarly intellectuality of former Ferrari pilot and present journalist Andrea de Adamich in the same race as daring Jochen Rindt, who lacked a wooden leg and a black eye-patch only to answer the image of a buccaneer.

There were the complex and the single-minded: ten times motor bike champion Mike Hailwood, who considered racing as the most important trifle in the world, and Gilles Villeneuve, who withdrew into his motor-home whenever he could to be spared the inevitable razzle-dazzle that accompanies the Grand Prix to concentrate on the one thing he lived and died for – racing. When Hailwood played the guitar or the clarinet in Chris Barber's jazzband or sang "Down by the riverside" with Chris and Pat Halcox, he showed another, much more harmless side to his existence. Things were immensely complicated, the world inscrutable, and so he once wept out of the blue during an interview because life is as it is.

To Villeneuve, however, who always drove beyond the limits of his cars, his Ferrari was the perfect medium of expressing himself. His total commitment made him the darling of the the crowd that groaned spellbound when he only set out for a practice lap.

There is room for charismatic personalities like feline and exotic Nelson Piquet, who is endowed with all the makings of high living such as beautiful girls, luxurious yachts, and Lear Jets, and inconspicuous and reliable craftsmen deliberately keeping a low profile, like Briton Derek Warwick or Belgian Thierry Boutsen as well.

There is scope for the eternal big boy like lanky German Hans-Joachim Stuck, who introduced the Bavarian yodel into the cockpit of a Brabham Alfa, roguish René Arnoux and wiry wag Arturo Merzario, whom possibly nobody ever saw without his cowboy hat. People like long-haired pop idol James Hunt, virile Swiss Clay Regazzoni, and handsome Parisian François Cevert all had their own peculiar ways of interpreting the playboy theme although Cevert's most famous playmate, Brigitte Bardot, failed to turn up in the paddocks, to the dismay of the curious.

There is that highly gifted actor, Nigel Mansell, strong and given to passionately pitying himself, who can stir up the emotions of the throng like nobody else, as well as the enigma Carlos Reutemann, who was to become governor of the province of Santa Fé in his native Argentina after his racing career. There is a man like triple world champion Jackie Stewart, who is still busy exploiting the bonanza of his former fame in many fields, whereas Paul Belmondo, son of actor Jean-Paul, invests millions of dollars in the dubious pleasure of seeing the wide rear wheels of the others vanishing into the distance.

There is the odd curriculum vitae of Nikolaus Lauda so full of incongruities that cannot be reconciled with one another. Six weeks after his fiery Nürburgring accident in 1976 he held up to ridicule whoever had already written his obituary, sitting in a racing car again in Monza. But then he voluntarily retired at Fuji in the rains, handing over the world championship to James Hunt on a silver tray, as it were.

There were the old heroes who had matured in the wild sixties, monuments that had somewhat outlived themselves at the beginning of the new decade. Jack Brabham retired in 1970 just in time to manage his sons' racing careers. He was known as "The Quiet Australian" but during his farewell celebration he suddenly stood up delivering a witty extempore 45-minute speech, which dumbfounded the people who had made a film about his life allowing for 45 seconds to include Brabham's last words.

Never was there a better ambassador of the sport than the sarcastic Londoner, Graham Hill. But in his last racing years he had to put up with the sobriquet of "Auntie Hill" having become an extra where he used to be a leading actor. Such is the irony fate dictates: In November 1975, nine months after he had forced himself to retire, he was killed when his plane crashed, a lot that also befell German journalist turned Grand Prix driver Harald Ertl in 1982 and highly talented Brazilian Carlos Pace in 1977.

There was lonesome warrior John Surtees, in his youth "Big John" for everybody, later "The Gray Wolf". In 1969 he commenced what he should rather have left altogether, namely building his own cars. Apart from Mike Hailwood's Formula Two championship in 1972 four fastest laps were the poor reward, and years after he had given up being a constructor in 1978 the 1964 world champion still sued sponsors who had never paid.

There were the ladies who followed the examples of legendary Czechoslovakian Elizabeth Junek and Italian Maria Teresa de Filippis to tackle the last stronghold of the males, only to capitulate, bitterly disappointed, such as plump Lella Lombardi, wild Divina Galica, ambitious Desiré Wilson, pretty Giovanna Amati.

And there is also a new set of young drivers bearing famous names and trying to carry on where their fathers left, like Damon Hill, Michael Andretti, and Christian Fittipaldi. Obviously the racing bug is handed down from generation to generation, sometimes more so, sometimes less. Talent and ambition as well as intrepidity and a strong character go with it. The skirmishes of the exponents are fought out with the most dangerous of all sports implements, although it has become ever more robust in recent years.

Profile and personality also showed when, in 1987, hot-blooded Briton Nigel Mansell and cool Brazilian Ayrton Senna left the Spa track in hostile harmony because both had laid claim to the same piece of road at the same time. Or when the scuffle between Senna's McLaren and Alain Prost's Ferrari at the Japanese Grand Prix decided the 1990 world championship in favour of the stubborn South American.

That man Senna: a sphinx, whimsical like a primadonna, perhaps the greatest of them all, particularly when it comes to demonstrating the ultimate limits of driving on a wet track. Even when he is playing down winning a race explaining in a soft voice why he ought not to have won at all he is throwing the gauntlet into his competitors' faces.

But rivalries could also smoulder under the surface, equally devastating for the underdog's ego. Jackie Stewart did win the 1973 German Grand Prix in the superior Tyrrell tandem beating his team mate François Cevert to the finish. On the very same evening, however, he intimated to his boss Ken Tyrrell that the Frenchman could have won the race had he only wanted to. A couple of weeks later he escorted Cevert to his grave, the young Parisian having been hacked to pieces in a brutal practice accident at Watkins Glen.

The potential hazard the Formula One pilot has to face is high, threatening then as now in spite of an amazingly long period without casualties. There used to be many: Jo Schlesser, Gerhard Mitter, Piers Courage, Jochen Rindt, Jo Siffert, Roger Williamson, Peter Revson, Helmut Koinigg, Mark Donohue, Tom Pryce, Ronnie Peterson, Patrick Depailler, Gilles Villeneuve, Ricardo Paletti and Elio de Angelis, only to name those who were killed in Grand Prix. All of them were young and hungry complying with Jim Clark's claim. But they were also colourful, each of them in his particular way.

LES PILOTES 1993-1969

«Les pilotes de Grand Prix d'aujourd'hui doivent être jeunes et affamés» a dit un jour Jim Clark en 1963. «Les caractères colorés d'hier ne vont plus dans notre siècle scientifique.» Ce qui, plus tard, se lit comme un communiqué combatif à des adeptes bougons du bon vieux temps n'est même que partiellement valable pour les générations qui suivent sa mort mystérieuse à Hockenheim le 7 avril 1968: même les pilotes de course représentent une tranche représentative de la société humaine, une panoplie de types dont le plus petit commun multiple est de pouvoir rouler plus vite en auto que d'autres.

On trouve là le brillant et le plutôt modeste, tel que l'Italien Elio de Angelis qui aurait tout aussi bien pu faire un bon pianiste si l'on en croit son apparence, sa virtuosité et ses manières, et son compatriote Vittorio Brambilla qu'ils nommaient le gorille de Monza, avec ses ongles sales et son talent à la joie débordante. Alors que vainqueur de la course sous la pluie à Zeltweg en 1975, il levait les bras dans un triomphe insouciant, sa March est venue heurter le parapet comme une balle de billard.

Il y a aussi les hommes d'une intellectualité brillante comme l'ancien pilote de Ferrari et journaliste actuel Andrea de Adamich dans la même course que l'audacieux Jochen Rindt, auquel il ne manquait plus que la jambe de bois et un bandeau sur l'œil à la Dayan pour qu'il s'identifie tout à fait au cliché du brigand. Même quand il roulait jusqu'au départ, cela devenait une scène très populaire quand il semait par-ci par-là une pirouette tellement il prenait plaisir à son métier. Là il y a ceux qui sont complexes et ceux qui font cela d'instinct et qui sont convaincus.

Mike Hailwood, dix fois champion de moto, pour lequel la course n'a toujours été qu'un détail des plus importants du monde et Gilles Villeneuve qui arrivait avec son mobilhome pour qu'on lui épargne tout le tremblement et tout le fourbi et pour pouvoir se concentrer sur ce pour quoi il vivait et il est mort: faire des courses. Quand Hailwood jouait de la guitare ou de la clarinette dans le jazzband de Chris Barber ou chantait avec Barber et Pat Halcox «Down by the riverside», il montrait ainsi d'autres possibilités d'existence bien plus inoffensives. Tout était compliqué, au fond, le monde était incompréhensible et ininterprétable et c'est ainsi qu'il a pleuré, une fois, lors d'une interview, tout simplement parce que sa vie était comme elle était.

Pour Villeneuve, par contre qui ressemblait à un garçon entêté auquel on aurait pris la trottinette et auquel on aurait donné un jouet bien plus dangereux, qui roulait toujours plus vite qu'il ne fallait, sa Ferrari était le seul medium de la représentation de soi. Les masses le sentaient et l'honoraient. Dès que le petit Franco-Canadien timide s'avançait pour un tour d'entraînement, un grand soupir se faisait entendre autour de la piste, à Monza un cri.

La personnalité charismatique d'un Nelson Piquet, qui, dans le cirque de la Formule I, a apporté un souffle d'exotisme avec ses yeux de braise et sa souplesse féline et auquel on a donné toutes les bénédictions d'une belle vie luxueuse avec filles, yachts et Lear Jet, fait tout aussi bien partie de la scène que l'artisan de bonne foi Thierry Boutsen, par exemple, ou Derek Warwick qui font de leur mieux, imperturbablement.

Cela donne du libre jeu à ce joueur de Hans-Joachim Stuck, ce Paganini du «practical joke» qui rendait la tyrolienne bavaroise possible et présentable même dans le cockpit d'une Brabham Alfa. Le malin coquin de René Arnoux et le guignol de Arturo Merzario, sec comme un coup de trique et tenace comme un vieux steak. Des hommes comme l'idole pop à la longue crinière James Hunt qui ne cassait jamais rien, le Tessinois viril Clay Regazzoni ou le beau Parisien et fils de bijoutier François Cevert rendaient les interprétations les plus variées de ce qu'est un playboy. Pourtant, on attendait toujours en vain dans les camps des pilotes la venue de la compagne de Cevert de l'époque, qui était Brigitte Bardot.

Là, il y a Nigel Mansell béni, fort et plaintif jusqu'à la limite du cabotinage et qui était capable, mieux que quiconque, de remuer les émotions de la foule comme personne d'autre, mais aussi le mystère Carlos Reutemann, plus tard gouverneur de la province de Santa Fé dans son pays natal d'Argentine. Là, c'est Jackie Stewart qui parcourt le monde, sous les mains duquel tout, mais alors absolument tout, se transforme en livre sterling, et qui exploite infatigablement la célébrité des années passées avec un sens des affaires levantin, tandis que Paul Belmondo, fils de l'acteur, fait engloutir au colosse de la Formule I des millions de dollars rien que pour le plaisir douteux de pouvoir regarder de derrière les roues arrière des autres, lors de quelques Grands Prix.

Là, c'est la carrière curieuse de Nikolaus Lauda qui s'oppose massivement à ce qu'on le mette dans une catégorie, quelle qu'elle soit Seulement une particule tirée de sa carrière pleine de contradictions: six semaines après son accident où il a été brûlé sur le Nürburgring en 1976, lui, dont la presse de boulevard avait annoncé la mort, se retrouve au volant d'une voiture de course à Monza, il est devenu un mythe mais aussi stigmatisé pour la vie. Six semaines plus tard, il brade son deuxième championnat du monde à James Hunt, quand, au Mont Fuji, sur une piste mouillée, une grande peur s'empare de lui et que Lauda sort de sa voiture après deux tours.

Là, il y avait les vieux, mûris dans les années sauvages, les années 60, monuments qui, au fond, s'étaient survécus au début de la nouvelle décennie. C'est en 1970 que Jack Brabham a réussi à faire le saut dans le privé et dans la direction de ses fils, juste à temps. On le nommait l'Australien tranquille parce qu'il ne desserrait pas les dents. Mais, quand il a pris congé, il s'est levé tout à coup et a tenu un discours très drôle pendant 45 minutes, au grand regret de ceux qui avaient tourné un film de sa vie pendant une heure et qui n'avaient gardé que 45 secondes pour ses dernières paroles.

Ou encore le Londonien sarcastique Graham Hill, ambassadeur de son sport, qui, à la fin de sa carrière, était devenu figurant et qui devait supporter le sobriquet de «Auntie Hill». Ironie du sort: en novembre 1975, neuf mois après s'être enfin décidé à se retirer à contre-cœur, Hill s'est écrasé en avion, tout comme en 1982, le préretraité du Grand Prix allemand Harald Ertl et, en 1977, le Brésilien Carlos Pace, qui avait encore beaucoup de projets dans son métier.

Ou le combattant solitaire John Surtees, dans sa jeunesse Big John pour tous, et plus tard pourtant nommé le loup gris. Ce qu'il a commencé en 1969 et ce qu'il a abandonné frustré, en 1978, c'est-à-dire faire partie des constructeurs de voitures, il aurait bien dû le laisser où c'était. Les quatre tours les plus rapides, c'est là le pauvre salaire et des années plus tard encore, le champion du monde de 1964 se disputait encore en justice avec des sponsors qui n'avaient jamais payé.

Il y avait les dames qui, à la suite de l'Italienne Maria Teresa de Filippis, se préparaient à l'attaque du dernier bastion du chauvinisme masculin et qui devaient laisser tomber avec déception: la ronde Lella Lombardi, la sauvage Divina Galica, l'ambitieuse Désiré Wilson, la jolie Giovanna Amati.

Et il y a là des porteurs de grands noms qui se démènent avec difficulté pour sortir de l'ombre que leur font leurs pères. Damon Hill, Michael Andretti, Christian Fittipaldi. Car la passion du sport automobile est héréditaire, quelquefois faiblement, quelquefois fortement. Le don et l'ambition, la force de caractère et la hardiesse en font partie. Si les protagonistes se rencontrent, il y a alors des tensions et des confrontations, combattues avec le plus explosif outil sportif, même s'il est devenu de plus en plus robuste au cours des dernières années.

Là aussi sont apparus le profil et la personnalité: comme le Britannique fougueux Nigel Mansell et le froid Brésilien Ayrton Senna, en 1987 à Spa, qui quittèrent le parcours dans un accord hostile parce que tous les deux avaient voulu arriver sur la même ligne en même temps. Ou encore la mêlée entre la McLaren de Senna et la Ferrari d'Alain Prost au Grand Prix du Japon en 1990, où le championnat du monde s'est décidé en faveur du Sud-Américain obstiné.

Justement parlons-en de ce Senna: un sphynx, lunatique comme une princesse, peut-être ou même très vraisemblablement le plus grand de tous, au plus tard quand il montre par temps de pluie les toutes dernières limites du faisable. Déjà avant qu'il ne prouve d'une voix douce par A plus B après chaque Grand Prix, lors de la conférence de presse, qu'il n'aurait en fait pas dû gagner, sa façon d'être avec les voitures de course devient une provocation et la preuve impertinente que le mieux est l'ennemi du bien.

Mais les rivalités pouvaient se passer aussi plus tranquillement, sous la surface et pourtant de façon tout aussi blessante pour celui qui devait en souffrir. Certes, Jackie Stewart a gagné le Grand Prix d'Allemagne en 1973 dans le tandem Tyrrell supérieur, contre son compagnon d'écurie François Cevert. Mais, le même soir, il confiait au chef d'équipe Ken Tyrrell que le Français aurait pu le battre s'il avait vraiment voulu. Quelques semaines plus tard, il l'escortait à son dernier repos car Cevert était décédé dans un brutal accident d'entraînement à Watkins Glen.

Le risque du métier des pilotes de Formule I, le prix potentiel pour le faste, le glamour et la gloire de ce sport, a été élevé dans ces années-là et l'est encore aujourd'hui. Jo Schlesser et Gerhard Mitter ont dû le payer eux aussi, Piers Courage et Jochen Rindt, Jo Siffert, Roger Williamson, Peter Revson, Helmut Koinigg, Mark Donohue, Tom Pryce, Ronnie Peterson, Patrick Depailler, Gilles Villeneuve, Ricardo Paletti et Elio de Angelis, jeunes et affamés, ils l'étaient tous, dans le sens de Jim Clarks. Et colorés – chacun à sa façon.

LOS PILOTOS 1993-1969

«Los pilotos de Grand Prix de hoy tienen que ser jóvenes y hambrientos», dijo Jim Clark en una ocasión en 1963. «Los caracteres variopintos de ayer ya no encajan en nuestra época científica». Lo que retrospectivamente parece una declaración de guerra a los refunfuñones patrocinadores del buen-tiempo-pasado, es entretanto válido, si bien sólo en parte, incluso para las generaciones posteriores a su misteriosa muerte en Hockenheim el 7 de abril de 1968: incluso los corredores constituyen una sección representativa de la sociedad humana, un panóptico de tipos con el mínimo común múltiplo de poder conducir más rápido que otros.

Aquí se reúnen el brillante y el más bien inofensivo, como el italiano Elio de Angelis, que, por su aspecto, virtuosidad y modales, hubiera llegado a ser un buen pianista; y su compatriota Vittorio Brambilla, al que llamaban el gorila de Monza, caracterizado esencialmente por las uñas sucias y por su capacidad de alegría pura y desfrenada. Cuando en 1975 en el Zeltweg salió vencedor de una carrera pasada por agua levantó irreflexivamente los brazos para proclamar su triunfo y su March se batió contra el guardarraíl como una bola de billar.

Hay hombres de intelectualismo gafoso como el otrora piloto de Ferrari, hoy periodista Andrea de Adamich, que había pilotado en la mis-ma carrera que el temerario Jochen Rindt, al que sólo le faltaban una pata de palo y un parche negro a la Moshe Dayán en el ojo para que le confundieran con el clisé de un pirata. Incluso del rodamiento previo a la salida hacía una entrada populista cuando intercalaba ya una que otra pirueta, de puro gusto por el oficio.

También tenemos al complejo y al impulsivo y bandido por convicción: el diez veces campeón de motociclismo Mike Hailwood, para quien el automovilismo era la bagatela más importante del mundo; y Gilles Villeneuve, que venía siempre con su *motor-home* para ahorrarse complicaciones y baraúndas y poder concentrarse en lo único que le interesaba, por lo que vivió y murió: correr en las carreras. Cuando Hailwood tocaba el clarinete o la guitarra en la Chris Barber Jazzband, o cuando cantaba «Down by the riverside» con Barber y Pat Halcox hacía exhibición de otras posibilidades, mucho más inofensivas, de su existencia. Todo era complicado, el mundo era en realidad incomprensible e indefinible, y una vez llegó a llorar durante una entrevista simplemente porque la vida es como es.

Para Villeneuve, por el contrario, que tenía el aspecto de un niño obstinado al que le han quitado el monopatín y, a cambio, le han dado un juguete mucho más peligroso; para él, que conducía siempre más rápido de lo que era posible, su Ferrari era el único medio de exponerse a sí mismo. Las masas lo sentían y le rendían honores por ello: tan pronto el pequeño francocanadiense hacía una vuelta de entrenamiento se llenaba de suspiros el circuito, de gritos si era el de Monza.

La carismática personalidad del corte de un Nelson Piquet, que había introducido en el circo de la Fórmula 1 un soplo de exotismo de mirada ardiente y elasticidad gatuna, abastecido con todas las bendiciones del suntuoso bienvivir —como mujeres, yate y Lear Jet— es tan parte de la escena como el honrado trabajador, como un Thierry Boutsen o un Derek Warwick, que dan impertérritos lo mejor de sí.

También hay sitio para el juguetón Hans-Joachim Stuck, aquel Paganini del chiste práctico que hacía posible y presentable el canto a la tirolesa incluso montado en el *cockpit* de su Brabham Alfa; para el taimado pícaro René Arnoux y para el payaso Arturo Merzario, flaco como un alambre y correoso como un bistec vetusto. Hombres como el melenudo *pop-idol* James Hunt, que por otra parte nunca renunciaba a nada; el viril Tessiner Clay Regazzoni o el hermoso hijo de un joyero parisino, François Cevert, aportaron las más diversas interpretaciones del tema playboy. Brigitte Bardot, por un tiempo compañera de Cevert, era siempre esperada, siempre en vano, en los *paddocks*.

Tenemos también al aventajado exibicionista Nigel Mansell, fuerte y quejica hasta tal extremo que parece un mal actor, uno capaz de agitar las emociones de las masas como nadie; y no olvidemos al misterioso Carlos Reutemann, que más tarde sería gobernador de la provincia de Santa Fé en su patria Argentina. Y el mundano Jackie Stewart, bajo cuyas sensibles manos todo se convierte en libras esterlinas, que descuartiza incansable la fama de los primeros años con un espíritu comercial levantino, mientras que Paul Belmondo —el hijo del actor— arroja millones de dólares a las fauces del Moloch Fórmula 1 por el dudoso placer de poder ver por detrás los anchos neumáticos de los demás en algunos —muy pocos— Grand Prix.

Y la curiosa carrera de Nikolaus Lauda, que se revela con todas sus fuerzas a ser archivado en algún cajón. Sólo una partícula de una carrera llena de contradicciones: seis semanas después de su accidente con fuego en el Nürburgring de 1976, ya dado por muerto por la prensa sensacionalista, se presenta en Monza sentado en su coche de carreras, convertido ya en mito, pero también marcado por el fuego para el resto de su vida. Otras seis semanas más tarde regaló su segundo Campeonato Mundial a James Hunt, cuando en el Mont Fuji se agitó un miedo sobrenatural sobre el circuito mojado y Lauda abandonó tras la segunda vuelta.

No olvidemos tampoco a los viejos monumentos madurados en los salvajes años sesenta que, en principio, se habían sobrevivido a sí mismos a comienzos de la nueva década. Jack Brabham dio en 1970, justo a tiempo, el salto a la vida privada y al *management* de sus hijos. Se le nombraba el silencioso australiano porque no despegaba los labios. Pero en su despedida se levantó de improviso y sostuvo un gracioso discurso de 45 minutos, para desgracia del equipo que había filmado para un programa de una hora sobre su vida y reservado 45 segundos para sus últimas palabras.

O el sarcástico inglés Graham Hill, mensajero de su deporte que, convertido en figurante al final de su carrera, tuvo que soportar el mote de tía Hill. Ironía del destino: en noviembre de 1975, diez meses después de haberse decidido de mala gana y tras larga lucha interior a abandonar, Hill sufrió un accidente de avión, al igual que en 1982 Harald Ertl, jubilado anticipado del Grand Prix, y en 1977 el brasileño Carlos Pace, al que todavía le quedaba mucho por hacer en su profesión.

O el luchador solitario John Surtees, de joven Big John para todos, más tarde el Lobo Gris. Lo que empezó en 1969 y abandonó, frustrado, en 1978, bien podía habérselo ahorrado: incorporarse a las filas de constructores de coches de carreras. Cuatro vueltas en primera línea fueron el raquítico resultado y todavía cuatro años más tarde querellaba en los tribunales el Campeón Mundial de 1964 con los patrocinadores que no habían pagado nunca.

Hablemos también de las damas que, siguiendo el ejemplo de la italiana Maria Teresa de Filippis, se mostraban dispuestas a asaltar el último bastión del chauvinismo masculino, y abandonaban decepcionadas: la redondita Lella Lombardi, la salvaje Divina Galica, la ambiciosa Desiré Wilson, la hermosa Giovanna Amati.

Hay asimismo una nueva generación portadora de grandes nombres, una generación dominada por el difícil propósito de salir de la sombra de sus padres: Damon Hill, Michael Andretti, Christian Fittipaldi. Pues la pasión por las carreras automovilísticas es hereditaria, si bien no siempre con el mismo grado de intensidad. Talento y ambición, fortaleza de carácter e intrepidez son inherentes a esta pasión. Si los exponentes se encuentran, surgen tensiones y confrontaciones que se zanjan con el más explosivo de todos los instrumentos deportivos, si bien en los últimos años se ha ido robusteciendo cada vez más.

También aquí se ponen en evidencia perfil y personalidad: como cuando el sangre caliente británico Nigel Mansell y el frío brasileño Ayrton Senna abandonaron en hostil discordia el circuito en 1987, en Spa, porque ambos habían reivindicado al mismo tiempo la misma trayectoria. O como cuando el cuerpo a cuerpo entre el McLaren de Senna y el Ferrari de Alain Prost en el Grand Prix de Japón de 1990 acabó fallando el Campeonato Mundial en favor del contumaz sudamericano.

Así es este Senna: una esfinge, caprichosa como una princesa del hielo, quizás —o sin quizás— el más grande de todos, por lo menos cuando presenta sobre mojado los límites más extremos de lo posible. Ya antes de demostrar con voz suave, al término de aquel Grand Prix, que él no debiera haber ganado, manejaba su coche de carreras con provocación y demostraciones de impertinencia por la perogrullada de que el mejor es enemigo de la indulgencia.

La rivalidad también podía transcurrir más silenciosamente bajo la superficie, pero igual de hiriente para el perjudicado. Cierto que Jackie Stewart ganó el Gran Premio de Alemania en 1973 en tándem de superioridad con Tyrrell contra su contrincante de acero François Cevert. Pero ya en la misma tarde confesó a su jefe de equipo Ken Tyrrell que el francés podía haber vencido si hubiera querido. Dos semanas más tarde, Stewart escoltaba a Cevert a su último reposo, pues éste había perdido la vida en un brutal accidente de entrenamiento en Watkins Glen.

El riesgo profesional de los pilotos de Fórmula 1, el precio potencial del esplendor, el *glamour* y la gloria de este deporte, era elevado en aquellos años, y es hoy tan amenazante como entonces. Un precio que también tuvieron que pagar Jo Schlesser y Gerhard Mitter, Piers Courage y Jochen Rindt, Jo Siffert, Roger Williamson, Peter Revson, Helmut Koinigg, Mark Donohue, Tom Pryce, Ronnie Peterson, Patrick Depailler, Gilles Villeneuve, Ricardo Paletti y Elio de Angelis, todos ellos jóvenes y hambrientos en el sentido de Jim Clark. Y variopintos, cada uno a su manera.

DRIVERS

2, 3

1 Jean Alesi (F)
Ferrari
Barcelona (E)

2 Gerhard Berger (A)
Ferrari
Donington (GB)

3 Karl Wendlinger (A)
Sauber Ilmor
Interlagos (BR)

4 Rubens Barrichello (BR)
Jordan Hart
Kyalami (ZA)

5 Fabrizio Barbazza (I), Minardi Ford
Luca Badoer (I), BMS Lola Ferrari

Kyalami (ZA)

6 Derek Warwick (GB),
Footwork Mugen - Honda
Martin Brundle (GB), Ligier Renault
Mark Blundell (GB), Ligier Renault

Montreal (CDN)

7 *Siegerehrung / Presentation ceremony /
Remise des prix / Homenaje a los Triunfadores:*
1. Ayrton Senna (BR), Marlboro McLaren Ford
2. Damon Hill (GB), Williams Renault
3. Michael Schumacher (D), Benetton Ford

Juan - Manuel Fangio (ARG) *gratuliert /
congratulates / félicite / felicitando a*

Ron Dennis (GB), *Team - Director McLaren /
McLaren team boss / directeur d'équipe
McLaren / director del equipo McLaren*

Interlagos (BR)

8, 9

10, 11

13

14

15

8   JJ. Lehto (SF)
    Sauber Ilmor
    Monaco

9   Christian Fittipaldi (BR)
    Minardi Ford
    Monaco

10 Riccardo Patrese (I)
    Benetton Ford
    Kyalami (ZA)

11 Michael Andretti (USA)
    Marlboro McLaren Ford
    Barcelona (E)

12 Michael Schumacher (D)
    Benetton Ford
    Barcelona (E)

13 Alain Prost (F)
    Williams Renault
    Interlagos (BR)

14 Damon Hill (GB)
    Williams Renault
    Interlagos (BR)

15 *Gruppenbild zum Saisonanfang /
    Start of season group photo /
    Photo de groupe au début de la saison /
    Fotografía en grupo al comienzo de la
    temporada*

    Kyalami (ZA)

DRIVERS

1   Martin Brundle (GB)
Benetton Ford
Monaco

2   Riccardo Patrese (I)
Williams Renault
Montreal (CDN)

3   Alain Prost (F)

*TV - Kommentator / TV commentator /
commentateur de télévision /
comentador de televisión*

Spa - Francorchamps (B)

4   Ukyo Katayama (J)
Larrousse - Venturi Lamborghini
Kyalami (ZA)

5   Ivan Capelli (I)
Ferrari
Barcelona (E)

6   Thierry Boutsen (B), Ligier Renault
Andrea de Cesaris (I), Tyrrell Ilmor

Monza (I)

7   Giovanna Amati (I)
Brabham Judd
Kyalami (ZA)

8   Christian Fittipaldi (BR)
Minardi Lamborghini
Spa - Francorchamps (B)

9   Karl Wendlinger (A)
March Ilmor
Kyalami (ZA)

10   Jean Alesi (F)
Ferrari
Imola (RSM)

11 Ayrton Senna (BR),
Marlboro McLaren Honda
(Sieger / winner / vainqueur / triunfador)

Weltmeister / World Champion /
Champion du monde / Campeón mundial
Nigel Mansell (GB), Williams Renault
(Zweiter / second / deuxième / segundo)

Gerhard Berger (A),
Marlboro McLaren Honda
(Dritter / third / troisième / tercero)

Hungaroring (H)

12 Michael Schumacher (D)
Benetton Ford
Kyalami (ZA)

13 *Weltmeister / World Champion /*
Champion du monde / Campeón mundial

Nigel Mansell (GB)
Williams Renault
Kyalami (ZA)

DRIVERS

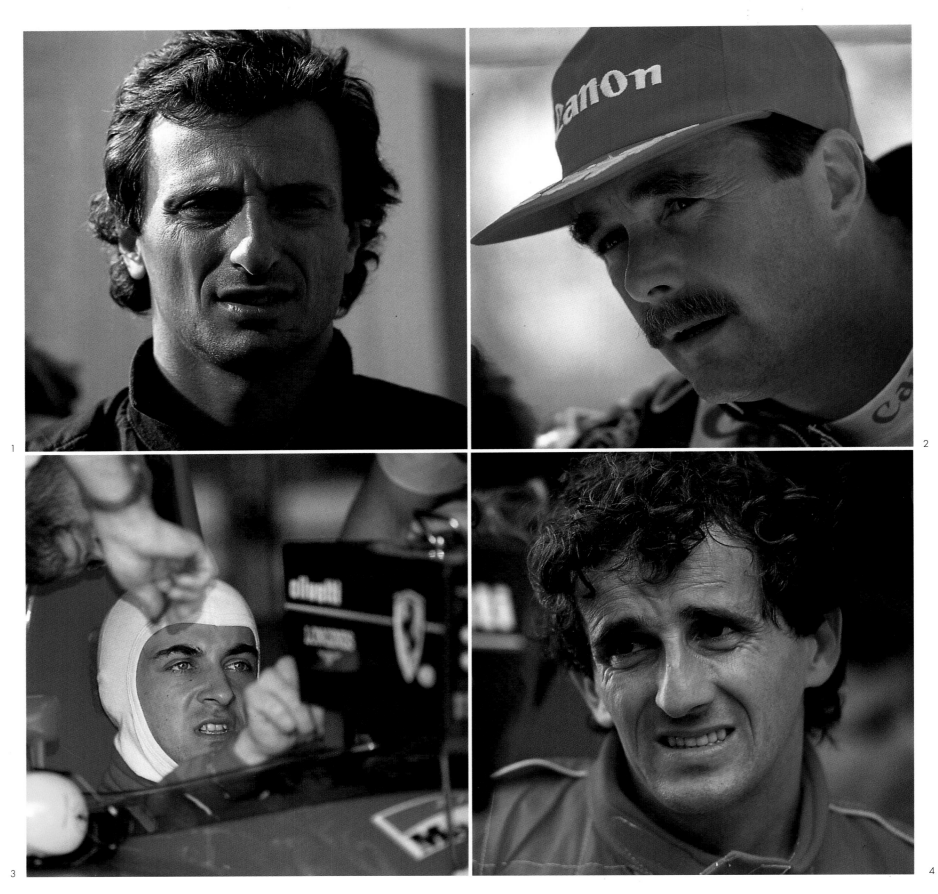

1 Riccardo Patrese (I)
Williams Renault
Spa - Francorchamps (B)

2 Nigel Mansell (GB)
Williams Renault
Magny - Cours (F)

3 Jean Alesi (F)
Ferrari
Phoenix (USA)

4 Alain Prost (F)
Ferrari
Estoril (P)

5 Mika Häkkinen (SF)
Lotus Judd
Magny - Cours (F)

6 JJ. Lehto (SF)
Dallara Judd
Magny - Cours (F)

7 Nelson Piquet (BR)
Benetton Ford
Interlagos (BR)

5

6

7

8

10

11

8 *Weltmeister / World Champion /*
   Champion du monde / Campeón mundial
   1991
   Ayrton Senna (BR), Marlboro McLaren Honda

   wird mit Champagner geduscht von
   is showered with champagne by
   est arrosé au champagne par
   recibiendo una ducha de champaña de
   Ron Dennis (GB), McLaren Team - Direktor /
   McLaren team boss / directeur de l'équipe
   McLaren / director del equipo McLaren

   Phoenix (USA)

9 Michael Schumacher (D)
   Benetton Ford
   Estoril (P)

10 *Weltmeister / World Champion /*
   Champion du monde / Campeón mundial
   Ayrton Senna (BR),
   Marlboro McLaren Honda

   Gerhard Berger (A),
   Marlboro McLaren Honda

   Interlagos (BR)

11 Gerhard Berger (A)
   Marlboro McLaren Honda
   Montreal (CDN)

DRIVERS

1 Martin Donnelly (GB)
Lotus Lamborghini
Phoenix (USA)

2 Jean Alesi (F)
Tyrrell Ford
Interlagos (BR)

3 Nelson Piquet (BR)
Benetton Ford
Interlagos (BR)

4 Alessandro Nannini (I)
Benetton Ford
Jerez (E)

5 Riccardo Patrese (I)
Williams Renault
Hockenheim (D)

6 Thierry Boutsen (B)
Williams Renault
Silverstone (GB)

7 Aguri Suzuki (J)
Lola Lamborghini
Silverstone (GB)

8 Satoru Nakajima (J)
Tyrrell Ford
Silverstone (GB)

9 Alex Caffi (I)
Arrows Ford
Hungaroring (H)

10 Stefan Johansson (S)
Onyx Ford
Phoenix (USA)

11 Alain Prost (F), Ferrari
Jackie Stewart (GB)

*beide 3 - fache Weltmeister /
both three - times world champion /
tous les deux trois fois champion du
monde /
ambos triple campeón mundial*

Phoenix (USA)

12 *Weltmeister / World Champion /
Champion du monde / Campeon mundial
1990*

Ayrton Senna (BR)
Marlboro McLaren Honda
Hockenheim (D)

13 Gerhard Berger (A)
Marlboro McLaren Honda
Silverstone (GB)

14 Nigel Mansell (GB), Ferrari
Ayrton Senna (BR),
Marlboro McLaren Honda

Estoril (P)

DRIVERS

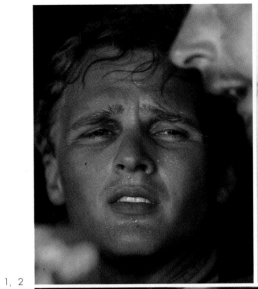

1   Johnny Herbert (GB)
    Benetton Ford
    Jacarepagua (BR)

2   Jean Alesi (F)
    Tyrrell Ford
    Monza (I)

3   Derek Warwick (GB)
    Arrows Ford
    Monaco

4   Stefano Modena (I)
    Brabham Judd
    Silverstone (GB)

5   Gerhard Berger (A)
    Ferrari
    Jacarepagua (BR)

6   Volker Weidler (D)
    Rial Ford
    Jacarepagua (BR)

7   Bernd Schneider (D)
    Zakspeed
    Jacarepagua (BR)

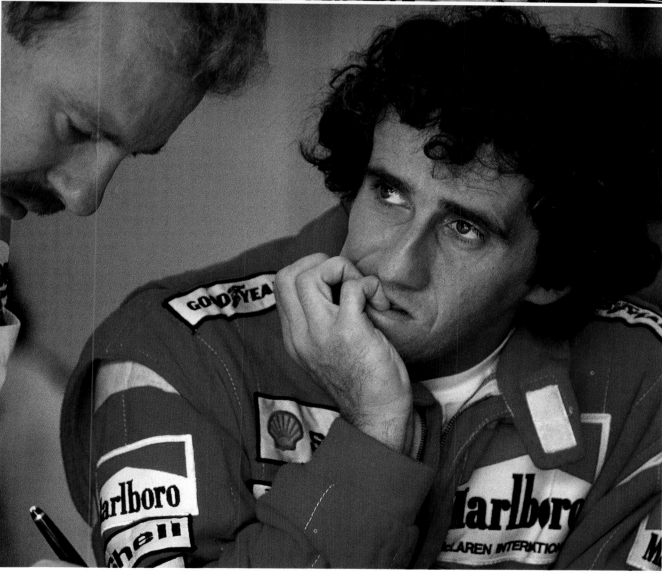

8 Ayrton Senna (BR)
Marlboro McLaren Honda
Jerez (E)

9 Riccardo Patrese (I)
Williams Renault
Silverstone (GB)

10 Nigel Mansell (GB)
Ferrari
Jacarepagua (BR)

11 *Weltmeister / World Champion/*
Champion du monde / Campeón mundial
1989

Alain Prost (F)
Marlboro McLaren Honda
Hungaroring (H)

DRIVERS

1, 2

4, 5

3

6

7

1 Thierry Boutsen (B)
   Benetton Ford
   Imola (RSM)

2 Michele Alboreto (I)
   Ferrari
   Monaco

3 Nelson Piquet (BR)
   Lotus Honda
   Monaco

4 Piercarlo Ghinzani (I)
   Bernd Schneider (D)
   Zakspeed

   Monaco

5 Stefan Johansson (S)
   René Arnoux (F)
   Ligier Judd

   Hungaroring (H)

6 Gerhard Berger (A)
   Ferrari
   Monaco

7 Alessandro Nannini (I)
   Benetton Ford
   Monaco

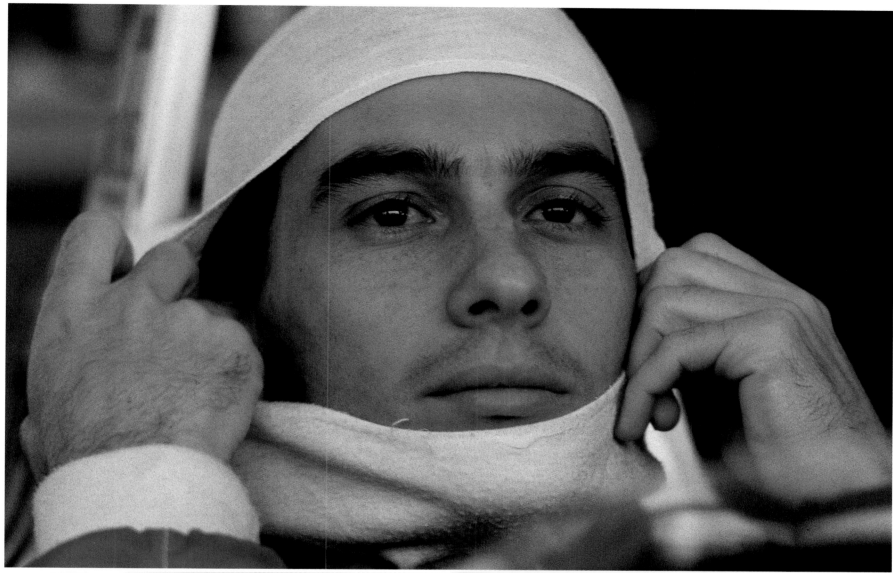

8 *Weltmeister / World Champion /*
Champion du monde / Campeón mundial
1988

Ayrton Senna (BR)
Marlboro McLaren Honda
Jerez (E)

9 Nigel Mansell (GB)
Riccardo Patrese (I)
Williams Judd

Jacarepagua (BR)

10 Alain Prost (F)
Marlboro McLaren Honda
Jacarepagua (BR)

1   Thierry Boutsen (B)
Benetton Ford
Silverstone (GB)

2   Martin Brundle (GB)
Zakspeed
Silverstone (GB)

3   Christian Danner (D)
Zakspeed
Monza (I)

4   Gerhard Berger (A)
Ferrari
Paul Ricard (F)

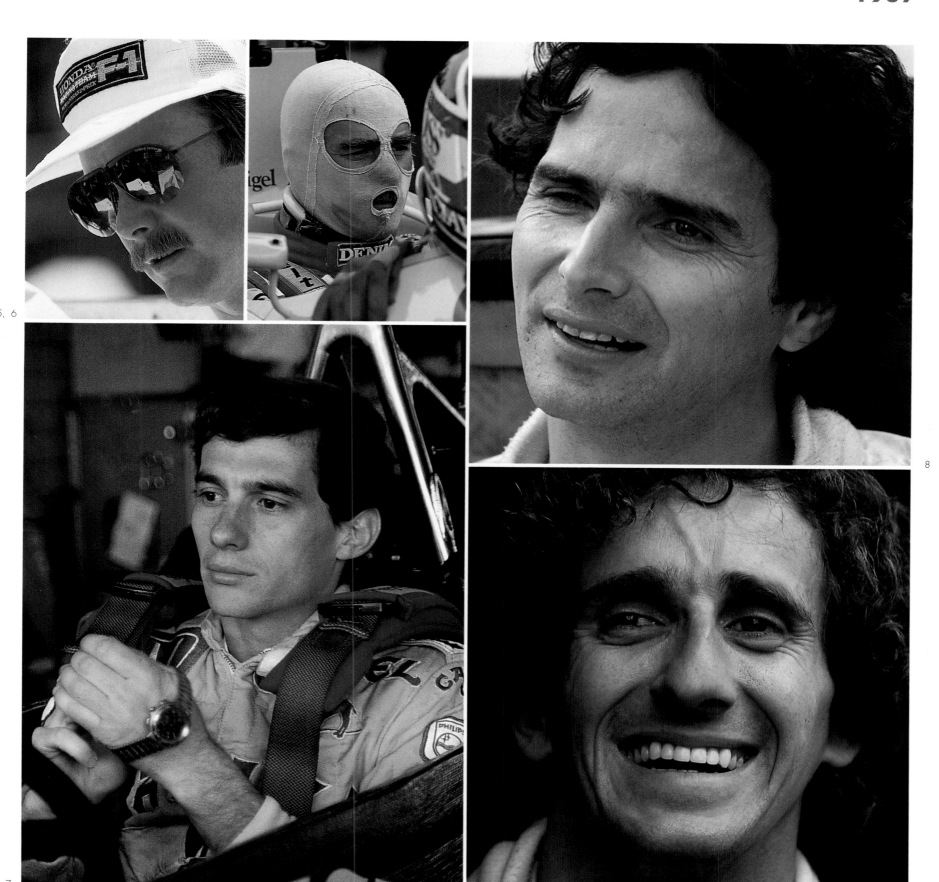

5   Nigel Mansell (GB)
    Williams Honda
    Monaco

6   Nigel Mansell (GB)
    Williams Honda
    Jerez (E)

7   Ayrton Senna (BR)
    Lotus Honda
    Zeltweg (A)

8   *Weltmeister / World Champion /*
    Champion du monde / Campeón mundial
    1987

    Nelson Piquet (BR)
    Williams Honda
    Monaco

9   Alain Prost (F)
    Marlboro McLaren TAG Porsche
    Imola (RSM)

DRIVERS

1   Jody Scheckter (ZA)
    TV Kommentator / TV commentator /
    commentateur de télévision /
    comentador de televisión

    Monaco

2   Jackie Stewart (GB)
    mit seinem Sohn Paul / with his son Paul /
    avec son fils Paul / con su hijo Paul

    Hungaroring (H)

3   Nelson Piquet (BR)
    Canon Williams Honda
    Hungaroring (H)

4   Stefan Johansson (S)
    Ferrari
    Brands Hatch (GB)

5   Nigel Mansell (GB)
    Canon Williams Honda
    Monza (I)

6   Theo Fabi (I)
    Benetton BMW
    Monza (I)

7   John Surtees (GB)
    Brands Hatch (GB)

8   Dan Gurney (USA)
    Hungaroring (H)

9   Stirling Moss (GB)
    Hungaroring (H)

10 Ayrton Senna (BR)
    JPS Lotus Renault
    Monza (I)

11 Christian Danner (D)
    Arrows BMW
    Paul Ricard (F)

12 Keke Rosberg (SF)
    Marlboro McLaren TAG Porsche
    Monaco

13 Jacques Laffite (F)
Ligier Renault
Paul Ricard (F)

14 Innes Ireland (GB)
Imola (RSM)

15 Elio de Angelis (I), Brabham BMW
Nigel Mansell (GB),
Canon Williams Honda

Jerez (E)

16 Marc Surer (CH)
Benetton BMW
Monaco

17 *Weltmeister / World Champion /*
Champion du monde / Campeón mundial
1986

Alain Prost (F)
Marlboro McLaren TAG Porsche
Paul Ricard (F)

18 Gerhard Berger (A)
Benetton BMW
Hockenheimring (D)

19 Team Williams
Nigel Mansell (GB)
Nelson Piquet (BR)
Canon Williams Honda

Imola (RSM)

20 Alain Prost (F)
Marlboro McLaren TAG Porsche
Hungaroring (H)

nach seinem Ausfall
after retiring from the race
aprés avoir abandonné la course
después de abandonar la carrera

DRIVERS

1, 2

3, 4

6, 7

8, 9

5

10, 11

12,

1   Thierry Boutsen (B)
    Arrows BMW
    Monaco

2   Gerhard Berger (A)
    Arrows BMW
    Monaco

3   Keke Rosberg (SF)
    Canon Williams Honda
    Monaco

4   Michele Alboreto (I)
    Ferrari
    Monza (I)

5   Ayrton Senna (BR)
    Lotus Renault
    Estoril (P)

6   Jonathan Palmer (GB)
    Zakspeed
    Estoril (P)

7   Stefan Johansson (S)
    Ferrari
    Estoril (P)

8   Stefan Bellof (D)
    Tyrrell Renault
    Spa - Francorchamps (B)

9   Manfred Winkelhock (D)
    Philippe Alliot (F)
    Skoal - Bandit RAM

    Estoril (P)

10 Elio de Angelis (I)
    Lotus Renault
    Estoril (P)

11 Patrick Tambay (F)
    Renault Elf
    Estoril (P)

12 Nelson Piquet (BR)
    Brabham BMW
    Zandvoort (NL)

14

13 Niki Lauda (A)
     Marlboro McLaren TAG Porsche
     Monaco

14 *Weltmeister / World Champion /*
     Champion du monde / Campeón mundial
     1985

     Alain Prost (F)
     Marlboro McLaren TAG Porsche
     Zandvoort (NL)

DRIVERS

3, 4

6

1, 2

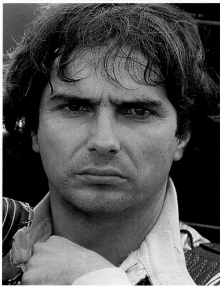

5

7, 8

1 Clay Regazzoni (CH)

Journalist / journalist / journaliste / periodista

Monza (I)

2 Stefan Bellof (D)
Tyrrell Ford
Dijon - Prenois (F)

3 Michele Alboreto (I)
Ferrari
Monza (I)

4 Keke Rosberg (SF)
Saudia Williams Honda
Monza (I)

5 Stefan Bellof (D)
Tyrrell Ford
Monaco

6 Manfred Winkelhock (D), ATS BMW
Derek Warwick (GB), Renault Elf

Zandvoort (NL)

7 Ayrton Senna (BR)
Toleman Hart
Zandvoort (NL)

8 Nelson Piquet (BR)
Brabham BMW
Brands Hatch (GB)

9

10

11

12

9 Niki Lauda (A)
Marlboro McLaren TAG Porsche
Zeltweg (A)

10 Alain Prost (F)
Marlboro McLaren TAG Porsche
Estoril (P)

11 Elio de Angelis (I)
Lotus Renault
Zandvoort (NL)

12 *Weltmeister / World Champion /
Champion du monde / Campeón mundial
1984*
Niki Lauda (A),
Marlboro McLaren TAG Porsche

Alain Prost (F),
Marlboro McLaren TAG Porsche

Estoril (P)

DRIVERS

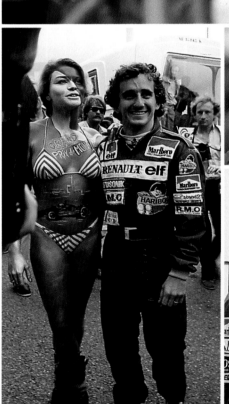

1 Alain Prost (F), Renault Elf
   Patrick Tambay (F), Ferrari
   Silverstone (GB)

2 Elio de Angelis (I)
   JPS Lotus Renault
   Zandvoort (NL)

3 Manfred Winkelhock (D)
   ATS BMW
   Zeltweg (A)

4 René Arnoux (F)
   Ferrari
   Imola (RSM)

5 Alain Prost (F)
   Renault Elf
   Monaco

6 Jacques Laffite (F)
   Saudia Williams Ford
   Monaco

7 Niki Lauda (A), Marlboro McLaren Ford

   John Watson (GB), Marlboro McLaren Ford
   (Sieger / winner / vainqueur / triunfador)

   René Arnoux (F), Renault Elf

   Long Beach (USA)

9

10

11, 12

8   *Weltmeister / World Champion /*
    Champion du monde / Campeón mundial
    1983

    Nelson Piquet (BR)
    Parmalat Brabham BMW
    Hockenheim (D)

9   Nelson Piquet (BR)
    Parmalat Brabham BMW
    Monaco

10 Keke Rosberg (SF)
    Saudia Williams Ford
    Hockenheim (D)

11 John Watson (GB)
    Marlboro McLaren Ford
    Monaco

12 Andrea de Cesaris (I)
    Marlboro Alfa Romeo
    Hockenheim (D)

DRIVERS

1   Manfred Winkelhock (D)
     ATS Ford
     Brands Hatch (GB)

2   Riccardo Patrese (I)
     Brabham Parmalat BMW
     Dijon - Prenois (F)

3   Elio de Angelis (I)
     JPS Lotus Ford
     Dijon - Prenois (F)

4   Didier Pironi (F), Ferrari
     Mauro Forghieri (I), Team Ferrari

     Zandvoort (NL)

5   Eddie Cheever (USA)
     Talbot Ligier Matra
     Long Beach (USA)

6   Niki Lauda (A)
     Marlboro McLaren Ford
     Long Beach (USA)

7   Gilles Villeneuve (CDN)
     Ferrari
     Long Beach (USA)

8   Michele Alboreto (I)
     Tyrrell Ford
     Dijon - Prenois (F)

9   Jacques Laffite (F)
     Talbot Ligier Matra
     Monaco

10   Keke Rosberg (SF), Saudia Williams Ford
     Niki Lauda (A), Marlboro McLaren Ford
     Gilles Villeneuve (CDN), Ferrari

     Long Beach (USA)

11   Marc Surer (CH)
     Arrows Ragno Ford
     Zolder (B)

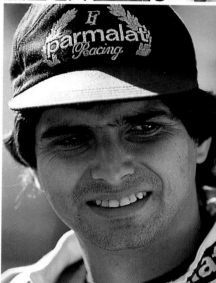

12 John Watson (GB)
Marlboro McLaren Ford
Monaco

13 Nelson Piquet (BR)
Brabham Parmalat Ford
Long Beach (USA)

14 Alain Prost (F)
Renault Elf
Monaco

15 Weltmeister / World Champion /
Champion du monde / Campeón mundial
1982

Keke Rosberg (SF)
Saudia Williams Ford
Zandvoort (NL)

DRIVERS

1 Gilles Villeneuve (CDN)
Ferrari
Monaco

2 René Arnoux (F)
Alain Prost (F)
Renault Elf

Long Beach (USA)

3 Slim Borgudd (S)
ATS Ford
Zeltweg (A)

4 Michele Alboreto (I)
Tyrrell Ford
Monaco

5 Derek Warwick (GB)
Brian Henton (GB)
Toleman Candy Hart

Zeltweg (A)

6 Carlos Reutemann (ARG)
Williams Saudia Leyland TAG Ford
Zeltweg (A)

7 Eddie Cheever (USA)
Talbot Ligier Matra
Paul Ricard (F)

8 Didier Pironi (F)
Ferrari
Paul Ricard (F)

9 Elio de Angelis (I)
Essex Lotus Ford
Zeltweg (A)

10 Mario Andretti (USA)
Marlboro Alfa Romeo
Long Beach (USA)

11 Jacques Laffite (F)
Talbot Ligier Matra
Zeltweg (A)

12 *Weltmeister/ World Champion/
Champion du monde / Campeón mundial
1981*

Nelson Piquet (BR)
Brabham Parmalat Ford
Monaco

13 John Watson (GB)
Marlboro McLaren Ford
Monaco

14 Alan Jones (AUS)
Saudia TAG Leyland Ford
Long Beach (USA)

15 Nigel Mansell (GB)
Essex Lotus Ford
Zeltweg (A)

DRIVERS

1 Patrick Depailler (F)
   Marlboro Alfa Romeo
   Jarama (E)

3 Alain Prost (F)
   Marlboro McLaren Ford
   Zeltweg (A)

2 Nelson Piquet (BR)
   Brabham Parmalat Ford
   Long Beach (USA)

4 Jochen Mass (D)
   Warsteiner Arrows Ford
   Monaco

5 Jean - Pierre Jabouille (F)
   Renault Elf
   Hockenheim (D)

6 Harald Ertl (D)
   ATS Ford
   Hockenheim (D)

7 Elio de Angelis (I)
   Essex Lotus Ford
   Monaco

8 Alan Jones (AUS)
   Saudia Leyland Williams Ford
   Jarama (E)

9 Carlos Reutemann (ARG)
   Saudia Leyland Williams Ford
   Long Beach (USA)

10 Jacques Laffite (F)
    Ligier Gitanes Ford
    Brands Hatch (GB)

11 René Arnoux (F)
    Renault Elf
    Monaco

12 *Weltmeister / World Champion /*
    Champion du monde / Campeón mundial
    1980

    Alan Jones (AUS)
    Saudia Leyland Williams Ford
    Long Beach (USA)

DRIVERS

1 Gilles Villeneuve (CDN), Ferrari
Alan Jones (AUS), Saudia Williams Ford
Jacques Laffite (F), Ligier Gitanes Ford

Zeltweg (A)

2 Alan Jones (AUS), Saudia Williams Ford

*Orangensaft statt Champagner, da Saudia
ein arabischer Sponsor ist / orange juice
instead of champagne because Saudia is an
Arabian sponsor / du jus d'orange au lieu
de champagne car Saudia est un sponsor
arabe / zumo de naranja en lugar de
champaña porque Saudia es un patrocinador árabe*

Zeltweg (A)

3 Nelson Piquet (BR),
Brabham Parmalat Alfa Romeo
Gordon Murray, *Designer / Designer /
Designer / Diseñador*
Bernie Ecclestone, *Teamchef / team boss /
directeur d'équipe / directór de equipo*

Jarama (E)

4 Niki Lauda (A),
Brabham Parmalat Alfa Romeo
Bernie Ecclestone

Monaco

5 Carlos Reutemann (ARG)
Martini Lotus Ford
Dijon - Prenois (F)

6 Mario Andretti (USA)
Martini Lotus Ford
Hockenheim (D)

7 Jacques Laffite (F)
Ligier Gitanes Ford
Hockenheim (D)

8

8 *Weltmeister / World Champion /*
Champion du monde / Campeón mundial
1979
Jody Scheckter (ZA), Ferrari

Gilles Villeneuve (CDN), Ferrari

Long Beach (USA)

DRIVERS

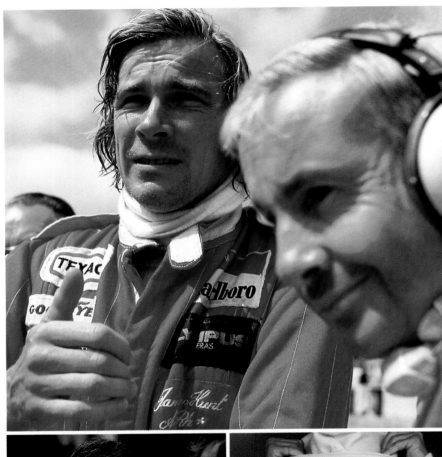

1 James Hunt (GB), Marlboro McLaren Ford
   Teddy Mayer (GB), *Teamchef / team boss / directeur d'équipe / director de equipo*
   Brands Hatch (GB)

2 Alan Jones (AUS)
   Saudia Williams Ford
   Brands Hatch (GB)

3 Jochen Mass (D)
   ATS Ford
   Jarama (E)

4 Patrick Depailler (F)
   Tyrrell Elf
   Monaco

5 Rolf Stommelen (D)
   Arrows Ford
   Jarama (E)

6 Hans Stuck (D)
   Tabatip Shadow Ford
   Jarama (E)

7 Jody Scheckter (ZA), Wolf Ford
   Jackie Stewart (GB)
   TV - Kommentator / TV commentator / commentateur de télévision / comentador de televisión
   Paul Ricard (F)

8 Ronnie Peterson (S)
   JPS Lotus Ford
   Jarama (E)

9, 13

14

10

11

12

15

9   Niki Lauda (A)
    Brabham Parmalat Alfa Romeo
    Hockenheim (D)

10 John Watson (GB)
    Brabham Parmalat Alfa Romeo
    Paul Ricard (F)

11 Didier Pironi (F)
    Elf Tyrrell Ford
    Jarama (E)

12 Clay Regazzoni (CH)
    Tabatip Shadow Ford
    Jarama (E)

13 Gilles Villeneuve (CDN)
    Ferrari
    Monaco

14 Emerson Fittipaldi (BR)
    Copersucar Ford
    Brands Hatch (GB)

15 *Weltmeister / World Champion /
    Champion du monde / Campeón mundial
    1978*

    Mario Andretti (USA)
    JPS Lotus Ford
    Jarama (E)

DRIVERS

1. Mario Andretti (USA)
   JPS Lotus Ford
   Long Beach (USA)

2. James Hunt (GB)
   Marlboro McLaren Ford
   Dijon - Prenois (F)

3. Jochen Mass (D)
   Marlboro McLaren Ford
   Monza (I)

4. Hans Stuck (D)
   Martini Brabham Alfa Romeo
   Hockenheim (D)

5. Jacques Laffite (F)
   Ligier Gitanes Matra
   Hockenheim (D)

6. Patrick Tambay (F)
   Ensign Ford
   Zeltweg (A)

7. Patrick Depailler (F)
   Ronnie Peterson (S)
   Elf Tyrrell FNCB Ford

   Long Beach (USA)

8 Jody Scheckter (ZA)
Wolf Ford
Hockenheim (D)

9 Carlos Reutemann (ARG)
Ferrari
Long Beach (USA)

10 Niki Lauda (A)
Ferrari
Hockenheim (D)

11 *Weltmeister / World Champion /
Champion du monde / Campeón mundial
1977*

Niki Lauda (A)
Ferrari
Monza (I)

DRIVERS

1 Niki Lauda (A)
Ferrari
Jarama (E)

2 Arturo Merzario (I)
Williams Ford
Zeltweg (A)

3 Hans Stuck (D)
March
Jarama (E)

4 Mario Andretti (USA), JPS Lotus Ford
Gunnar Nilsson (S), JPS Lotus Ford

Brands Hatch (GB)

5 Niki Lauda (A)
Ferrari
Brands Hatch (GB)

6 Clay Regazzoni (CH)
Ferrari
Nürburgring (D)

7 Clay Regazzoni (CH)
Niki Lauda (A)
Ferrari

Nürburgring (D)

8

9, 10

11, 12

8 *Weltmeister / World Champion/*
Champion du monde / Campeón mundial
1976

James Hunt (GB)
Marlboro Texaco McLaren Ford
Monaco

9 Patrick Depailler (F)
Elf Tyrrell Ford
Nürburgring (D)

10 Ronnie Peterson (S)
March Ford
Nürburgring (D)

11 Jody Scheckter (ZA)
Elf Tyrrell Ford
Nürburgring (D)

12 Alan Jones (AUS)
Surtees Durex Ford
Brands Hatch (GB)

DRIVERS

1 James Hunt (GB), Hesketh Ford
Mario Andretti (USA), Parnelli Ford

Monaco

2 John Watson (GB)
Ronnie Peterson (S)
JPS Lotus Ford

Nürburgring (D)

3, 4 Vittorio Brambilla (I)
March Beta Ford
Zeltweg (A)

5 Jochen Mass (D),
Marlboro Texaco McLaren Ford
Mike Hailwood (GB)

Monaco

6 Mark Donohue (USA)
FNCB Penske Ford

Monaco

7 Mark Donohue (USA)
FNCB Penske Ford

interviewt von Jackie Stewart
being interviewed by Jackie Stewart
interviewé par Jackie Stewart
entrevistado por Jackie Stewart

Monaco

8 Carlos Pace (BR), Martini Brabham Ford
Clay Regazzoni (CH), Ferrari
Bernie Ecclestone, Martini Brabham
Teamchef / team boss /
directeur d'équipe / director de equipo

Zolder (B)

9 Graham Hill (GB), Embassy Lola Ford
Tony Brise (GB), Embassy Lola Ford

Nürburgring (D)

10

11

12

10 *Fahrerbesprechung*
    Drivers' briefing
    Briefing des pilotes
    Intercambio de impresiones entre los
    pilotos

    Monaco

11 Niki Lauda (A), Ferrari
    Udo Jürgens (A)
    (Sänger / singer / chanteur / cantante)

    Zeltweg (A)

12 *Weltmeister / World Champion /*
    Champion du monde / Campeón mundial
    1975

    Niki Lauda (A)
    Ferrari
    Zeltweg (A)

DRIVERS

1, 2

3, 4

5

6

10

7, 8

9, 1

1 Carlos Reutemann (ARG)
   Brabham Ford
   Dijon - Prenois (F)

2 John Watson (GB)
   Brabham Hexagon Ford
   Monza (I)

3 Patrick Depailler (F)
   Tyrrell Elf Ford
   Nivelles (B)

4 Carlos Pace (BR)
   Brabham Ford
   Dijon - Prenois (F)

5 Clay Regazzoni (CH), Ferrari
   Ronnie Peterson (S), JPS Lotus Ford
   Niki Lauda (A), Ferrari

   Dijon - Prenois (F)

6 Jean - Pierre Jarier (F)
   UOP Shadow Ford
   Dijon - Prenois (F)

7 Mike Hailwood (GB)
   Yardley McLaren Ford
   Jarama (E)

8 James Hunt (GB)
   March Ford
   Jarama (E)

9 Niki Lauda (A)
   Ferrari
   Jarama (E)

12

10 Graham Hill (GB)
    Embassy Lola Ford
    Dijon - Prenois (F)

11 Arturo Merzario (I)
    Iso Marlboro Ford
    Dijon - Prenois (F)

12 *Weltmeister / World Champion /*
    Champion du monde / Campeón mundial
    1974

    Emerson Fittipaldi (BR)
    Marlboro Texaco McLaren Ford
    Monza (I)

13 *Weltmeister / World Champion /*
    Champion du monde / Campeón mundial
    1974

    Emerson Fittipaldi (BR)
    Marlboro Texaco McLaren Ford
    Zeltweg (A)

14 Clay Regazzoni (CH)
    Ferrari
    Nürburgring (D)

15 Jody Scheckter (ZA)
    Elf Tyrrell Ford
    Brands Hatch (GB)

DRIVERS

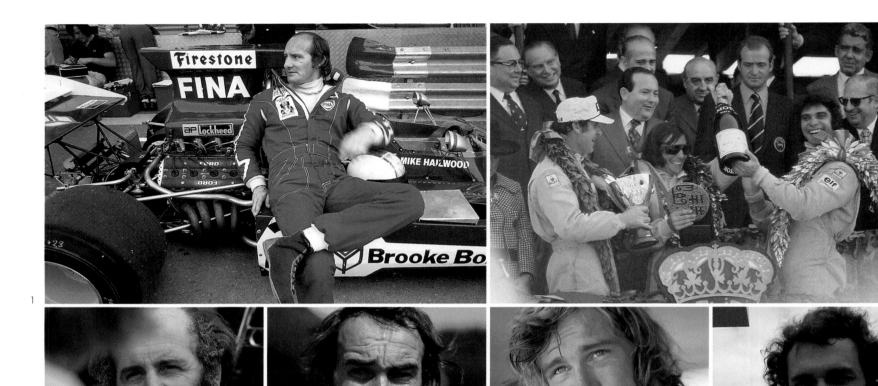

1 Mike Hailwood (GB)
Brooke Bond
Oxo Surtees Ford
Monaco

2 George Follmer (USA), UOP Shadow Ford
Emerson Fittipaldi (BR), JPS Lotus Ford
François Cevert (F), Elf Tyrrell Ford

Montjuich (E)

3 Denis Hulme (NZ)
Yardley McLaren Ford
Montjuich (E)

4 Clay Regazzoni (CH)
Marlboro BRM
Zeltweg (A)

5 James Hunt (GB)
March Ford
Zeltweg (A)

6 Jochen Mass (D)
Surtees Ford
Nürburgring (D)

7 Ronnie Peterson (S)
Emerson Fittipaldi (BR)
Colin Chapman (GB)
*Teamchef / team boss /
directeur d'équipe / director de equipo*

JPS Lotus Ford

Zolder (B)

9

8

10

8 *Weltmeister / World Champion /*
   Champion du monde / Campeón mundial
   1973

   Jackie Stewart (GB)
   Elf Tyrrell Ford
   Silverstone (GB)

9 *Weltmeister / World Champion /*
   Champion du monde / Campeón mundial
   1973

   Jackie Stewart (GB)
   Elf Tyrrell Ford
   Zandvoort (NL)

10 François Cevert (F), Elf Tyrrell Ford
    Jackie Stewart (GB), Elf Tyrrell Ford

    Montjuich (E)

DRIVERS

1 Mike Hailwood (GB),
Brooke Bond Oxo Surtees Ford
Niki Lauda (A), STP March Ford
Ronnie Peterson (S), STP March Ford

Jarama (E)

2 Denis Hulme (NZ)
Peter Revson (USA)
Yardley McLaren Ford

Monza (I)

3 Jackie Stewart (GB)
Elf Tyrrell Ford
Monaco

4 Jacky Ickx (B)
Ferrari
Nürburgring (D)

5 *Fahrerbesprechung*
Drivers' briefing
Briefing des pilotes
Intercambio de impresiones entre los pilotos

Lauda, Pace, Hulme, Hailwood, Reutemann,
Surtees, Hill, Galli, Wisell, Regazzoni,
Amon, E. Fittipaldi

Monza (I)

6 Graham Hill (GB)
Brabham Ford
Monaco

7 Brian Redman (GB)
McLaren Ford
Nürburgring (D)

8 Ronnie Peterson (S)
STP March Ford
Monaco

9 Carlos Reutemann (ARG)
Brabham Ford
Monza (I)

10 Jacky Ickx (B)
Ferrari
Monaco

11 Chris Amon (NZ)
Matra Simca
Clermont - Ferrand (F)

12 *Weltmeister / World Champion /
Champion du monde / Campeón mundial
1972*

Emerson Fittipaldi (BR)
JPS Lotus Ford
Brands Hatch (GB)

DRIVERS

1 Clay Regazzoni (CH)
   Ferrari
   Monaco

2 Emerson Fittipaldi (BR)
   Gold Leaf Lotus Ford
   Monaco

3 Graham Hill (GB)
   Brabham Ford
   Monaco

4 Rolf Stommelen (D)
   Surtees Ford
   Monaco

5

5 Weltmeister / World Champion /
Champion du monde / Campeón mundial
1971

Jackie Stewart (GB)
Elf Tyrrell Ford
Montjuich (E)

DRIVERS

1 Jacky Ickx (B)
Ferrari
Zeltweg (A)

2 Jacky Ickx (B)
Ferrari
Jarama (E)

3 Pedro Rodríguez (MEX)
Yardley BRM
Spa - Francorchamps (B)

4 Jack Brabham (AUS)
Brabham Ford
Hockenheim (D)

5 Jackie Stewart (GB)
March Elf Ford
Hockenheim (D)

6 Dan Gurney (USA)
McLaren Ford
Zandvoort (NL)

7   *Weltmeister / World Champion /*
Champion du monde / Campeón mundial
1970

Jochen Rindt (A)
Gold Leaf Lotus Ford
Hockenheim (D)

8   Jochen Rindt (A)
Gold Leaf Lotus Ford
Brands Hatch (GB)

9   Jochen Rindt (A)
Nina Rindt (SF)
Colin Chapman (GB)
Teamchef / team boss /
directeur d'équipe / director de equipo

Gold Leaf Lotus Ford

Zeltweg (A)

10   Jochen Rindt (A)
Nina Rindt (SF)
Colin Chapman (GB)

Clermont - Ferrand (F)

DRIVERS

1 Graham Hill (GB)
   Gold Leaf Lotus Ford
   Monza (I)

2 Jo Siffert (CH)

   und Teamchef
   and team boss
   et le directeur d'équipe
   y el director de equipo
   Rob Walker

   Lotus Ford

   Monaco

3 Jochen Rindt (A)
   Gold Leaf Lotus Ford
   Silverstone (GB)

4 Jacky Ickx (B)
   Brabham Ford
   Monza (I)

5

5   *Weltmeister / World Champion /*
    Champion du monde / Campeón mundial
    1969

    Jackie Stewart (GB)
    Matra Elf Ford
    Zandvoort (NL)

„Die Form folgt der Funktion": Selten gilt dieses versteckte Postulat vorbehaltloser als in der Formel 1. Wer immer einen Rennwagen konzipiert, sieht sich eingezwängt in das magische Dreieck zwischen den Bedürfnissen der Technik, der Aerodynamik und der Sicherheit. Überdies meldet sich die Werbung energisch zu Wort, die sich gleichwohl mit einem Minimum an Ausstellungsfläche begnügen muß, an rasch bewegter zumal. Da hilft lediglich der radikale Kompromiß. Wie er in den letzten 25 Jahren jeweils aussah, war eine Frage der Zeit – auch der historischen. Unabänderlich blieb, daß sich bis zu 70 Prozent des Luftwiderstands gegen die fetten Räder der Grand Prix-Monoposti stemmen. Der eigentliche Spiel-Raum der Techniker liegt also dazwischen. Nach den schlanken und glatten Projektilen der späten Sechziger mit ihrem gebrechlichen Flügelwerk trug man gewissermaßen mehr Bauch. Jegliches Luftleitwerk war fest mit dem Rumpf verbunden oder Teil der Karosserie.

Abwechslung in drohendes Einerlei trug bereits 1970 die konsequente Keilform des Lotus 72, die sich schließlich durchsetzte. 1977 wies Lotus Vor- und Querdenker Colin Chapman erneut den Weg. Die Ära der Wing Cars begann. Der klassische Flügel-Wagen, der sich mit Querbeschleunigungen bis zu 4 g am Boden festzulutschen vermochte: ein schmales Monocoque, der Tank als tragendes Element hinter dem Piloten, das Cockpit dadurch nach vorne verschoben, vergleichsweise aufrechte Sitzposition, flankiert von Wasser- und Öl-kühler, die von umgekehrten seitlichen Profilen umschlossen waren, um vehementen Unterdruck zu erzeugen. Der Fahrtwind unterströmte sie unbehindert, da die Feder/Dämpfer-Einheiten nach innen aus dem Weg geräumt wurden. Der Frontspoiler wurde häufig entbehrlich, der hintere auf ein Minimum reduziert. Schürzen aller Arten überbrückten den Abstand zur Fahrbahn und steigerten damit den Abtrieb. Die Fahrer indessen wurden geschunden durch irrwitzige Kurven-geschwindigkeiten und granitharte Chassis. Für die Saison 1983 setzte die Motorsport-Behörde FISA dem Flügel-Spuk ein Ende und verordnete dem Grand-Prix-Wagen einen glatten Unterleib. Beim Großen Preis von Holland kreierte McLaren-Konstrukteur John Barnard mit dem MP4/1E die Flaschenhals-Mode: Vor der Hinterachse ver-jüngt sich der voll umkleidete Wagenkörper, damit der Luftstrom das Heckleitwerk ohne viele Turbulenzen anlaufen kann.

Ein Einschnitt, wenn auch keine Revolte, oft kopiert und manchmal übertroffen: daß der Tyrrell 019 vom Grand Prix von San Marino 1990 an die Nase hoch, den Frontspoiler jedoch tief trug. Die Idee hatte der damalige Tyrrell-Designer Harvey Postlethwaite, aber sie wurde ihm auch vom Windtunnel in den Computer diktiert. Längst hatte sich der Windkanal-Arbeiter gegenüber dem Techniker emanzipiert: Seinen Job, sagte Williams-Experte Adrian Newey einmal selbstbe-wußt, sehe er als genauso wichtig an wie den seines Kollegen Patrick Head, der für die Gesamtkonzeption des Fahrzeugs verantwortlich sei. Der Beweis: Die aktive Aufhängung der Williams-Rennwagen, die den Abstand zur Straße unter allen Umständen konstant hält, optimiert nicht zuletzt ihre Aerodynamik.

Form follows function – the Formula One car is possibly the epitome of that insight. Whoever conceives a racing car sees himself squeezed into the magic triangle between the needs of technology, aerodynamics, and safety. Moreover there are the claims of advertising, which has to put up with a minimum of display space and a fast moving one to boot, the only solution being radical compromise. What that looked like in the last quarter of a century depended on the respective state of science. Inevitably up to 70 percent of air resistance braces itself against the enormous wheels of the cars so that the only scope left for the engineer is between them. After the slender and smooth projectiles of the late sixties with their delicate wing configurations the cars sported more belly, as it were. Whatever spoilers there were had to be firmly rooted in the trunk or were integral parts of the bodywork.

The exception to the rule was the Lotus 72 of 1970, whose wedge form would set the pace for future designs to carry the day in the long run. In 1977 Colin Chapman again showed the way ushering in the era of the wing car, the principle behind it being that the whole section mounted alongside the chassis, which had coolers integrated into it, would produce negative lift, in addition to the downforce provided by conventional front and rear wings. The latter, however, became increasingly superfluous as the distance to the road was bridged by skirts. That did not make life easier for the drivers, who had to put up with rock-hard chassis and exorbitant cornering speeds. For the 1983 season racing's governing body FISA eventually ruled out the wing design administering flat bellies to the Formula One car. At the Dutch Grand Prix McLaren chassis expert John Barnard introduced the bottleneck fashion with his hastily completed trend-setting MP4/1E interim model, whose fully covered rear tapered towards the back axle to have the airstream hit the wing with a minimum of turbulences.

A landmark rather than a revolt was that Harvey Postlethwaite's 1990 Tyrrell 019 carried its nose high, its front spoiler, however, low so as to improve the airflow at the front. No longer did the aerodynamicist feel inferior to the technician. Williams wizard Adrian Newey points out that he considers his job equally important to his colleague Patrick Head's, who looks after the overall concept of the car, the proof being that active suspension is basically an aerodynamic device, keeping the distance between car and tarmac constant under all circumstances. But ineluctably 25 years of Grand Prix history are also full of flops and failures, of wrong ways and blind alleys. To err is human, after all, even in that mega-million business Formula One.

DESIGN / VOITURES DE FORMULE 1

«La forme suit la fonction». Il est rare que ce postulat caché soit valable avec moins de restrictions que dans la Formule 1. Toute personne qui conçoit une voiture de course se trouve forcé de concilier les besoins de la technique, de l'aérodynamique et de la sécurité. Il n'y a ici que le compromis radical qui puisse faire quelque chose. Son apparence dans les 25 dernières années était une question de temps, ainsi que du temps historique. Reste constant le fait que jusqu'à 70% de la résistance de l'air pousse contre les grosses roues des Monoposti de Grand Prix. La marge de manœuvre des techniciens se trouve entre ces deux points. Après les projectiles minces et lisses de la fin des années soixante avec leurs ailes fragiles, on a porté comme qui dirait un peu plus de ventre. Les spoilers étaient fixement raccordés au corps ou à une partie de la carrosserie.

Un changement dans cette uniformité menaçante représentait déjà en 1970 la forme pointue constante de la Lotus 72 qui, finalement, s'imposa par la suite. En 1977, Lotus remonta la direction à Colin Chapman, avant-gardiste et penseur original. Ce fut le début de l'ère des Wing Cars. La voiture classique à ailes, qui était capable de se coller au sol grâce à des accélérations transversales pouvant atteindre 4g: une monocoque étroite, le réservoir, élément porteur, derrière le pilote et de ce fait, le cockpit repoussé vers l'avant, en position assise droite, flanqué du radiateur à eau et à huile qui étaient entourés de profils latéraux retournés pour produire une sous-pression. Le vent passait par en-dessous sans les gêner car on avait enlevé les unités de suspension et d'amortissement pour les placer vers l'intérieur. Le spoiler avant devenait de plus en plus indispensable et à l'arrière, réduit au strict minimum. Des tabliers de toutes sortes réduisaient la distance de la chaussée et augmentaient ainsi la force d'appui au sol. Pendant ce temps, les pilotes étaient maltraités par des vitesses démentes en virage et des châssis durs comme du granit. Pour la saison 1983, l'autorité du sport automobile a mis fin au fantôme de l'aile et a ordonné au Grand Prix un bas-ventre lisse. Au Grand Prix de Hollande, John Barnard, le constructeur de McLaren a créé avec le MP4/1E la mode du goulot de bouteille: devant l'axe arrière, la carrosserie s'amincit afin que l'air glisse sans turbulences.

Un tournant même si ce n'est pas une révolte, souvent copié et parfois dépassé: la Tyrrell 019 du Grand Prix de San Marino, en 1990, a le nez haut mais le spoiler avant bas. C'est l'ancien designer de Tyrrell, Harvey Postlethwaite, qui avait eu l'idée mais elle lui avait été dictée dans l'ordinateur par la soufflerie. Il y avait longtemps que l'ouvrier de la soufflerie s'était émancipé par rapport au technicien. Adrian Newey disait un jour, très conscient de lui-même, qu'il considérait que son job était tout aussi important que celui de son collègue Patrick Head responsable de toute la conception du véhicule. La preuve: la suspension active de la voiture de course Williams qui maintient constante la garde au sol dans toutes les circonstances optimise en même temps son aérodynamisme.

DISEÑO / COCHES DE FÓRMULA 1

«La forma se adapta a la función»: pocas veces tiene este postulado una validez tan incondicional como en la Fórmula 1. Quien quiera concebir un Fórmula 1, se verá constringido en el mágico triángulo de las exigencias entre la técnica, la aerodinámica y la seguridad. Además la publicidad pide enérgicamente la palabra y tiene que contentarse con un mínimo de superficie expositiva —que para colmo se mueve velozmente—. Aquí sólo ayuda el compromiso radical. Tal compromiso en los últimos 25 años era una cuestión de tiempo, también de historia. Lo único invariable es que hasta el 70 por ciento de la resistencia contra el aire se acumula en las obesas ruedas de los *monoposti* de Grand Prix y entre campo de acción de los técnicos. Tras los delgados y planos proyectiles de finales de los sesenta se empezó a concentrar el volumen en el vientre. Aquel estabilizador aerodinámico estaba fijamente unido al tronco o a parte de la carrocería.

La forma de cuña de Lotus aportó en 1970 una variación de agresiva uniformidad, que fue la que se impuso. En 1977 con el estrafalario precursor Colin Chapman comenzó la era de los *wing cars*. El clásico bólido de ala que se adhería al suelo con una fuerza centrífuga de hasta 4g: un estrecho *monocoque*, el tanque como soporte detrás del piloto, el *cockpit* desviado hacia delante, asiento en posición relativamente vertical, flanqueado por los radiadores de agua y aceite rodeados por perfiles laterales contrarios para crear un vehemente efecto adhesivo. El viento corría por debajo sin obstáculos pues las unidades de resorte y amortiguamiento se habían instalado en el interior. El *spoiler* frontal era imprescindible, el posterior reducido al mínimo. Carenados de todo tipo distancias a la pista y elevaban la fuerza salida de arranque. Los conductores eran desollados por dementes velocidades de curva y duros chasis como el granito. Para 1983, la administración del automovilismo FISA puso fin a la chorrada del ala inferior y prescribió un abdomen liso a los coches de Grand Prix. En el Gran Premio de Holanda, el constructor de McLaren John Barnard creó la moda del cuello de botella con su MP4/1E: antes del eje trasero se estrecha el cuerpo del coche para que la corriente de aire pueda circular sin tantas turbulencias.

Una novedad, aunque no una revolución, copiada y a veces mejorada: a partir del Grand Prix de San Marino de 1990, el Tyrrell 019 llevaba la nariz alta, pero el *spoiler* frontal bajo. La idea proviene del diseñador de entonces de la Tyrrell, Harvey Postlethwaite, aunque le había sido dictada en el ordenador por el túnel aerodinámico. El especialista del túnel aerodinámico ya se había emancipado hacía tiempo del técnico: su trabajo, aseguró el experto de Williams Adrian Newey, le parecía tan importante como el de su colega Patrick Head, responsable de la concepción conjunta del vehículo. La prueba: la suspensión activa de los coches de carreras Williams, que mantiene constante la distancia al suelo en cualquier circunstancia, contribuye en último término a una óptima aerodinámica.

DESIGN

1 Jean Alesi (F)
   Ferrari F 93 B V-12

2 Alessandro Zanardi (I)
   Castrol Lotus 107 B / Ford V-8 HB

3 Ayrton Senna (BR)
   Marlboro McLaren MP 4-8 / Ford V-8 HB

4 Ukyo Katayama (JAP)
   Tyrrell 020 C / Yamaha V-10

5 **Alain Prost (F)**
   Canon Williams FW 15 C /
   Renault R 55, V-10

6 Riccardo Patrese (I)
   Camel Benetton B 193 B / Ford V-8 HB

7   Mark Blundel (GB)
Gitanes Blondes Ligier JS 39 /
Renault R 55, V-10

9   Christian Fittipaldi (BR)
Minardi M 193 / Ford V-8 HB

11   Thierry Boutsen (B)
Sasol Jordan 193 / Hart V-10

8   Karl Wendlinger (A)
Sauber C 12 / Ilmor V-10

10   Erik Comas (F)
Larrousse LH 93 / Lamborghini V-12

12   Derek Warwick (GB)
Footwork FA 14 / Mugen - Honda V-10

| | 1989 | 1990 | 1991 | 1992 |

1 Ferrari F1 - 89, Nigel Mansell (GB)

2 Camel Lotus 101 Lotus Judd,
Nelson Piquet (BR)

3 Brabham BT 58 Judd, Stefano Modena (I)

4 **Marlboro McLaren M 4/5 Honda,**
Ayrton Senna (BR)

5 Tyrrell 018 Ford, Michele Alboreto (I)

6 Williams FW 13 Renault,
Riccardo Patrese (I)

1 Ferrari F 641-2 V-12, Alain Prost (F)

2 Camel Lotus 102 Lamborghini V-12,
Derek Warwick (GB)

3 Brabham BT 59 Judd V-8,
David Brabham (AUS)

4 **Marlboro McLaren M P4/5 B
Honda V-10,** Gerhard Berger (A)

5 Tyrrell 019 Ford V-8 DFR, Jean Alesi (F)

6 Williams FW 13 B Renault V-10,
Thierry Boutsen (B)

1 Ferrari F1-91, Alain Prost (F)

2 Lotus 102 B Judd, Mika Hakkinen (SF)

3 Brabham BT 60 Y Yamaha,
Mark Blundell (GB)

4 **Marlboro McLaren MP 4-6 Honda
Ayrton Senna (BR)**

5 Tyrrell 020 Honda, Stefano Modena (I)

6 Williams FW 14 Renault,
Nigel Mansell (GB)

1 Ferrari F 92 A, Jean Alesi (F)

2 Lotus 102 D Ford, Mika Hakkinen (SF)

3 Brabham BT 60 B Judd, Damon Hill (GB)

4 Marlboro McLaren MP 4/7 Honda,
Ayrton Senna (BR)

5 Tyrrell 020/B Ilmor 2175 A V-10,
Andrea de Cesaris (I)

6 **Williams FW 14 B Renault,
Nigel Mansell (GB)**

/4

nna (BR)

(GB)

bo,

kal der Konstrukteure / constructors'championship / Championnat des constructeurs / Campeonato de constructores

1984   1985   1986   1987   1988

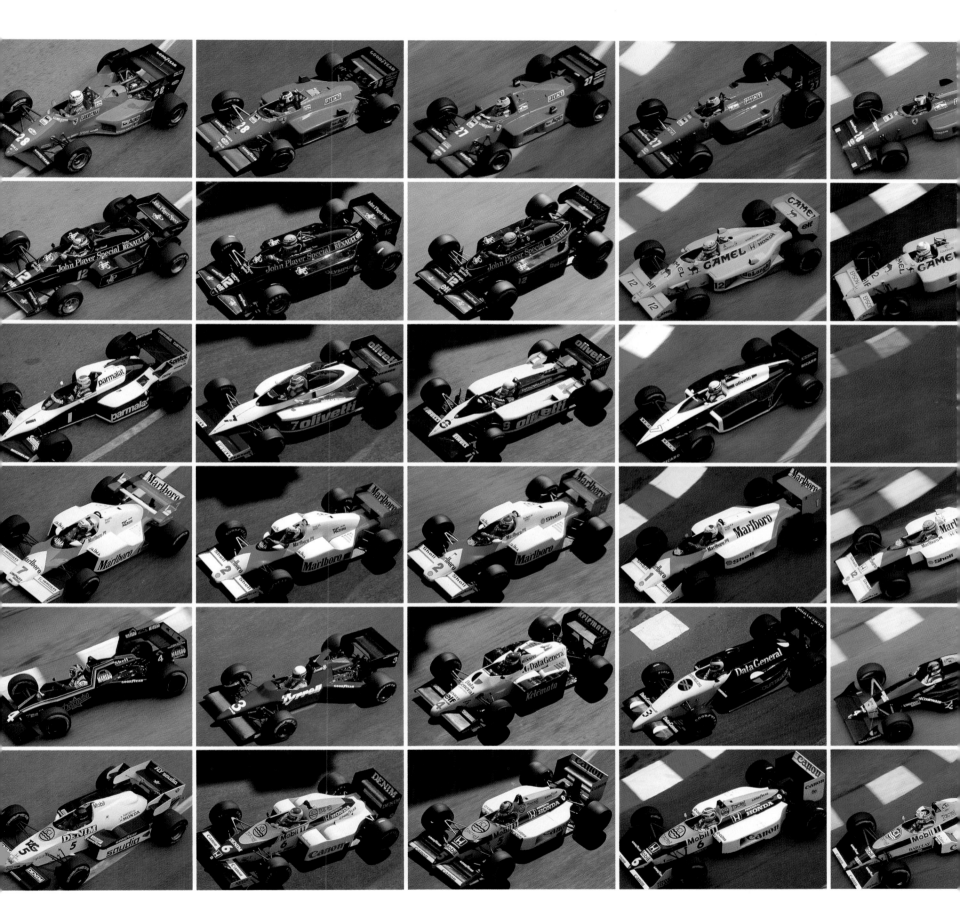

1984
Ferrari Turbo 126 C4, René Arnoux (F)
PS Lotus 95 T Renault Turbo, Nigel Mansell (GB)
Olivetti Brabham BT 53 BMW Turbo, Nelson Piquet (BR)
Marlboro McLaren MP 4/2 TAG Porsche Turbo, Alain Prost (F)
Tyrrell 012 Ford, Stefan Bellof (D)
audia Williams FW 09/09 B Honda Turbo, acques Laffite (F)

1985
1 Ferrari Turbo 156/85, Stefan Johansson (S)
2 JPS Lotus 97 T Renault Turbo, Ayrton Senna (BR)
3 Olivetti Brabham BT 54 BMW Turbo, Nelson Piquet (BR)
4 **Marlboro McLaren MP 4/2 B TAG Porsche Turbo, Alain Prost (F)**
5 Tyrrell 014 Ford, Martin Brundle (GB)
6 Williams FW 10 / FW 10 B Honda Turbo, Keke Rosberg (SF)

1986
1 Ferrari Turbo F1 - 86, Michele Alboreto (I)
2 JPS Lotus 98 T Renault Turbo, Ayrton Senna (BR)
3 Olivetti Brabham BT 55 BMW Turbo, Elio de Angelis (I)
4 Marlboro McLaren MP 4/2 C TAG Porsche Turbo, Keke Rosberg (SF)
5 Tyrrell 015 Ford, Philippe Streiff (F)
6 **Williams FW 011 Honda Turbo,** Nigel Mansell (GB)

1987
1 Ferrari Turbo F1 - 87, Michele Alboreto (I)
2 Camel Lotus T 99 Honda Turbo, Ayrton Senna (BR)
3 Brabham BT 50 BMW Turbo, Riccardo Patrese (I)
4 Marlboro McLaren MP 4/3 TAG Porsche Turbo, Alain Prost (F)
5 Tyrrell 016 Ford, Jonathan Palmer (GB)
6 **Williams FW 011 B Honda Turbo, Nelson Piquet (BR)**

1988
1 Ferrari Turbo F1 - 87 / 88 C, Gerhard Berger (A)
2 Camel Lotus T 100 Honda T Satoru Nakajima (J)
3 - - -
4 **Marlboro McLaren MP Honda Turbo, Ayrton**
5 Tyrrell 017 Ford, Julian Baile
6 Williams FW 012 B Judd, Nigel Mansell (GB)

1	Ferrari 1976	2	Brabham Parmalat BMW 1984	3	Tyrrell - Ford 1984	4	Tyrrell - Ford 1976
5	Brabham Parmalat BMW 1983	6	JPS - Lotus - Ford 1976	7	Brabham - Alfa Romeo 1976	8	Marlboro McLaren - TAG 1984
9	RAM - Hart 1984	10	RAM - Hart 1984	11	Marlboro Texaco McLaren - Ford 1976	12	JPS - Lotus - Ford 1982
13	*Boxentafel / Pit board / tableau de stand / tablero de jaula*	14	ATS - BMW 1984	15	Renault - Elf 1985	16	Renault - Elf 1979
17	Arrows - BMW 1984	18	Arrows - BMW 1984	19	Tolemann - Hart 1984	20	Williams - Ford 1976
21	Spirit - Hart 1984	22	Ensign - Ford 1976	23	Benetton - Alfa Romeo 1984	24	Hesketh - Ford 1976

Vorherige Seite / Previous page / Page précédente / Página anterior : Benetton BMW Turbo, Gerhard Berger (A), Hungaroring (H) 1986

Georges Follmer (USA)
UOP Shadow Ford
Paul Ricard (F) 1973

1

1   JPS Lotus 72 D Ford
    Emerson Fittipaldi (BR)
    Zandvoort (NL) 1973

2   March 701 Ford
    Jo Siffert (CH)
    Zeltweg (A) 1970

3   March 711 Ford
    Ronnie Peterson (S)
    Zandvoort (NL) 1971

4   March 721 Ford
    Monaco 1971

5   March 721 Ford
    Ronnie Peterson (S)
    Jarama (E) 1971

6   Surtees TS7 - Ford
    John Surtees (GB)
    Monza (I) 1970

7   BRM P 153
    Monaco 1970

2, 3

4, 5

9

6

10

7, 8

15, 11

12

16, 17

8, 14

8   Skoal - Bandit RAM
    Manfred Winkelhock (D)
    Estoril (P) 1985

9   De Tomaso 505 - 38 Ford
    Piers Courage (GB)
    Frank Williams (GB), *Team Manager /*
    directeur d'équipe / director de equipo

    Monaco 1970

10 Matra Simca
    Chris Amon (NZ)
    Monza (I) 1971

11 UOP Shadow Ford
    Tom Pryce (GB)
    Zeltweg (A) 1975

12 BRM P 153
    Jo Siffert (CH)
    Silverstone (GB) 1971

13 Hesketh 308 Ford
    Nürburgring 1975

14 Warsteiner Hesketh 308 Ford
    Zeltweg (A) 1975

15 Wolf WR1
    Jody Scheckter (ZA)
    Hockenheim (D) 1977

16 Marlboro Alfa Romeo 179
    Patrick Depailler (F)
    Long Beach (USA) 1980

17 Marlboro Alfa Romeo 179
    Bruno Giacomelli (I)
    Monza (I) 1981

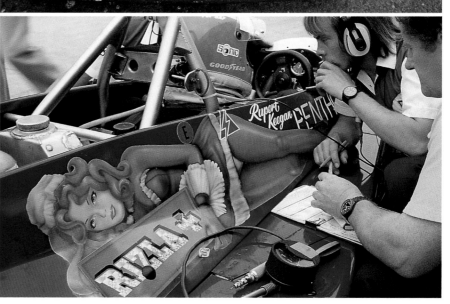

1   STP March 711 Ford
    Monaco 1971

2   Colani Eifelland March 721 Ford
    Rolf Stommelen (D)
    Jarama (E) 1972

3   Shadow Samson Ford
    Jan Lammers (NL)
    Long Beach (USA) 1979

4   Hesketh 308 BAF Ford
    Rupert Keegan (GB)
    Hockenheim (D) 1977

5

5 Hesketh 308 Ford
Guy Edwards (GB)
Brands Hatch (GB) 1976

Wo andere ihre Haut zu Markte trugen und in wechselnder Loyalität Farbe bekannten, blieb das Ferrarirot konstant – wie die Treue seiner Fans. Nur: diese wurde manchmal auf eine harte Probe gestellt. Nachdem die Baureihen 312/F1 und 312/B1 und 2 nur sporadische Siege an die Fahne mit dem Pferd geheftet hatten, leitete der B3 von 1973 auch formal über zu den kantig-klotzigen T-Modellen, so genannt, weil das Getriebe quer („trasversale") eingebaut war. Mit dem 312/T stellte sich der Erfolg ein wie nie zuvor in der Geschichte der Marke, die beiden Weltmeisterschaften mit Niki Lauda 1975 und 1977 sowie, gewissermaßen als Gipfel der Ferrari-Hausse im Zweijahrestakt, das Doppel-Championat 1979 durch Jody Scheckter und Gilles Villeneuve mit dem zuverlässigen T4. Die Ära der zierlicher konzipierten Turbo-Ferrari, zwischen dem 126/C von 1981 und dem F1-87/88C von 1988, blieb unergiebig. Den Saugern der folgenden Jahre im modischen Eierhandgranaten-Look gebührte vor allem eine Auszeichnung für den Belcanto ihrer Zwölfzylinder, dem Flop F92A von 1992, der anmutete wie ein Jetfighter auf vier Rädern, ein Preis für seine aggressive Schönheit. Im übrigen verharrten die roten Renner aus Maranello im Wartestand – wie die wechselnd farbigen des einstmals schärfsten Rivalen aus Hethel in der englischen Grafschaft Norfolk.

Seit dem Jahr der Lotus-Blüte 1978, als Mario Andretti mit dem Wing Car Lotus 79 die Ferrari-Hegemonie aufbrach, hatte man magere acht Grand Prix gewonnen, einen mehr, als der Amerikaner damals für seine Meisterschaft anhäufte. Mit dem frühen Tode Colin Chapmans am 16.12.1982 war das Unternehmen seines umtriebigen Impresarios und Übervaters beraubt. Von allen als Superhirn und genialer Neuerer anerkannt, war Chapman gleichwohl eine tragische Figur. Immer wieder leitete er Trends in die Wege, die andere aufgriffen und vollendeten. Das galt für die Flügel-Autos Lotus 78 und 79. Das galt ebenso für den Lotus-Keil 72 von 1970 mit seinem geschlossenen Bug und seitlichen Kühlern. McLaren-Konstrukteur Gordon Coppuck verwandelte dieses Konzept seinem M 23 an und machte die Kopie damit zum Hauptakteur in sechs Jahren Grand Prix-Historie, während etwa 1973 die Fahrer der sargschwarzen Lotus 72 sich selbst und einander im Wege standen: Emerson Fittipaldi und Ronnie Peterson brachten es zusammen auf sieben Grand Prix-Siege, Tyrrell-Pilot Jackie Stewart reichten fünf für den Titel. Ein Jahr zuvor hatte der spätere Formel 1-Makler Bernie Ecclestone den Brabham-Rennstall übernommen, den Gründervater und dreimaliger Weltmeister Jack Brabham Ende 1970 seinem Konstrukteur und Freund Ron Tauranac anvertraut hatte. Erst Ende der achtziger Jahre stieß er ihn wieder ab, des kränkelnden Unternehmens müde und überdrüssig geworden. Zu lange lagen die Jahre des zweiten Brabham-Booms nach den Championaten von 1966 und 1967 zurück, längst war Nelson Piquet, Brabham-Weltmeister von 1981 und 1983, zu neuen Ufern aufgebrochen. In beiden Fällen reichten dem Brasilianer drei Siege, beim erstenmal mit dem Brabham BT 49 C des Konstrukteurs Gordon Murray, der den Kreisbogen zum stilistischen Credo erhoben, das

Prinzip des Wing Cars indessen so perfektioniert hatte, daß der Wagen am Ende keinen vorderen Flügel mehr benötigte, beim zweitenmal mit dem pfeilförmig-grazilen BT 52, der um den BMW Vierzylinder-Turbo herum gebaut war. Vorzugsweise war man eigene, häufig originelle Wege gegangen, mit dem BT 34 von 1971 zum Beispiel, der „Hummerzange", deren Kühler vorn nach links und rechts ausgelagert worden waren. Oder mit dem „Staubsauger" BT 46, der sich beim Großen Preis von Schweden 1978 mit einem Gebläse an der Straße festsog, daß den nachfolgenden Piloten die Steine um die Ohren flogen. Oder dem BT 55 von 1986, Entwicklungskosten 6,8 Millionen Pfund, der sich tief wie kein zweiter über dem Boden kauerte, weil Murray das BMW-Triebwerk fast liegend eingebaut hatte. Was dabei herauskam, läßt sich auf eine kurze Formel bringen: nichts. 1988 erschien die Schrift an der Wand, als Brabham für ein Jahr pausierte, mit dem Ende der Saison 1992 indessen landete, was 1962 hoffnungsvoll begonnen hatte, auf dem Sperrmüll der Formel 1-Geschichte.

Dergleichen Irrungen und Wirrungen blieben der Tyrrell-Organisation erspart, schon weil der gute Name und die knorrige Führerfigur des ehemaligen Holzhändlers Ken Tyrrell Dauer im Wechsel garantierten. Als wenig anhänglich indessen erwies sich das Schlachtenglück: Die ersten Tyrrell-Jahre waren entschieden die besten. Bereits in ihrer zweiten Saison trugen 1971 seine breiten blauen Rennwagen mit den markanten Frontverschalungen – ihre Chassisnummern 001 und 002 wurden in der Branche wie Namen aufgenommen – Jackie Stewart zu seiner zweiten Weltmeisterschaft. Kurz und stämmig und von einem mächtigen Ansaugkamin gekrönt war der 006, mit dem dem Schotten 1973 der dritte Streich glückte. Dann aber begab sich Tyrrell-Designer Derek Gardner auf den Holz-Weg: Sein dreiachsiger P34 von 1976 und 1977 mit vier gelenkten Vorderrädern auf 10-Zoll-Felgen drohte eine Zeitlang eine veritable Sechs-Welle auszulösen, verkümmerte aber schließlich zu Kuriosum und Stilblüte, obwohl ihm in Anderstorp 1976 ein Doppelsieg mit Jody Scheckter und Patrick Depailler gelang. Er beanspruche das Preisgeld für die ersten drei Plätze, sagte Ken Tyrrell damals – die ersten 12 Räder hätten zu seinen Autos gehört. Dann aber verging ihm das Lachen. Mit Derek Gardner, der nach dem P34-Fiasko Hut und Reißbrett nehmen mußte, sei auch Tyrrells Fortune gegangen, sagten viele. Seit jenem Großen Preis von Schweden verteilten sich drei Tyrrell-Siege schütter über 17 Jahre und immer jungfräulicher wurde das Blau seiner Wagen, immer riesiger der Schriftzug Tyrrell in den Niederungen des Mißerfolgs Mitte der achtziger Jahre. 1990, als der Tyrrell 019 plötzlich den Bug hochnäsig in den Fahrtwind reckte, winkte Licht am Ende des Tunnels, zumal sich Ken Tyrrell mit Hilfe von McLaren-Boß Ron Dennis für die nächste Saison den Honda-Zehnzylinder gesichert hatte. Aber das schien nur so.

Amidst changing colour schemes Ferrari red has remained constant – like the loyalty of its fans. But again and again they had to weather hard times. There were, for instance, only a few victories to the credit of the 312/F1 and 312/B1 and 2 models. Then, however, there was light at the end of the tunnel when the 1973 B3 appeared, anticipating the angular T models, called like that because the gearbox was installed transversally. With the 312/T came success like never before in the history of the marque culminating in Niki Lauda's two championships in 1975 and 77 and and a third one in 1979 for Jody Scheckter, runner-up Gilles Villeneuve also driving the reliable T4 which, however, was already eclipsed in the second half of the season by the Williamses. The era of the nimbler-looking turbo Ferraris, from the 1981 126/C to the F1-87/88C of 1988, was graced by 15 victories altogether. The normally aspirated cars of the following years, which were in keeping with the prevailing fashion in that they looked like egg-shaped handgrenades, excelled in terms of the belcanto of their twelve cylinders, whereas the 1992 F92A turned out to be a dud, deserving, however, a prize for its aggressive beauty. In the last couple of years the red cars from Maranello have been also-rans, like the garishly coloured ones of their once toughest rival Lotus from Hethel in the English county of Norfolk.

Since 1979, when Mario Andretti interrupted the Ferrari hegemony with a Lotus walkover, Lotus cars have scored a poor eight victories, one more than Andretti amassed in his championship year. A severe blow was inflicted to the British team when its mastermind, Colin Chapman, prematurely died on December 12th, 1982. He was a tragical figure nonetheless, time and again initiating trends that were consummated by others. That went for his wing cars Lotus 78 and 79, and, earlier already, for his wedge-shaped 72 with its closed front and lateral radiators upon which was modelled Gordon Coppuck's McLaren M 23. This car was to be the leading protagonist in six years of Grand Prix history while in 1973, for instance, the drivers of the black and gold Lotus 72 stood in the way of each other, with Emerson Fittipaldi and Ronnie Peterson accumulating seven victories between them, whereas Tyrrell pilot Jackie Stewart needed five only to win the title. In the year before, Bernie Ecclestone had bought the Brabham stable entrusted by founding father and triple world champion Jack Brabham to his engineer and friend Ron Tauranac in the end of 1970. Only towards the end of the eighties did Ecclestone sell the sickly enterprise again. Many years had passed since the second Brabham boom after the 1966 and 1967 championships, and Nelson Piquet, Brabham world champion in 1981 and 1982, had set off for new ventures long ago. In both cases he had been able to make do with three wins only, first in Gordon Murray's BT 49 C, whose salient feature was the circular arc, later in the graceful arrow-shaped BT 52 built around the compact BMW four cylinder turbo engine. Quite often there had been a peculiar Brabham approach, one example being the "Lobster Claw" BT 34 of 1971, its twin radiators mounted ahead of the front wheels. Another one was the "hoover" car BT 46 with a large fan installed at the back with a sealed-off chassis underside to create an aerodynamic downforce, but also blowing debris from the track straight into other drivers' faces at Anderstorp 1978. Another unorthodox Brabham experiment ended in a fiasco after 6.8 million pounds had been squandered: the 1986 BT 55, its BMW engine tilted 18 degrees to the left to achieve an ideal roll centre and a lower centre of gravity as the car was extremely shallow. In 1988 the writing on the wall appeared when Brabham had to take a one-year break, and with the end of the 1992 season came to nought what had hopefully begun in 1962.

Trials and tribulations of this description never affected the Tyrrell organization, always centred upon its somewhat larger-than-life and charismatic leader Ken Tyrrell. Fortune, however, was fickle, the first Tyrrell years being much more rewarding than later ones. In their second season already his blue cars with their distinctive snub noses carried Jackie Stewart to his second championship. Their chassis numbers 001 and 002 were talked about like names in the business. Tyrrell's 006, the Scot's championship winning tool in 1973, was short and stubby, an enormous funnel looming behind the driver's head. Then, however, designer Derek Gardner was on the wrong track introducing the P34 six-wheeler in 1976 which, for quite a while, seemed the way to go at least with Tyrrell landing double victory at Anderstorp with Jody Scheckter and Patrick Depailler. Ken is said to have said that he claimed the prize money for the first three as the first twelve wheels over the line belonged to his cars. However, laughter was rarely heard in the Tyrrell organization ever after. Derek Gardner was fired and many said that with his defection luck left the former timber merchant for good. Ever since that Swedish Grand Prix there have been three Tyrrell victories scattered over 17 years, and the more of the original blue there was on his cars in the disastrous middle eighties, the bigger became the Tyrrell logo on their flanks indicating that Ken was possibly spending a lot of his own money . There seemed to be a ray of hope when, in 1990, the Tyrrells sported Harvey Postlethwaite's high noses and the team, with help from Ron Dennis, managed to secure Honda ten cylinder engines for the next season. But then things looked bleak again.

Alors que d'autres n'ont pas cessé de changer de couleur, le rouge de Ferrari est resté constant, comme la fidélité de ses fans. Seulement, celle-ci a souvent été mise à l'épreuve, et rudement. Après les victoires sporadiques des séries de construction 312/F1, 312/B1 et 2, la B3 de 1973 a joué un rôle de transition qui a donné plus tard les modèles T, anguleux et grossiers, appelés ainsi parce que la boîte de vitesse était transversale. C'est alors que le succès se montra, comme jamais auparavant dans l'histoire de la marque, avec la 312/T, les deux championnats du monde de Niki Lauda en 1975, en 1977, et, en plus, l'apogée de la hausse Ferrari pour ainsi dire, à un rythme de tous les deux ans, le championnat double en 1979 de Jody Scheckter et de Gilles Villeneuve avec la fidèle T4. L'ère de la Ferrari turbo, conçue dans une certaine finesse, entre la 126/C de 1981 et la F1-87/88C de 1988 restait improductive. Une mention honorable revenait de droit aux modèles des années suivantes qui avaient un look de grenade ovoïde, pour le belcanto de leurs 12 cylindres, le flop F92A de 1992 qui plaisait comme un jetfighter sur quatre roues, un prix pour sa beauté agressive. Du reste, les coureurs rouges de Maranello sont restées en attente tout comme leurs rivales d'Hethel, aux couleurs changeantes, autrefois les plus inflexibles, dans le comté anglais de Norfolk.

Depuis l'année de la fleur de Lotus en 1978, lorsque Mario Andretti fit prendre le départ à l'hégémonie Ferrari avec la voiture à ailerons Lotus 79, on n'avait gagné que huit maigres Grands Prix, un de plus que ce que l'Américain avait accumulé à l'époque pour son championnat. Avec la mort prématurée de Colin Chapman, le 16.12.1982, l'entreprise avait perdu son père et un imprésario énergique. Reconnu par tous comme étant un super-cerveau et un novateur génial, Chapman était aussi un personnage tragique. Il ne cessait pas de mettre des modes en route dont d'autres s'emparaient pour les mener à bien. C'était le cas des voitures à ailerons Lotus 78 et 79. C'était tout aussi valable pour la Lotus cunéiforme 72 de 1970 avec son nez fermé et ses radiateurs latéraux. Gordon Coppuck, le constructeur de chez McLaren, transforma ce plan dans sa M23 et la copia; elle devint l'actrice principale de six ans d'histoire du Grand Prix tandis qu'en 1973, les pilotes de la Lotus 72, noire comme un cercueil, se trouvaient bien embarrassés: Emerson Fittipaldi et Ronnie Peterson remportèrent ensemble sept fois le Grand Prix. Cinq ont été suffisants à Jackie Stewart, pilote de chez Tyrrell, pour obtenir le titre. Un an auparavant, Bernie Ecclestone, celui qui deviendra plus tard l'agent d'affaires de la formule I, avait repris l'écurie Brabham que Jack Brabham, fondateur et triple champion du monde, avait confié à son constructeur et ami Ron Tauranac, fin 1970. Ce n'est qu'à la fin des années 80 qu'il s'en est défait, fatigué et dégoûté de cette firme maladive. Il y avait eu trop d'années de passées depuis le deuxième boom Brabham et les championnats de 1966 et 1967; il y avait longtemps que Nelson Piquet, le champion du monde de chez Brabham, de 1981 et 1983, était parti pour d'autres rivages. Dans les deux cas, trois victoires ont suffi au Brésilien, la première fois avec

la Brabham BT 49 C du constructeur Gordon Murray qui, ayant fait de l'arc de cercle un credo stylistique, avait perfectionné le principe de la voiture à ailerons tant et si bien qu'à la fin, la voiture n'avait plus besoin d'ailes avant; la deuxième fois avec la BT 52, gracile et en forme de flèche, construite tout autour du turbo BMW quatre cylindres. On avait préféré prendre des chemins personnels et souvent originaux, avec la BT 34 de 1971 par exemple, la «pince de homard», dont les radiateurs avant avaient été changés de place et mis à gauche et à droite; ou avec «l'aspirateur» BT 46 au Grand Prix de Suède en 1978 qu'un ventilateur faisait complètement adhérer à la route de telle sorte que les pierres sifflaient autour des oreilles des pilotes qui se trouvaient derrière; ou encore, la BT 55 de 1986, frais de réalisation: 6,8 millions de livres, qui s'aplatissait sur le sol comme aucune autre parce que Murray avait installé le moteur de la BMW en longueur. Ce qui en résulta est très simple: rien. En 1988, on vit venir les choses lorsque Brabham fit une pause d'un an et à la fin de la saison 1992, ce qui avait été commencé en 1962 avec espoir fut réduit à néant.

De tels errements et tourments ont été épargnés à l'organisation Tyrrell déjà rien que par le fait que le bon nom et la figure de chef vigoureuse de l'ancien marchand de bois, Ken Tyrrell garantissaient la stabilité dans le changement. Pourtant, la chance dans la bataille s'est montrée moins fidèle. Les premières années de Tyrrell ont été décidément les meilleures. Dès la deuxième saison, ses larges voitures de course bleues aux coffrages frontaux prononcés (leurs numéros de châssis 001 et 002 ont été repris dans cette branche comme des noms) ont mené Jackie Stewart à son deuxième championnat. La 006, courte et trapue, était couronnée d'un puissant conduit d'aspiration et c'est avec elle que l'Ecossais a réussi son troisième coup en 1973. Mais après, Derek Gardner, le designer de chez Tyrrell, a fait fausse route. Sa P34 de 1976 et 1977, trois axes avec quatre petites roues avant montées sur des jantes de 10 pouces, a menacé un instant de déclencher une véritable vague de six roues, mais a disparu finalement pour devenir une curiosité et une fleur de rhétorique bien qu'elle soit parvenue à une double victoire de Jody Scheckter et Patrick Depailler à Anderstorp en 1976. Ken Tyrrell disait à l'époque qu'on lui devait l'argent du prix des trois premières places, les 12 premières roues ayant appartenu à ses voitures. Mais il a dû cesser de rire par la suite. Avec Derek Gardner, qui, après le fiasco de la P34, a dû ramasser ses billes, beaucoup ont dit que la fortune de Tyrrell s'était envolée. Depuis ce Grand Prix de Suède, Tyrrell a obtenu trois victoires échelonnées sur 17 ans et le bleu de ses voitures s'est trouvé de moins en moins utilisé; le nom de Tyrrell se retrouva de plus en plus parmi les perdants au milieu des années 80. En 1990, lorsque la Tyrrell 019 a relevé son nez dans le vent, la lumière pointait à la sortie du tunnel, d'autant plus que Ken Tyrrell, avec l'aide du boss de chez McLaren, Ron Dennis, s'était assuré la Honda dix cylindres pour la saison suivante. Mais ce n'était qu'une apparence.

Donde otros cambiaban de piel como un camaleón y de color como de lealtad, Ferrari permaneció constante —como la fidelidad de sus *fans*—. Sólo que esta fidelidad sufrió alguna que otra prueba de fuego. Después de que las series 312/f1 y 312/b1 y 2 se habían apuntado sólo victorias esporádicas, el B3 de 1973 inició la transición a los aristados y macizos modelos T, así llamados porque la caja de cambios había sido instalada transversalmente. Con el 312/T se lograron más éxitos que nunca en la historia de la marca, como los dos Mundiales con Niki Lauda en 1975 y 1977, y, en cierto modo la apoteosis de la casa Ferrari en ritmo bianual, el doble Campeonato de 1979 con Jody Scheckter y Gilles Villeneuve con los seguros T4. La era de las construcciones de concepción delicada de los Ferrari turbo, entre el 126/C de 1981 y el F1-87/88C de 1988, permaneció infecunda. Las aspiradoras de los años siguientes con su *look* de granadas ovoides a la moda se merecen una condecoración por el belcanto de sus doce cilindros; el fracaso F92A de 1992, con el aspecto de un *Jetfighter* sobre cuatro ruedas, se merece un premio por su belleza agresiva. Por lo demás, los bólidos rojos de Maranello se quedaron estancados en estado de espera, como los de cambiantes colores del que fuera el rival más duro de Hethel, en el condado inglés Norfolk.

Desde 1978, el año del florecimiento de la Lotus, cuando Mario Andretti inauguró la hegemonía Ferrari con el *wing car* Lotus 79, se habían ganado 8 Grand Prix, uno más de los que el americano consiguiera amontonar entonces para su Campeonato. Con la temprana muerte de Colin Chapman el 16.12.1982 se quedó la empresa sin su intrigante empresario y padre superior. Chapman, reconocido por todos como supercerebro y genial innovador, era una figura trágica. Una y otra vez abría el camino a nuevas tendencias que otros recogían y perfeccionaban. Esto es aplicable a los coches de ala Lotus 78 y 79. También es válido para el Lotus 72 en forma de cuña de 1970 con su morro cerrado y los radiadores en posición lateral. El constructor de McLaren Gordon Coppuck transformó este concepto en su M 23, convirtiendo la copia en el actor principal de seis años de historia del Grand Prix, mientras que en 1973, por ejemplo, los corredores de los negrísimos Lotus 72 se ponían la zancadilla mutuamente: Emerson Fittipaldi y Ronnie Peterson consiguieron reunir siete victorias de Grand Prix, el piloto de la Tyrrell Jackie Stewart sólo necesitó cinco para el título. Un año antes, Bernie Ecclestone —más tarde se convertiría en agente de Fórmula 1— tomó a su cargo el equipo de la Brabham que el fundador y tres veces Campeón del Mundo Jack Brabham había confiado a finales de 1970 a su constructor y amigo Ron Tauranac. No fue hasta fines de los ochenta que le expulsó, cansado y aburrido de la achacosa empresa. Atrás quedaban los años del segundo boom Brabham tras los Campeonatos de 1966 y 1967, tiempo hacía ya que Nelson Piquet, el Campeón Mundial de Brabham de 1981 y 1983, había arribado a nuevos puertos. En ambos casos le bastaron al brasileño tres victorias para el Campeonato. La primera vez, con el Brabham BT 49 C del constructor Gordon Murray que había erigido el arco de círculo a credo estilístico perfeccionando así el principio del *wing car* de tal manera que, al final, el coche podía prescindir del alerón delantero. La segunda vez, con el grácil BT 52 en forma de flecha, construido entorno al cuatro cilindros turbo de BMW. Preferentemente se apostaba por soluciones propias, a menudo originales, como sucedió con el BT 34 de 1971, «la tenaza», cuyos radiadores habían sido desplazados a la posición delantera, a derecha e izquierda. O con la «aspiradora» BT 46, que en el Gran Premio de Suecia de 1978 se adhería al suelo con tal fuelle, que los pilotos de atrás tenían que apartarse de las piedras volantes. O el BT 55 de 1986, costes de producción 6,8 millones de libras, que se acuclillaba sobre el suelo más bajo que ningún otro, pues Murray había instalado el motor casi acostado. El resultado se puede reducir a una simple fórmula: nada. En 1988, cuando Brabham hizo una pausa de un año, colofonó el fin de la temporada arrojando al basurero de la historia de la Fórmula 1 lo que con tanta ilusión había empezado en 1962.

La organización Tyrrell se ahorraba semejantes errores y extravíos, simplemente porque el buen nombre y la robusta figura dirigente de Ken Tyrrell, otrora maderero, eran garantía de duración en el cambio. De menos duración, sin embargo, fue la fortuna en la guerra: los primeros años Tyrrell fueron los mejores. Sus anchos coches azules con los característicos revestimientos frontales —sus números de chasis 001 y 002 tenían el rango de nombres en el ramo— llevaron ya en su segunda temporada, en 1971, a Jackie Stewart a su segundo Campeonato Mundial. Corto y robusto y coronado por una poderosa chimenea aspirante era el 006 que propició en 1973 la tercera victoria del escocés. Pero después, el diseñador de la Tyrrell Derek Gardner se adentró en el camino equivocado: su tres ejes P34 de 1976 y 1977, con cuatro ruedas delanteras direccionales con llantas de 10 pulgadas amenazó durante un tiempo con desatar la moda de seis ruedas, pero finalmente quedó reducido a curiosidad y florecimiento estilístico, aunque logró en 1976, en Anderstorp, una doble victoria con Jody Scheckter y Patrick Depailler. Revindica el dinero del premio por los tres primeros puestos, decía entonces Ken Tyrrell, pues las 12 primeras ruedas pertenecían a sus coches—. Pero no tardó en marchitársele la sonrisa. Con Derek Gardner, que tras el fiasco del P34 tuvo que tirar la toalla y el tablero de dibujo, también voló la fortuna de Tyrrell, decían muchos. Después de aquel Gran Premio de Suecia, la Tyrrell consiguió aún tres victorias esparcidas a lo largo de 17 años, y el color azul de sus coches se iba volviendo cada ves más vírgen, la secuencia Tyrrell cada vez más grande en la depresión de fracasos de mediados de los ochenta. En 1990, cuando el Tyrrell 019 de repente levantó arrogante el morro con el viento favorable, brilló la luz al fondo del túnel, más aún teniendo en cuenta que Ken Tyrrell, con ayuda del *boss* de McLaren Ron Dennis, se había asegurado el Honda diez cilindros para la temporada siguiente. Pero eran sólo apariencias.

DESIGN

1, 2, 3

4

5

6

7

1 Ferrari 312
   Clay Regazzoni (CH)
   Monaco 1971

2 Ferrari 312 T
   Clay Regazzoni (CH)
   Zeltweg (A) 1975

3 Ferrari 312 T 4
   Gilles Villeneuve (CDN)
   Jarama (E) 1979

4 Ferrari 126 C 2
   Gilles Villeneuve (CDN)
   Long Beach (USA) 1982

5 Ferrari 126 C 4
   René Arnoux (F)
   Monaco 1984

6 Ferrari F 1 - 87
   Gerhard Berger (A)
   Spa - Francorchamps (B) 1987

7 Ferrari 641
   Alain Prost (F)
   Hockenheim (D) 1990

8 Ferrari 312 B Cockpit
Jacky Ickx (B)
Zandvoort (NL) 1971

9 Ferrari 641 Cockpit
Nigel Mansell (GB)
Monaco 1990

10 Ferrari
Hockenheim (D) 1987

11 Ferrari 641
Estoril (P) 1990

12 Ferrari F 89
Jerez (E) 1989

13 Ferrari 641
Alain Prost (F)
Jerez (E) 1990

DESIGN

1 Ferrari 643
Silverstone (GB) 1991

2 Ferrari F 92 A
Kyalami (ZA) 1992

3 Ferrari Emblem am Auto / Ferrari emblem
on the car / Les emblème Ferrari sur la
voiture / Emblema de Ferrari en el vehículo
Imola (RSM) 1989

4 Ferrari Fan Silvio Ferri
Hockenheim (D) 1991

5 Ferrari Emblem, Batterie / Ferrari emblem
on the battery / Les emblème Ferrari sur la
batterie / Emblema de Ferrari en la batería
Monaco 1992

6 Ferrari Emblem an Niki Laudas
Kopfhörern /
Ferrari emblem on Niki Lauda's
headphones /
Les emblème Ferrari sur le casque de
Niki Lauda /
Emblema de Ferrari en los audífonos
de Niki Lauda

Magny - Cours 1992

7 Ferrari F 92 A
Monaco 1992

8 Ferrari F 92 A
Imola (RSM) 1992

9 Ferrari F 92 A
Kyalami (ZA) 1992

10 Ferrari F 93 A
Monaco 1993

11 Ferrari F 93 A
Imola (RSM) 1993

12 Ferrari F 93 A
Monaco 1993

13 Ferrari F 92 A
Monaco 1992

14 Ferrari F 93 A
Monaco 1993

15 Ferrari F 93 A
Monaco 1993

16 Ferrari F 93 A
Kyalami (ZA) 1993

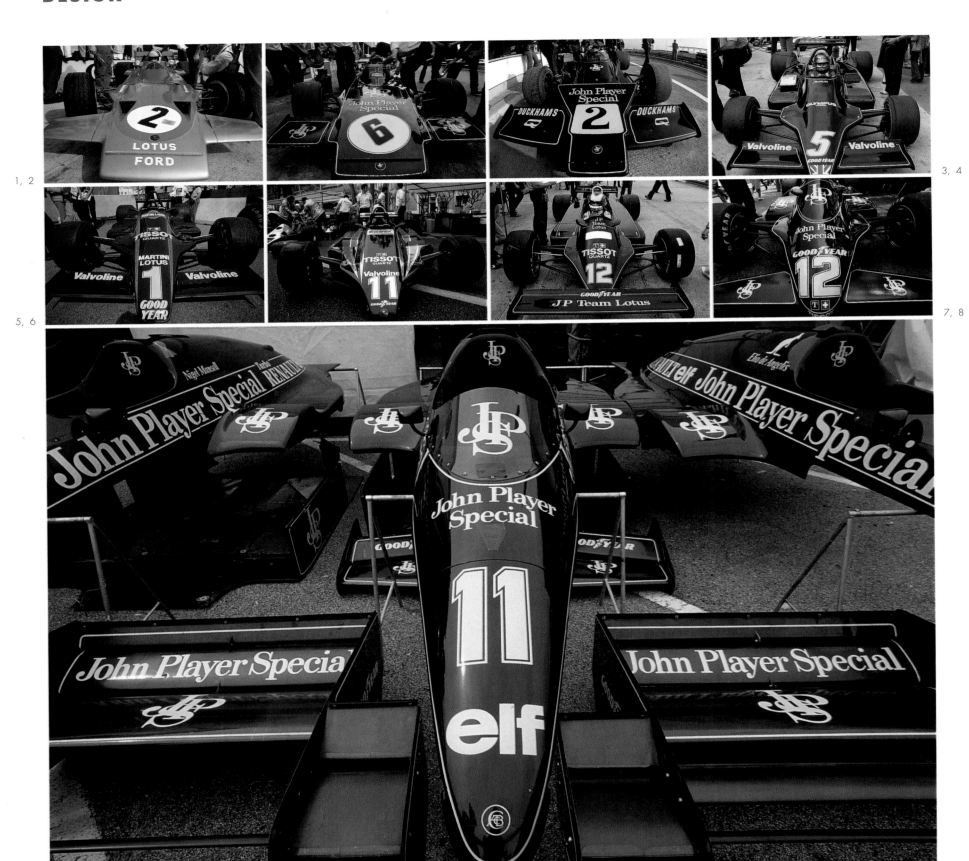

1   Gold Leaf Lotus Ford
    Jochen Rindt (A)
    Hockenheim (D) 1970

2   JPS Lotus Ford
    Emerson Fittipaldi (BR)
    Monza (I) 1972

3   JPS Lotus Ford
    Jacky Ickx (B)
    Jarama (E) 1974

4   JPS Lotus Ford
    Mario Andretti (USA)
    Brands Hatch 1978

5   Martini Lotus Ford
    Long Beach (USA) 1979

6   Essex Lotus Ford
    Monaco 1980

7   Lotus Essex JPS Ford
    Österreichring (A) 1981

8   Lotus JPS Ford
    Monaco 1982

9   Lotus JPS Renault Turbo
    Dijon - Prenois 1984

10   JPS Lotus Ford
     Emerson Fittipaldi (BR)
     Le Castellet (F) 1973

11   JPS Lotus Renault Turbo
     Elio de Angelis (I)
     Brands Hatch (GB) 1984

12   Lotus Essex JPS Ford
     Nigel Mansell (GB)
     Österreichring (A) 1981

13   JPS Lotus Renault Turbo
     Ayrton Senna (BR)
     Le Castellet (F) 1986

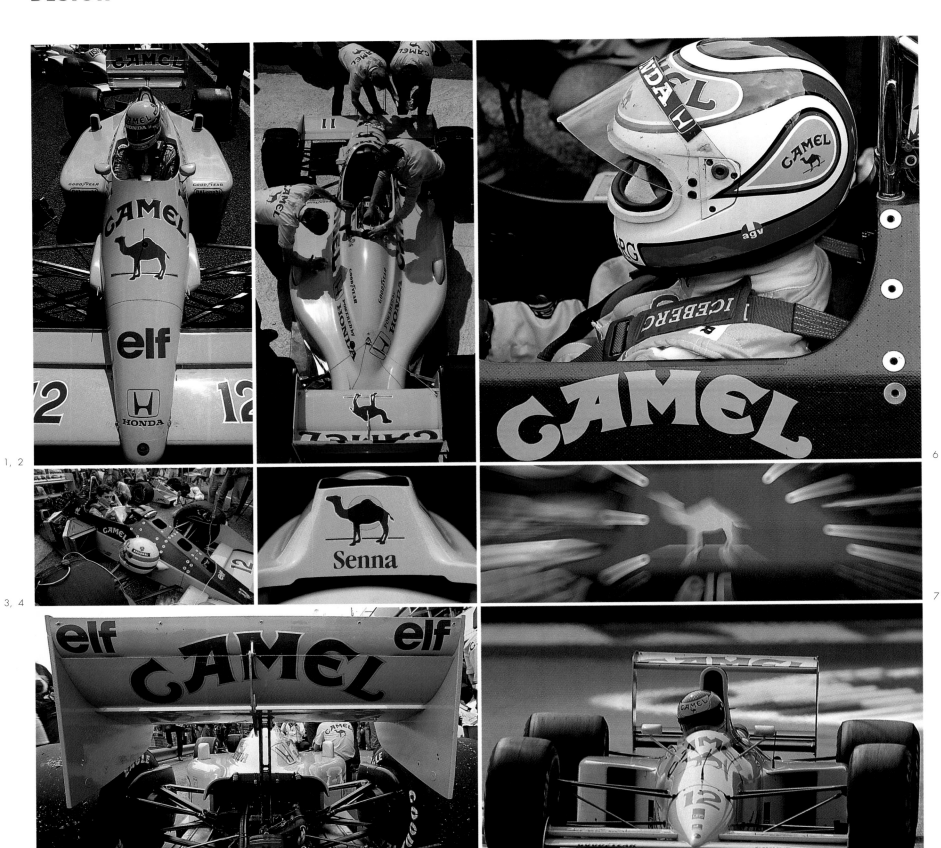

1   Ayrton Senna (BR)
    Camel Lotus T 99 Honda Turbo
    Spa - Francorchamps (B) 1987

2   Camel Lotus T 99 Honda Turbo
    Monza (I) 1987

3   Ayrton Senna (BR)
    Camel Lotus T 99 Honda Turbo
    Monza (I) 1987

4   Camel Lotus T 99 Honda Turbo
    Imola (RSM) 1987

5   Camel Lotus T 99 Honda Turbo
    Imola (RSM) 1987

6, 7   Nelson Piquet (BR)
    Camel Lotus T 100 Honda Turbo
    Spa - Francorchamps (B) 1988

8   Martin Donnelly (GB)
    Camel Lotus T 102 Lamborghini V-12
    Monza (I) 1990

10, 11

13

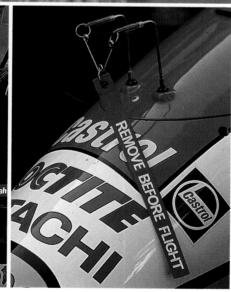

15, 16

9   Mika Häkkinen (SF)
    Lotus 102 B Judd V-8
    Monaco 1991

10 Lotus 102 B Judd V-8
    Interlagos (BR) 1991

11 Lotus 102 D Ford
    Montreal (CDN) 1992

12 Johnny Herbert (GB)
    Lotus 102 D Ford
    Mexico 1992

13 Johnny Herbert (GB)
    Lotus 102 D Ford
    Mexico 1992

14 Alessandro Zanardi (I)
    Castrol Lotus 107 B Ford
    Montreal (CDN) 1993

15, 16 Castrol Lotus 107 B Ford
        Monaco 1993

1   Denny Hulme (NZ)
    (Fahrer, driver, pilote, piloto)

    Weltmeister / World Champion /
    Champion du monde / Campeón mundial
    1959, 1960, 1966
    Jack Brabham (AUS)
    Brabham Repco - BT 19

    Nürburgring (D) 1966

2   Rolf Stommelen (D)
    Brabham BT 33 Ford
    Zeltweg (A) 1970

3   Graham Hill (GB)
    Brabham BT 34 Ford
    Monza (I) 1971

4   Wilson Fittipaldi (BR)
    Brabham BT 42 Ford
    Nürburgring (D) 1973

5   Carlos Reutemann (ARG)
    Brabham BT 44 Ford
    Jarama (E) 1974

6   Hans - Joachim Stuck (D)
    Martini Brabham BT 45 B Alfa Romeo
    Dijon - Prenois (F) 1977

7 Nelson Piquet (BR)
Brabham Parmalat Ford
Dijon - Prenois (F) 1981

8 Nelson Piquet (BR)
Brabham Parmalat BMW Turbo
Zandvoort (NL) 1983

9 Nelson Piquet (BR)
Brabham Parmalat BMW Turbo
Zeltweg (A) 1983

1, 2

3

4

5

6

7

8

1 Brabham Parmalat BMW BT 50
 Nelson Piquet (BR)
 Zolder (B) 1982

2 Brabham Parmalat BMW BT 50
 Nelson Piquet (BR)
 Dijon - Prenois (F) 1982

3 Brabham Parmalat BMW BT 52
 Nelson Piquet (BR)
 Paul Ricard (F) 1983

4 Brabham Parmalat BMW BT 53
 Nelson Piquet (BR)
 Brands Hatch (GB) 1984

5 Brabham Olivetti BMW BT 55
 Derek Warwick (GB)
 Brands Hatch (GB) 1986

6 Brabham Olivetti BMW BT 55
 Riccardo Patrese (I)
 Imola (RSM) 1986

7 Spa - Francorchamps (B) 1985

8 Brabham Olivetti BMW BT 55
 Derek Warwick (GB)
 Monza (I) 1986

9 Brabham Yamaha BT 60 Y
   Martin Brundle (GB)
   Imola (RSM) 1991

10 Brabham Yamaha BT 60 Y
    Monaco 1991

11 Brabham Judd BT 60 B
    Damon Hill (GB)
    Hockenheim (D) 1992

DESIGN

1 Elf Tyrrell 005 Ford
   François Cevert (F)
   Brands Hatch (GB) 1972

2 Elf Tyrrell 003 Ford
   Jackie Stewart (GB)
   Barcelona (E) 1971

3 Elf Tyrrell P 34 Ford
   Jody Scheckter (ZA)
   Brands Hatch (GB) 1976

4 Tyrrell 010 Ford
   Michele Alboreto (I)
   Imola (RSM) 1981

5 Elf Tyrrell P 34 Ford
   Anderstorp (S) 1976

6 Elf Tyrrell 008 Ford
   Patrick Depailler (F)
   Monaco 1978

7 Systime Tyrrell 012 Ford
   Stefan Johansson (S)
   Brands Hatch (GB) 1984

8 Delonghi Tyrrell 012 Ford
   Stefan Bellof (D)
   Brands Hatch (GB) 1984

9 Tyrrell 014 Renault
   Martin Brundle (GB)
   Spa - Francorchamps (B) 1985

10 Elf Tyrrell 015 Renault
   Philippe Streiff (F)
   Brands Hatch (GB) 1986

11 Tyrrell 016 Ford
   Philippe Streiff (F)
   Spa - Francorchamps (B) 1987

12 Elf Tyrrell 019 Ford
   Jean Alesi (F)
   Hockenheim (D) 1990

13 Tyrrell 020 Honda
   Stefano Modena (I)
   Monaco 1991

14 Tyrrell 020 C Yamaha
   Ukyo Katayama (J)
   Montreal (CDN) 1993

McLAREN / WILLIAMS / BENETTON

Kein Zweifel: Die eiligste Dreifaltigkeit in der Formel 1 der frühen neunziger Jahre ist die von McLaren, Williams und Benetton. Nur: Die Wege, die in der totalen Herrschaft der Großen Drei über den Rest der Grand Prix-Welt mündeten, verliefen ganz verschieden. Am süffigsten liest sich zweifellos die McLaren-Saga, obzwar durchaus nicht frei von Rückschlägen, Reinfällen und Rohrkrepierern. Sie zerfällt in drei Kapitel: der Pionier, die Nachlaßverwalter, der Neuerer.

Der Pionier: Bruce McLaren selbst, Rennfahrer von Rang und 1966 Mann der ersten Stunde. Als er am 2. Juni 1970 beim Testen in Goodwood sein früh vollendetes Leben ließ, herrschten Trauer und Konsternation. Aber die Schau ging weiter. Die Nachlaßverwalter: Männer wie Phil Kerr und Teddy Mayer, der das Team mit den beiden Weltmeisterschaften für Emerson Fittipaldi 1974 und James Hunt 1976 auf Gordon Coppucks Erfolgs-Keil M 23 ersten Gipfeln zuführte. Aufstieg und Fall: Ende der Siebziger war die Sollbruchstelle zum Unsäglichen erreicht, McLaren 1979 Siebenter in der Konstruktorenwertung. Der Neuerer: Mister McLaren der Zweite, Ron Dennis. Mit ihm kamen 1980 Frühjahrsputz und Revirement, der neue Stil für die verbleibenden Jahre des Jahrtausends.

Und mit ihm kam Star-Designer John Barnard. Am 6. März 1981 stellte er der Presse in Silverstone bei strömendem Regen sein klug erdachtes Modell MP4 vor, Werkstoff fürs Monocoque: Kohlefaserlaminate. An den MP4 und seine Abkömmlinge knüpft sich eine Chronik der Superlative: bis 1992 sieben Fahrerchampionate und sechs Konstruktorentitel, aber auch etwa 15 von 16 möglichen Grand Prix-Siegen 1988. Dabei ist Dennis eher bewahrender Denkungsart: Erst spät mochte er sich zu High Tech-Tops wie aktiver Aufhängung und automatischem Getriebe durchringen. 1993 aber, nachdem ihm alle sein Technologie-Defizit und eine verspätete und verfehlte Motorenwahl hämisch angekreidet hatten, war er einfach wieder da. Und auch der große Ayrton Senna kam aus dem Nichts seines selbst auferlegten Exils und gewann drei von den ersten sechs großen Preisen. Wie der von Ron Dennis wurde der Name Frank Williams anfänglich als kleine Münze gehandelt im Umkreis der Grand Prix. Ein Aufsteiger aus der Formel 2 mit ein paar respektablen Ergebnissen auf seinem Konto, gewiß. Die Formel 1 jedoch – das war eine andere Welt. Da würde er zeigen müssen, was in ihm steckte. Das tat Williams, aber der Aufstieg war lang und dornig. Und er begann schlimm, als sein Pilot und Freund Piers Courage beim Großen Preis von Holland 1970 in der Magnesiumhölle des Monoposto verbrannte, den Williams für den Argentinier Alejandro de Tomaso einsetzte. Noch heute erinnert ein verstaubter Zwilling des Unglücksautos in de Tomasos Sportwagenschmiede in Modena an den schwarzen Tag von Zandvoort. Immer am Rande des Ruins, griff der drahtige Brite auch später nach allem, was vier fette Räder hatte und verfügbar war: dem Politoys, dem March 721, dem ISO, der Erbmasse aus dem Rennstall des beleibten und exzentrischen Lords Alexander Hesketh, als dieser Lust und Laune an der Formel 1 verloren hatte und auch ein paar Pfunde – Sterling, versteht sich.

Clay Regazzonis Sieg in Silverstone im Juli 1979 auf dem Williams FW 07 war dann die Schwalbe, die den Sommer jenes Jahres machen sollte und des nächsten: 1980 wurde Alan Jones Weltmeister auf Williams, ebenso knapp wie Keke Rosberg 1982. Längst waren Frank Williams und sein Hauskonstrukteur Patrick Head zusammengewachsen zu einem formidablen Gespann. Daß Williams seit dem 8. März 1986 nach einem Autounfall unweit des Kurses von Le Castellet an den Rollstuhl gekettet ist, änderte an seiner magischen Präsenz im Grand Prix-Sport überhaupt nichts. Nur muß alles Spätere als Triumph der reinen Ambition gesehen werden, eines Willens ohne Körper, wie es der österreichische Journalist Helmut Zwickl ohne jede makabre Ironie genannt hat.

1987 rang Williams-Pilot Nelson Piquet seinen Teamkollegen Nigel Mansell mit knapper Not nieder. 1992 indessen konnte niemand mehr dem kampfstarken Briten das Wasser reichen- und dem Williams FW 14B, mit dem das Techniker-Duo Patrick Head und Adrian Newey die hohe Kunst der Technologie um die drei Parameter denkendes Fahrwerk, Getriebeautomatik und Traktionskontrolle so auf die Spitze getrieben hatte, daß sich die Motorsport-Legislative FISA zur Intervention gezwungen sah.

Der Grand Prix-Rennwagen, den der englische Groß-Spediteur Ted Toleman 1981 zum höheren Ruhme seines Unternehmens in die Welt setzte, war eine Gleichung mit drei Unbekannten: dem neuen Chassis seines fähigen Designers Rory Byrne, dem neuen Vierzylinder Turbo-Aggregat des Tuners Brian Hart, den Pneus von Pirelli, Neuling auf dem Reifenmarkt der Formel 1. Sie erwies sich lange Zeit als unlösbar, auch wenn der kleine Italiener Teo Fabi 1985 mit dem Toleman TG 185 die Pole Position auf den Asphalt des Nürburgrings radierte. Unbestritten jedoch blieb, daß sich Byrnes Chassis zwar wunderlich von allen anderen abhoben, aber zu den besten des ganzen Feldes zählten, so gut, daß die Toleman häufig auf einen Reifenwechsel verzichten konnten, wo die meisten Teams nachfassen mußten. Byrne hatte ein Händchen für so etwas, optimierte indessen auch seine Autos in dem exklusiv genutzten Windtunnel des Royal Military College zu Shrivenham. Daran änderte auch nichts, daß der Rennstall im Januar 1986 in den Besitz des italienischen Kleiderfabrikanten Luciano Benetton überging. Seither tragen Byrnes Boliden das schrille Bunt der United Colors of Benetton und, seit 1991, die Nase ganz besonders hoch. Wenn er etwas mache, sagt Teamchef Flavio Briatore, dann richtig. Und so verfügt man 1993 über ein aktives Fahrwerk, ein halbautomatisches Getriebe sowie Fords stärkstes Stück mit pneumatischen Ventilen. Benetton-Siege haftet immer etwas Besonderes an: Der in Mexico 1986 war Gerhard Bergers erster, der in Japan 1989 Alessandro Nanninis einziger, die in Japan und Australien 1990 sowie Canada 1991 Nelson Piquets letzte und der in Belgien 1992 Michael Schumachers erster von gewiß vielen...

McLAREN / WILLIAMS / BENETTON

The fastest threesome in contemporary Grand Prix racing undoubtedly is McLaren, Williams and Benetton. The ways, however, that have led to their total supremacy have been entirely different. At first sight the McLaren saga seems to be the most attractive one in spite of not being exempt from crises and drawbacks. It falls into three chapters: the pioneer, his curators, the innovator.

The pioneer was Bruce McLaren himself, a first-rate racing driver and, in 1966, founding father of his own enterprise. Sadness and consternation prevailed when he lost his young life testing a CanAm car at Goodwood on June 2nd, 1970. But the show had to go on. The curators: men like Phil Kerr and Teddy Mayer, whose era culminated in Emerson Fittipaldi and James Hunt winning the first two championships for the Colnbrook-based team in 1974 and 1976 respectively with Gordon Coppuck's wedge-shaped M 23. But rise was inevitably followed by fall, and near the end of the seventies McLaren was affected by an all-time low, being seventh in the 1979 constructors' championship. Then, however, arrived Mister McLaren the Second, Ron Dennis, whose vigorous takeover was to set the pace for the remainder of the millenium.

With Dennis came star designer John Barnard, introducing his sophisticated MP4 model to the press at Silverstone on March 6th, 1981, the circuit awash with rain. Extensive use of carbon fibre had been made raising quite a few eyebrows, which did not prevent the MP4 and its derivatives starring in a unique success story which featured seven drivers' and six constructors' championships so far as well as feats like 15 out of 16 potential Grand Prix victories in 1988. For all that Ron Dennis has always been conservative, hesitant, for instance, to introduce high technology tops such as active suspension and automatic gearbox. At the beginning of the 1993 season, however, after the augurs of the sport had predicted another McLaren depression the red and white cars came back with a vengeance, and so did Ayrton Senna, who had seemed to take a year off like his arch-rival Alain Prost the season before, winning three out of the initial six Grand Prix. Frank Williams' path to the peak of Formula One was arduous and thorny, his little outfit pitiably underfinanced and plagued by creditors for many years. He had done quite well in Formula Two, but Formula One was a different world. And it turned out to be a cruel one when his driver and friend Piers Courage was burnt to death at the 1970 Dutch Grand Prix in the magnesium hell of the car entered by Williams for Argentinian Alejandro de Tomaso. Even today a dusty twin of that vehicle preserved in de Tomaso's Modena sports car factory reminds the visitor of that black day at Zandvoort. Throughout the seventies Frank Williams tried his luck with whatever had four fat wheels, his own Politoys and ISO, a March 721, the remains from the racing stable of corpulent and eccentric Lord Hesketh after His Lordship had decided to give up the costly venture Formula One for good.

Clay Regazzoni's Silverstone victory in July 1979 with the FW 07 eventually smoothed the way for more as Alan Jones presented Williams with his first world championship in 1980 and Keke Rosberg with his second in 1982, by a narrow margin, though. In years full of trials and tribulations Frank and his designer Patrick Head had grown together into a formidable team. That he has been confined to a wheelchair ever since a car accident near the Paul Ricard circuit on March 8th, 1986, has not changed his mesmeric presence in Grand Prix racing a jot. The meteoric rise of the Williams name in the period to come must, however, be seen as the triumph of sheer ambition, of a will without a body, as Austrian journalist Helmut Zwickl put it without any macabre irony.

The 1987 victory of Williams pilot Nelson Piquet over his team mate Nigel Mansell was close indeed. But in 1992 the pugnacious Briton was untouchable, and so was the Williams FW 14B, built around the parameters active suspension, automatic gearbox and traction control like his 1993 successor FW 15C by technical director Patrick Head and aerodynamicist Adrian Newey. So devastating the Williams hegemony had become by then that racing's governing body FISA intervened banning electronic driving aids from 1994 on.

In 1981 carrier tycoon Ted Toleman called into being a Grand Prix team to promote the wider interest of his company at an international level. The car he had constructed by his capable designer Rory Byrne was an equation with three unknowns: a brand-new chassis, a new four cylinder turbo engine built by Brian Hart, tyres from Pirelli, a newcomer to the then Formula One tyre market. For a long time it proved difficult to solve, although wee Italian Teo Fabi was on pole for the 1985 German Grand Prix at Nürburgring with the Toleman TG 185. Soon it went without saying that Byrne's chassis looked odd, but were among the very best on the grid so that Toleman cars could often cover a Grand Prix distance shod with the same set of tyres while others had to change. Byrne had a knack for this but also made ample use of the Royal Military College wind tunnel at Shrivenham. This did not even change when the team was taken over in January 1986 by Italian clothes magnate Luciano Benetton. Ever since Byrne's cars have been in the lavish United Colors of Benetton and, from 1991 on, carried their noses particularly high. Things must be done properly, says team boss Flavio Briatore. And so his 1993 drivers have at their disposal an active suspension and a semi-automatic gearbox as well as being the first to have Ford's best HB engine with pneumatic valves, to the dismay of fellow Ford customer Ron Dennis. Benetton victories always have a special tinge: Mexico 1986 being Gerhard Berger's first, Japan 1989 Alessandro Nannini's only one, Japan and Australia 1990 as well as Canada 1991 Nelson Piquet's last and Belgium 1992 Michael Schumachers first of certainly many ...

Cela ne fait aucun doute: la sainte Trinité en formule I du début des années 90 est celle de McLaren, Williams et Benetton. Mais les chemins qui ont permis aux trois Grands de gouverner le reste du monde des Grands Prix, ont été tout à fait différents. C'est bien la saga McLaren qui est sans doute la plus succulente à lire, même si elle n'est pas sans retours de bâton, pièges et flops. Elle se découpe en trois chapitres: le pionnier, les administrateurs de l'héritage, le novateur.

Le pionnier: Bruce McLaren lui-même, pilote de course de rang, et, en 1966, l'homme de la première heure. Quand, aux essais de Goodwood, le 2 juin 1970, il laissa derrière lui une vie achevée très tôt, le deuil et la consternation ont régné. Mais le show a continué. Les administrateurs de l'héritage: des hommes comme Phil Kerr et Teddy Mayer. Celui-ci a mené l'équipe tout en haut, avec les deux championnats du monde: Emerson Fittipaldi en 1974 et James Hunt en 1976 sur la M23, le modèle à succès de Gordon Coppuck. Ascension et chute: à la fin des années 70, le point de rupture obligatoire était atteint, McLaren, septième au classement des constructeurs. Le novateur: Mister McLaren II, Ron Dennis.

Et le designer vedette, John Barnard, arrive avec lui. Le 6 mars 1981, à Silverstone, il présentait à la presse, sous une pluie battante, sa MP4, modèle intelligemment conçu, le matériau du monocoque: du laminé à la fibre de carbone. Il y a une chronique des superlatifs qui se rattache au modèle MP4 et à ses rejetons: jusqu'en 1992, il y a eu sept championnats de pilotes et six titres de constructeurs, mais environ aussi 15 victoires de Grand Prix possibles sur 16. Dennis est en cela plutôt constant dans sa façon de penser. Ce n'est que bien plus tard qu'il a réussi à se décider pour les techniques de pointe comme la suspension active et la boîte de vitesse automatique. Mais en 1993, après l'échec qu'il a essuyé à cause de tout son déficit technologique et d'un choix de moteur tardif et manqué, il est tout simplement revenu. Et le grand Ayrton Senna lui aussi, est revenu du néant de l'exil dans lequel il s'était envoyé lui-même et a gagné trois des six premiers Grands Prix. Tout comme celui de Ron Dennis, le nom de Frank Williams ne valait pas cher dans le cercle des Grands Prix au début. Certes, c'était quelqu'un qui avait de l'ambition et quelques résultats à son actif gagnés en Formule II. Mais la formule I, c'était un autre monde! Il devait montrer ce qu'il avait dans le ventre. C'est ce que fit Williams, mais l'ascension fut longue et pleine d'embûches. Et elle commença affreusement lorsque son pilote et ami Piers Courage brûla vif au Grand Prix de Hollande en 1970 dans l'enfer de magnésium de son monoplace alors que Williams lui avait fait faire la course à la place de l'Argentin Alejandro de Tomaso. Aujourd'hui encore, un jumeau poussiéreux de la voiture accidentée rappelle ce jour noir à Zandvoort, dans l'atelier de voitures de sport de De Tomaso à Modène. C'est toujours quand ils étaient au bord de la ruine que ce fil de fer de Britannique a toujours repris tout ce qui avait quatre roues et était disponible: la Politoys, la March 721, la ISO, le patrimoine de l'écurie d'Alexander Hesketh, lord excentrique et corpulent qui avait perdu le goût de la formule I et quelques livres … sterling, s'entend.

La victoire de Clay Regazzoni à Silverstone en juillet 1979 sur la Williams FW 07 a été alors l'hirondelle qui a fait le printemps de cette année-là et aussi du suivant: en 1980, Alan Jones a été champion du monde sur Williams, de façon tout aussi limite que Keke Rosberg en 1982. Il y avait longtemps que Frank Williams et son constructeur personnel, Patrick Head, s'étaient associés pour faire une formidable paire. Le fait que Williams, à la suite d'un accident automobile près du circuit de Paul Ricard ait été cloué dans un fauteuil roulant depuis le 8 mars 1986, n'a absolument rien empêché à sa présence magique dans le sport du Grand Prix. Seulement, tout ce qui vient plus tard, doit être considéré comme le triomphe d'une ambition pure, d'une volonté sans corps, comme l'a appelée le journaliste autrichien Helmut Zwickl, sans ironie macabre.

En 1987, le pilote de chez Williams, Nelson Piquet, a réussi de peu à battre son coéquipier Nigel Mansell. Pourtant, en 1992, plus personne n'arrivait à la cheville du Britannique combatif et de la Williams FW 14B avec laquelle le duo de techniciens Patrick Head et Adrian Newey avait porté au paroxysme le grand art de la technologie autour de trois paramètres: un châssis pensant, une boîte de vitesse automatique et un contrôle de traction, de telle sorte que la législation du sport automobile, la Fisa, s'est vue devoir intervenir.

La voiture de course de Grand Prix, que le grand transporteur Ted Toleman a mis au monde en 1981 et qui a été la très grande célébrité de son entreprise, était une équation à trois inconnues: le nouveau châssis de son designer très capable, Rory Byrne, le nouveau moteur turbo quatre cylindres du régleur Brian Hart, les pneus de chez Pirelli, nouveau venu sur le marché des pneus de formule I. On a longtemps été incapable de résoudre cette équation même si le petit Italien Teo Fabi gommait la Pole Position sur l'asphalte du Nürburgring en 1985 avec la Toleman TG 185. Mais il restait indiscutable que les châssis de Byrne se distinguaient d'entre tous et qu'ils faisaient bien partie des meilleurs, tant et si bien que les Toleman pouvaient plus souvent renoncer que les autres à un changement de pneus. Byrne s'y connaissait, par contre, et entre-temps, il s'employait à rendre ses voitures de plus en plus parfaites dans le tunnel aérodynamique du Royal Military College de Shrivenham qu'il pouvait utiliser exclusivement. Mais cela n'empêcha pas l'écurie de passer aux mains du fabricant de vêtements italiens, Luciano Benetton. Quand je fais quelque chose, dit le chef d'équipe Briatore, je le fais bien. Et c'est ainsi que depuis 1993, on dispose d'un châssis actif, d'une boîte de vitesse semi-automatique ainsi que de la pièce la plus puissante de Ford avec des soupapes pneumatiques. Il y a toujours quelque chose de particulier aux victoires de Benetton. Celle de Mexico en 1986 a été la première de Berger, celle du Japon en 1989 a été la seule de Nannini, celles du Japon et d'Australie en 1990 et celle du Canada en 1991, les dernières de Piquet et celle de Belgique en 1992 a été la première de Schumacher, certainement la première de nombreuses qui vont suivre.

McLAREN / WILLIAMS / BENETTON

Sin duda: la rapidísima trinidad de los primeros años del noventa de la Fórmula 1 está formada por McLaren, Williams y Benetton. Sólo los caminos, que desembocaban en el dominio absoluto de los Tres Grandes sobre el resto en el mundo de la Fórmula 1, tenían recorridos muy diversos. La saga McLaren era sin duda la más agradable al paladar, si bien tampoco estaba libre de reveses, chascos y fiascos. Esta saga se divide en tres capítulos: el pionero, los administradores del legado, el innovador.

El pionero: el propio Bruce McLaren, corredor de rango y hombre de la primera hora en 1966. Cuando el 2 de junio de 1970 perdió la vida prematuramente durante una prueba en Goodwood imperaban duelo y consternación. Pero la fiesta continuó. Los administadores del legado: hombres como Phil Kerr y Teddy Mayer, llevaron al equipo a dos Campeonatos Mundiales encumbrando a Emerson Fittipaldi en 1974 y a James Hunt en 1976 con la exitosa cuña M 23 de Gordon Copuck. Auge y decadencia: a finales de los setenta el punto débil se había convertido en una herida abierta, la séptima en la valoración de los constructores. El inovador: Mister McLaren II, Ron Dennis. Con él vinieron el encalado de primavera en 1980 y el *revirement*, el nuevo estilo para los siguientes años del siglo.

Y con él vino la *star* del diseño John Barnard. El 6 de marzo de 1981 presentó a la prensa, bajo una lluvia torrencial en Silverstone, su ingenioso modelo MP4, materia báscia para el monocoque: láminas de fibra de carbono. El MP4 y su descendencia están relacionados con una crónica de superlativos: siete Campeonatos de pilotos y seis Títulos de constructores hasta 1992, pero también 15 victorias de las 16 posibles en el Grand Prix de 1988. Y siendo Dennis más bien de ideología conservadora, no sería hasta más tarde que se lanzara a *high-tech-tops* como la suspensión activa y el cambio automático de marchas. Pero en 1993, después de que todos le habían reprochado solapadamente el déficit tecnológico y la elección, atrasada y equivocada, de motor, volvió a ser el de antes. Y también el gran Ayrton Senna volvió de la nada de su exilio autoimpuesto y ganó tres de los seis primeros Grandes Premios. Al igual que el de Ron Dennis, el nombre de Frank Williams era calderilla en el círculo del Grand Prix. Un aspirante venido de la Fórmula 2 con un par, cierto, de resultados respetables en el bolsillo. Pero la Fórmula 1 era otra cosa. Ahí tenía que demostrar lo que llevaba dentro. Y lo hizo, pero el ascenso de Williams fue duro y espinoso. El comienzo fue catastrófico. Durante el Gran Premio de Holanda de 1970, su piloto y amigo Piers Courage ardió en el infierno de magnesio del monoplaza que Williams había destinado al argentino Alejandro de Tomaso. Todavía hoy, en el yunque de coches deportivos de Tomaso, un polvoriento gemelo de aquel auto siniestro recuerda el funesto día de Zandvoort. Siempre al borde de la ruina, el flexible británico echaba mano de todo lo que tuviera cuatro ruedas gordas y estuviera disponible: el Politoys, el March 721, el ISO, la masa hereditaria del equipo del excéntrico y corpulento Lord Alexander Hesketh, cuando éste había perdido el humor y el gusto por la Fórmula 1 y también un par de libras —esterlinas, se sobreentiende—. La victoria de Clay Regazzoni en Silverstone en julio de 1979 con el Williams FW 07 fue la golondrina que hizo verano aquel año y también el siguiente, Alan Jones, se subió al palmarés del Mundial de 1980 en un Williams, tan por los pelos como Keke Rosberg en 1982. Ya hacía tiempo que Frank Williams y su constructor Patrick Head se habían fusionado en una yunta formidable. El que Williams esté atado a una silla de ruedas desde el 8 de marzo de 1986, tras sufrir un accidente no lejos del circuito Le Castellet, no cambió absolutamente nada en su mágica presencia en el deporte de Grand Prix. Sólo que todo lo posterior tendría que ser visto como triunfo de la pura ambición, de una voluntad sin cuerpo, como lo formulara el periodista austríaco Helmut Zwickl sin el menor tono de ironía macabra.

En 1987 en enconada disputa venció el piloto de la Williams Nelson Piquet a su colega de equipo Nigel Mansell. En 1992 ya nadie le llegaba al combativo británico a las suelas de los zapatos; ni al Williams FW 14B, con el que el dúo de técnicos Patrick Head y Adrian Newey había llevado a tales alturas el gran arte de la tecnología entorno a los tres parámetros: suspensión activa, cambio automático de marchas y control de tracción, que la organización legislativa del deporte del motor, FISA, se vio obligada a intervenir.

El coche de carreras de Grand Prix que el gran agente de transporte Ted Toleman trajo al mundo en 1981 para mayor gloria de su empresa, se trataba de una ecuación de tres desconocidos: el nuevo chasis de su competente diseñador Rory Byrne, el nuevo agregado del turbo cuatro cilindros del sintonizador Brian Hart, el *Pneus* de Pirelli, novato en el mercado de neumáticos de la Fórmula 1. La ecuación demostró no tener solución durante largo tiempo, si bien el pequeño italiano Teo Fabi grabó la *pole position* sobre el asfalto del Nürburgring en 1985 con el Toleman TG 185. Lo que estaba fuera de discusión es que si bien el chasis de Byrne tenía un aspecto bastante raro, era el mejor de todos, tan bueno, que los Toleman podían prescindir de un cambio de gomas cuando la mayoría de los equipos tenían que repetir rancho. Byrne era un manitas para estas cosas, y entretanto optimizaba sus coches en exclusivo en el túnel aerodinámico del Royal Military College de Shrivenham. En ello no influyó el hecho de que el equipo pasara en enero de 1986 a manos del fabricante de ropa, el italiano Luciano Benetton. Desde entonces, los bólidos de Byrne llevan los llamativos colores de United Colors of Benetton. Cuando él hacía algo, decía el jefe de equipo Flavio Briatore, lo hacía bien. Y así, desde 1993 disponemos de suspensión activa, un cambio semiautomático de marchas, así como la flor y la nata de la Ford con válvulas neumáticas. Las victorias de Benetton tienen siempre algo especial: la de México en 1986 fue la primera de Gerhard Berger; la de Japón en 1989, la única de Alessandro Nannini; las de Japón y Australia en 1990 y la de Canadá en 1991, la última de Nelson Piquet; y la de Bélgica en 1992, la primera —seguro que de muchas— de Michael Schumacher.

DESIGN

1

2, 3

4, 6

5, 7

8

1 McLaren Ford
   Barcelona (E) 1970

2 Yardley McLaren Ford
   Peter Revson (USA)
   Barcelona (E) 1973

3 Marlboro Texaco McLaren Ford
   Emerson Fittipaldi (BR)
   Anderstorp (S) 1974

4 Yardley McLaren Ford
   Mike Hailwood (GB)
   Jarama (E) 1974

5 Marlboro Texaco McLaren Ford
   Emerson Fittipaldi (BR)
   Zolder (B) 1975

6 Marlboro McLaren Ford
   Patrick Tambay (F)
   Brands Hatch (GB) 1978

7 Marlboro McLaren Ford
   John Watson (GB)
   Zolder (B) 1980

8 Im Fahrerlager
   In the paddock
   Dans le paddock
   En el campamento de los pilotos

   Silverstone (GB) 1983

9 Marlboro McLaren Ford
    Monaco 1978

10 Marlboro McLaren TAG Porsche
     Brands Hatch (GB) 1984

11 Marlboro McLaren Honda
     Spa - Francorchamps (B) 1990

DESIGN

1 Marlboro McLaren MP 4/5 B Honda
Imola (RSM) 1990

2 Marlboro McLaren MP 4/6 Honda
Montreal (CDN) 1991

3 Marlboro McLaren MP 4/6 Honda
Phoenix (USA) 1991

4 Marlboro McLaren MP 4/7 Honda
Monaco 1992

5 Marlboro McLaren MP 4/6 Honda
Ayrton Senna (BR)
Barcelona (E) 1991

6 Marlboro McLaren MP 4/7 Honda
Silverstone (GB) 1992

7 Marlboro McLaren MP 4/7 Honda
Monaco 1992

8 Marlboro McLaren MP 4/6 Honda
   Silverstone (GB) 1991

9 - 12 Marlboro McLaren MP 4/8 Ford
        Monaco 1993

1 Williams FW 07 - B
Alan Jones (AUS)
Hockenheim (D) 1980

2 Williams FW 07 - B
Alan Jones (AUS)
Hockenheim (D) 1980

3 Williams FW 08 - C
Keke Rosberg (SF)
Le Castellet (F) 1983

4 Williams FW 07 - C
Long Beach (USA) 1981

5, 6

7, 8

9

5   Williams FW 09 / 09 - B
     Keke Rosberg (SF)
     Brands Hatch (GB) 1984

6   Williams FW 10 / 10 - B
     Nigel Mansell (GB)
     Monaco 1985

7   Williams FW 08 - C
     Nelson Piquet (BR)
     Le Castellet (F) 1986

8   Williams FW 012 - B
     Nigel Mansell (GB)
     Estoril (P) 1988

9   Williams FW 13 - B
     Spa - Francorchamps (B) 1990

1

2

3

4

1 Williams Renault FW 14
Riccardo Patrese (I)
Hungaroring (H) 1991

2 Williams Renault FW 14
Riccardo Patrese (I)
Monaco 1991

3 Williams Renault FW 14
Riccardo Patrese (I)
Magny - Cours (F) 1991

4 Williams Renault FW 14
Nigel Mansell (GB)
Barcelona (E) 1992

5

6, 7

8, 9

10

5 Williams Renault FW 15 C
   Monaco 1993

6 Williams Renault FW 15 C
   Interlagos (BR) 1993

7 Williams Renault Team
   Imola (RSM) 1993

8 Williams Renault FW 15 C
   Alain Prost (F)
   Kyalami (ZA) 1993

9 Williams Renault FW 15 C
   Alain Prost (F)
   Imola (RSM) 1993

10 Williams Renault FW 15 C
    Alain Prost (F)
    Barcelona (E) 1993

DESIGN

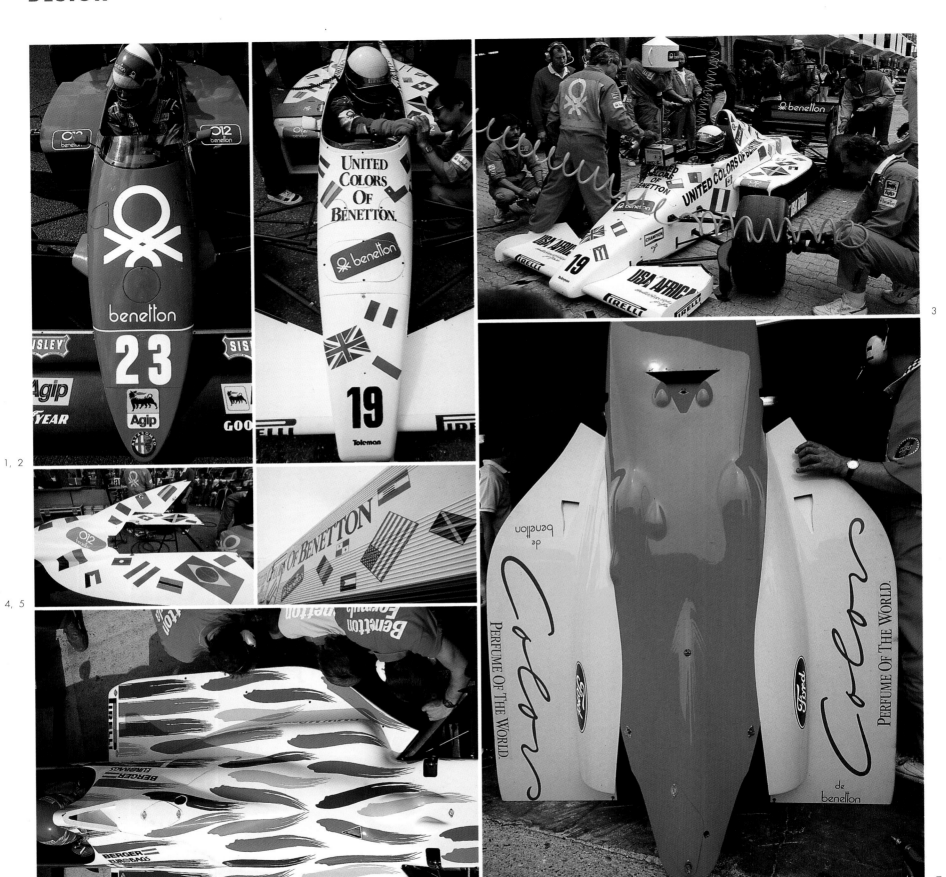

1 Benetton Alfa Romeo Turbo
   Eddie Cheever (USA)
   Spa - Francorchamps (B) 1985

2 Benetton Alfa Romeo Turbo
   Teo Fabi (I)
   Monaco 1985

3 Benetton Alfa Romeo Turbo
   Teo Fabi (I)
   Le Castellet (F) 1985

4 Benetton Alfa Romeo Turbo
   Monaco 1985

5 *Benetton Formel 1 - Transporter*
   Benetton Formula 1 car transporter
   Camion de transport de voiture Formule 1
   de Benetton
   Camión de transporte de vehículos de
   fórmula 1 de Benetton

6 Benetton BMW Turbo
   Gerhard Berger (A)
   Hungaroring (H) 1986

7 Benetton Ford
   Imola (RSM) 1987

8   Benetton - Alfa Romeo Turbo
    Eddie Cheever (USA)
    Monaco 1984

9   Benetton BMW - Turbo
    Gerhard Berger (A)
    Monaco 1986

10 Benetton Ford - Turbo
    Teo Fabi (I)
    Monaco 1987

11 Benetton Ford
    Nelson Piquet (BR)
    Monaco 1990

12 Camel Benetton Ford
    Nelson Piquet (BR)
    Monaco 1991

13 Camel Benetton Ford
    Michael Schumacher (D)
    Monaco 1992

14 Benetton Ford
    Thierry Boutsen (B)
    Paul Ricard (F) 1988

DESIGN

1 Benetton Alfa Romeo Turbo
   Zandvoort (NL) 1983

2 Benetton BMW Turbo
   Le Castellet (F) 1986

3 Benetton Ford Turbo
   Monaco 1987

4 Camel Benetton Ford
   Monza (I) 1992

5 Benetton Ford
   Silverstone (GB) 1990

6 Camel Benetton Ford Turbo V-8
   Hungaroring (H) 1991

7 Benetton Ford
   Monaco 1992

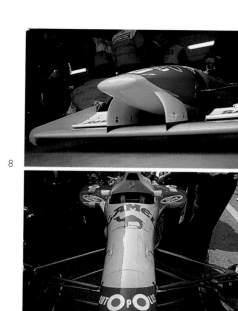

8

9

10

11

12

8 Camel Benetton Ford
Monaco 1991

9 Camel Benetton Ford
Monaco 1991

10 Camel Benetton Ford
Monaco 1992

11 Camel Benetton Ford
Michael Schumacher (D)
Kyalami (ZA) 1993

12 Camel Benetton Ford
Michael Schumacher (D)
Barcelona (E) 1993

In einem Punkte ähnelt der Grand Prix-Sport der Londoner Dauer-inszenierung von Agatha Christies Erfolgs-Klamotte „Die Mausefalle": Das Stück bleibt dasselbe, die Akteure wechseln – bis auf wenige. In den letzten 25 Jahren waren es in der Formel 1 rund 50, die gingen, oder kamen und gingen, oder kamen, manchmal als Hauptdarsteller, meistens als Komparsen. Für fast alle geriet die Glitzerwelt der Großen Preise zum Friedhof der Illusionen und zum Groschengrab: Nur in der Raumfahrt und an der Börse wird man in noch kürzerer Zeit noch mehr Geld los.

Beispiel British Racing Motors: Seit 1951 tief im ergiebigen Mut-terboden des englischen Nationalismus verwurzelt, brachte BRM aus den sechziger Jahren vor allem das rostige Renommee von Graham Hills Weltmeisterschaft 1962 mit. 1971 verlor das Team innerhalb von drei Monaten seine beiden Fahrer Pedro Rodriguez und Jo Siffert an den Renntod. 1972 verzettelte man sich zwar, angespornt durch eine Marlboro-Entwicklungshilfe von zwei Millionen Schweizer Franken, in eine Armada von fünf Wagen, aber BRM-Pilot Jean-Pierre Beltoise gewann auch den Großen Preis von Monaco – bei sintflutartigem Regen. Dann jedoch begann die qualvolle Agonie der Zwölfzylinder aus dem verschlafenen Städtchen Bourne. Sie dauerte bis 1977. Wenn BRM-Boß „Big" Louis Stanley am Ende mit seiner Gattin Jean die Boxengasse herunterflanierte, wirkten die beiden wie Denkmäler aus einer anderen Zeit – wie ihre Rennwagen, erst rundlich, dann einfach nur noch skurril gestaltet, die heute in Tom Wheatcrofts Donington Collection auf dem Altenteil stehen.

Beispiel March, im April 1969 von den vier Herren Max Mosley, Alan Rees, Graham Coaker und Robin Herd frohgemut aus der Taufe gehoben, am Ende der Saison 1992 still verblichen, drei Grand Prix-Siege. Der scheinbar revolutionäre 721X, an dem Herd 1972 das Getriebe vor der Hinterachse und damit fast alles Gewicht zum Schwerpunkt hin angesiedelt hatte, erwies sich als Papiertiger, der in praxi nie die Krallen ausfuhr. Ein Dreiachser mit vier angetriebenen Hinterrädern als Antwort auf Ken Tyrrells P34 machte Mitte der Siebziger zwar fleißig seine Hausaufgaben, erschien aber zum Glück nie zum Dienst auf den Grand Prix-Pisten. Als March mit dem kleinen und kompakten Modell 881 Adrian Neweys 1988 plötzlich wieder für vordere Ränge taugte, stand das finanzielle Menetekel bereits an der Wand. Gleichwohl hatte sich die im englischen Bicester ansässige Monoposto-Manufaktur um den Motorsport verdient gemacht – als Grossist für Rennwagen aller Arten zwischen Formel Atlantic und Indycar. Was dem heutigen FIA-Präsidenten Max Mosley einfällt, wenn er an die Jahre mit March zurückdenkt? Viel Arbeit, sagt er, und lächelt, und die Angst, am Ende des Monats die Löhne nicht auszah-len zu können.

Beispiel Renault, Verweildauer im Grand Prix-Geschäft zwischen 1977 und 1985, mitten in der Turbo-Ära also, Lehrstück zugleich, daß sich trotz markiger Absichtsbekundungen und der nach oben hin un-begrenzten Ressourcen der französischen Régie Nationale nicht alle erklärten Ziele so einfach erzwingen lassen: Zwischen Jean-Pierre

Jabouilles erstem Sieg in Dijon 1979 und Alain Prosts letztem in Zeltweg 1983 gönnte man sich 13 weitere Erfolge und damit einen Renault-Sieg in jedem achten Rennen. Die Fahrer- und Konstruk-torenweltmeisterschaften aber machten andere unter sich aus. Vielleicht litt man unter dem Ferrari-Syndrom: zu viele Häuptlinge, zu wenige Indianer.

Beispiel Alfa Romeo: Der Versuch der Mailänder, ab 1979 da anzuknüpfen, wo die legendären Alfetta 1951 aufgehört hatten, zeitigte katastrophale Resultate, und als Vorstand und Gewerkschaften in seltener Einmütigkeit die Wut über die verlorenen Lire-Milliarden packte, hatte es 1985 sein Bewenden mit dem verkrüppelten Comeback. Da war der rührige Austrokanadier Walter Wolf mit seinen viel geringeren Mitteln weitaus ökonomischer umgegangen: Er kaufte 1976 den vormaligen Lotus-Bediensteten Peter Warr als Team-Manager ein, den Williams-Kostgänger und Doktor der Philosophie Harvey Postlethwaite als Konstrukteur und den unter Ken Tyrrells Fuchtel leicht abgeklärten Jody Scheckter als Fahrer und stellte im Zeitraffertempo den Wolf WR 1 auf die Goodyear-bereiften Räder. Als dieser 1977 postwendend den Grand Prix von Argentinien gewann und später noch zwei weitere dazu, wähnte Walter Wolf, die Formel 1 liege ihm zu Füßen. Das tat die aber keineswegs, und so war der vielseitige und risikofreudige Unternehmer mit dem Ende der Saison 1979 seines neuen Spielzeugs überdrüssig. Selbst in der prunksüchtigen Welt der Großen Preise hinterließ er eine klaffende Lücke oder gar deren zwei, wo nämlich sein privater Lamborghini Countach und sein Jetranger gestanden hatten, alles in apartem Blaugold wie seine Rennautos.

Ein Unstern waltete unterdessen und auch später über dem Kennzei-chen „D" wie Deutschland, und fast immer konnte man sagen warum. Über dem Eifelland des Mayener Caravan-Bauers Günther Hennerici, einem verkappten March 721, hatte der Formenträumer Luigi Colani 1972 ein Füllhorn von unausgegorenen Ideen ausgegossen, die den steifen Sachzwängen der Realität nicht standhielten. Die Rennställe des pfälzischen Felgen-Fabrikanten Günter Schmid, ATS zwischen 1977 und 1984, Rial 1988 und 1989, wurden von Personalquerelen gebeutelt, Rennleiter und halbe Belegschaften gaben einander die Klinke in die Hand, nur Kontinuität mochte nie einkehren. Erich Zakowski hingegen wollte zuviel auf einmal, ein Eifel-Ferrari ohne die Mittel zum Mythos. Zwei Punkte in Imola 1987 – da winkte, so schien es, Licht am Ende des Tunnels für Team Zakspeed (1985 - 1989). Seine verbleibenden 26 Grand Prix indessen hagelten auf das kleine, aber propere Aufgebot Zakowskis nieder wie Daueraufträge des Unerträg-lichen im 14-Tage-Rhythmus. Alle aber wurden sie zum Opfer der Mercedes-Legende, in der geschrieben steht, man habe zu kommen, zu sehen und zu siegen. Heute werden dem vielversprechenden Team des Eidgenossen Peter Sauber Gunst und Geld des Stuttgarter Kon-zerns zuteil. Vielleicht nimmt man es sogar eines Tages in die Familie auf wie Saubers Silberpfeile in der Gruppe C. Der Erfolg hat nämlich viele Väter – manchmal stellt sich sogar der richtige ein…

In one respect Grand Prix racing resembles the seemingly imperishable London theatre production of Agatha Christie's whodunnit "The Mousetrap": the play remains the same, the actors change. In the last 25 years about 50 Formula One teams went, or came and went, or went, some as leading protagonists, the majority as extras. In most cases the glittering world of the Grand Prix turned out to be a cemetery of illusions, devouring enormous amounts of money in no time, second to space travel and the stock exchange only.

This is what happened to British Racing Motors, for instance: Firmly rooted in the fertile soil of British nationalism since 1951, BRM arrived in the seventies with the somewhat rusty renown of Graham Hill's 1962 championship. Tragedy struck when, in 1971, the team's drivers Pedro Rodriguez and Jo Siffert were killed within three months of each other. In 1972, encouraged by a Marlboro allowance of two million Swiss francs, BRM entered an armada of five cars, Jean-Pierre Beltoise winning the Monaco Grand Prix tiptoeing his path through a veritable deluge with the assurance of a sleepwalker. Then, however, began the painful agony of the twelve cylinder cars from the sleepy little town of Bourne. It was to last until 1977. When BRM boss "Big" Louis Stanley and his wife Jean strutted up and down the pitlane in the final phase, they looked like monuments from another time — as did their cars, first plump, then just strangely shaped, which are on view in Tom Wheatcroft's Donington Collection today.

This is what happened to March, founded in April 1969 by the four gentlemen Max Mosley, Alan Rees, Graham Coaker and Robin Herd, expired in peace at the end of the 1992 season with three Grand Prix victories to the make's credit: Herd's seemingly revolutionary 1972 model 721X, its final drive behind the gearbox to reduce the polar moment of inertia, never stood by its promise, nor did a six-wheeler with which the Bicester company responded to Ken Tyrrell's 1976 P34 and which never made its way to the circuits. In 1988 March was competitive again with Adrian Newey's small and compact 881 model. But then the writing was already on the wall in financial terms. For all that March deserved well of racing being a supermarket for cars of all descriptions from Formula Atlantic to Indycars for many years. If you ask the present FIA president, Max Mosley, what comes into his mind thinking back to his time at March he will say, smiling: "Lots of work and, towards the end of the month, the fright not to be able to pay our employees' wages."

This is what happened to Renault, involved as a team from 1977 until 1985, i.e. in the turbo era, a case history perfectly suited to illustrate that you cannot sway luck with firm intention and a huge budget: Between Jean-Pierre Jabouille's first Renault win in 1979 at Dijon and Alain Prost's last one at Zeltweg in 1983 there admittedly were thirteen more victories, but the championships were disputed by others. Perhaps the Régie's Grand Prix effort suffered from the Ferrari syndrome: too many chiefs, not enough Indians.

This is what happened to Alfa Romeo: The attempt of the Milan state enterprise to carry on in 1979 where the legendary Alfetta had left off in 1951 produced disastrous results, and so its abortive comeback was discontinued in 1985 when the managing committee and the trade unions chafed at the loss of billions of lire in rare unanimity. By way of comparison, energetic Austro-Canadian Walter Wolf made much better use of much smaller means employing former Lotus man Peter Warr as team manager, ex-Williams engineer and doctor of philosophy Harvey Postlethwaite as constructor, and slightly mellowed Tyrrell recruit Jody Scheckter as driver in 1976 and putting his Wolf WR 1 on its Goodyear-shod wheels remarkably quickly. When Scheckter won its inaugural race in Argentina on January 9th, 1977, as well as the Monaco and the Canadian rounds, Wolf jumped to the conclusion that the Grand Prix world lay at his feet. That is exactly what it did not, and so the versatile and venturesome entrepreneur was fed up with his new plaything at the end of the 1979 season. Even in the ostentatious microcosm of Formula One he left a gap or two, at least where his private Lamborghini Countach and his Jetranger helicopter had stood, all in his smart dark blue and gold colours.

Less spectacular were the German attempts to attain fame in the highest echelon of motor racing, and you could always say why. The design poet, Luigi Colani, had emptied a cornucopia full of half-baked ideas over Caravan builder Günther Hennerici's 1972 Eifelland. So the car only worked after it had been bought by an English businessman and converted back into the March 721 which it had originally been, in the capable hands of John Watson. The two racing stables of wheel manufacturer Günter Schmid, ATS between 1977 and 1984 and Rial from 1988 to 1989, were afflicted by continuous staff problems and the perpetual change of team managers so that they lacked the continuity it takes to be successful in this sport. Erich Zakowski, however, wanted too much at a time, an Eifel Ferrari without the means to be a myth. Two points at Imola in 1987 – that seemed to spell the breakthrough for Team Zakspeed (1985 - 1989). But in its remaining 26 Grand Prix Zakowski's small but neat outfit went from bad to worse, its white-haired boss finding it difficult indeed to accept defeat after a rewarding career in saloon and sports car racing. Like the others he had fallen a victim to the Mercedes legend, which says that you have to come, to see, and to win. Today the promising team of Swiss Peter Sauber enjoys the benefit of being supported in pecuniary and in moral terms by the Stuttgart giant. Maybe it will even be accepted as a member of the family one day like Sauber's silver arrows in Group C. So far Sauber has come and seen, but he has yet to win…

Sur un point, le sport, du Grand Prix ressemble à une mise en scène permanente londonienne du vieux succès d'Agatha Christie: «La Souricière». La pièce reste la même, les acteurs changent, sauf quelques-uns. Dans la formule 1 des 25 dernières années, une cinquantaine sont partis, sont venus et repartis, ou sont venus, quelquefois en ayant le rôle principal et la plupart du temps le second rôle. Pour presque tous, le monde scintillant des Grands Prix est devenu le cimetière des illusions et une tombe de quatre sous. Il n'y a que dans l'espace et à la bourse que l'on peut perdre encore plus d'argent en un temps plus restreint.

Un exemple: British Racing Motors: depuis 1951, enraciné dans la terre mère et généreuse du nationalisme anglais, BRM a surtout tiré des années 60 la renommée rouillée du championnat du monde de Graham Hill en 1962. En 1971, l'équipe a perdu en trois mois ses deux pilotes Pedro Rodriguez et Jo Siffert, morts sur le circuit. En 1972, on s'est bien éparpillé, incité par une aide au développement Marlboro de deux millions de francs suisses dans une armada de cinq voitures, mais le pilote de chez BRM, Jean-Pierre Beltoise, gagna aussi le Grand Prix de Monaco sous une pluie diluvienne. Pourtant, l'agonie horrible des douze cylindres commença dans la petite ville endormie de Bourne. Elle a duré jusqu'en 1977. Quand le boss de BRM, «Big» Louis Stanley, descendait l'aire des boxes en flânant en compagnie de son épouse Jean, ils donnaient tous les deux l'impression de venir d'une autre époque, comme leurs voitures de course, tout d'abord rondelettes, puis tout simplement bizarres; elles se trouvent maintenant dans la collection de Donington appartenant à Tom Wheatcroft, dans le coin des antiquités.

L'exemple de la March, présentée dans la joie par quatre messieurs: Max Mosley, Alan Rees, Graham Coaker et Robin Herd, en avril 1969, et, à la fin de la saison de 1992, elle a doucement disparu: trois victoires de Grands Prix. La 721X apparemment révolutionnaire dans laquelle Herd avait placé en 1972 la boîte de vitesse devant l'axe arrière et avait réussi ainsi à obtenir presque tout le poids sur le centre de gravité, n'est pas devenue ce qu'elle aurait pu être. Un trois axes avec quatre roues arrières motrices en réponse à la P34 de Ken Tyrrell au milieu des années 70; il a bien fait ses devoirs, mais heureusement qu'il n'est pas apparu au service des pistes du Grand Prix. Quand March s'est retrouvé bon pour les premiers rangs, tout à coup, en 1988, avec le petit modèle 881 compact d'Adrian Newey, la débâcle financière était déjà à l'ordre du jour. N'importe, la manufacture anglaise de monoplaces dont le siège était à Bicester s'était beaucoup engagée dans le sport automobile comme grossiste en voitures de course en tout genre entre la Formel Atlantic et l'Indycar. Que vient à l'esprit de l'actuel président de la FIA, Max Mosley, quand il repense aux années passées avec March? Beaucoup de travail, dit-il en souriant, et la peur de ne pas pouvoir payer les salaires de fin de mois.

Renault, par exemple, qui est resté dans le Grand Prix entre 1977 et 1985, donc au milieu de l'ère des turbos, c'est aussi une leçon: tous les objectifs ne peuvent pas être toujours aussi facilement atteints malgré des déclarations d'intention précises et les ressources illimitées de la Régie Nationale française. Entre la première victoire de Jean-Pierre Jabouille à Dijon en 1979 et la dernière d'Alain Prost à Zeltweg en 1983, on s'est offert 13 autres victoires et cela a donné ainsi une victoire de Renault toutes les huits courses. Mais il y en a d'autres qui se sont arrangés entre eux pour les championnats du monde de pilotes et de constructeurs. Peut-être est-ce que l'on souffrait trop du syndrome de Ferrari: trop de chefs, pas assez d'indiens.

Alfa Romeo par exemple: quand les Milanais ont essayé de reprendre, à partir de 1979, là où les Alfetta avaient arrêté en 1951, cela a entraîné des résultats catastrophiques et, quand la direction et les syndicats, dans une rare unanimité, enragèrent devant cette perte de milliards de lires, on en resta là, en 1985, avec un comeback atrophié. Par contre, Walter Wolf, l'Austro-Canadien énergique avait employé ses moyens plus modestes avec bien plus de parcimonie. Il acheta en 1976 l'ancien employé de Lotus, Peter Warr, comme manager de l'équipe, le pensionnaire de Williams et docteur en philosophie, Harvey Postlethwaite, comme constructeur, et Jody Scheckter, un peu apathique sous la coupe de Ken Tyrrell comme pilote et mit en un temps accéléré la Wolf WR 1 sur des roues aux pneus Goodyear. Quand celle-ci gagna le Grand Prix d'Argentine par retour du courrier en 1977, et deux autres supplémentaires plus tard, Walter Wolf a cru à tort que la Formule 1 était à ses pieds. Mais cela ne se passa pas comme cela et c'est ainsi qu'à la fin de la saison 1979, l'entrepreneur aux multiples facettes, amoureux du risque, en a eu assez de son nouveau jouet.

Une mauvaise étoile se trouvait à ce moment-là, et un peu plus tard encore sur le signe «D» comme Deutschland et on pouvait presque toujours dire pourquoi. Le rêveur de formes, Luigi Colani, avait déversé en 1972 une corne d'abondance d'idées non élaborées qui ne résistaient pas aux dures lois de la réalité sur le constructeur de caravanes de Mayen, dans l'Eifel, Günther Hennerici et par là, sur une March 721 tronquée. Les écuries de Günter Schmidt, fabricant de jantes dans le Palatinat, ATS entre 1977 et 1984, Rial 1988 et 1989 ont été secouées par des querelles au sein du personnel, des directeurs de course et des moitiés d'équipes n'arrêtaient pas de défiler et la continuité ne parvenait pas à revenir. Par contre, Erich Zakowski en voulait trop à la fois, une Ferrari Eifel sans les moyens pour accéder au mythe. Deux points à Imola en 1987: une lueur apparaissait à l'horizon pour l'équipe Zakspeed (1985-1989). Ses 26 Grands Prix restants grêlèrent sur le petit mais correct déploiement de voitures de Zakowski. Mais tous ont été victimes de la légende de Mercedes dans laquelle il est écrit que l'on doit venir, voir et vaincre. Aujourd'hui, la faveur et l'argent du konzern de Stuttgart sont attribués à l'équipe prometteuse de Peter Sauber. On adoptera peut-être même un jour comme la flèche d'argent de Sauber dans le groupe C. En effet, le succès a beaucoup de pères. Quelquefois, c'est même le bon qui apparaît…

En un punto se parece el deporte del Grand Prix a la representación permanente de la exitosa comedia de Agatha Christie «La ratonera»: la pieza es siempre la misma, los actores cambian —exceptuando a unos pocos—. En los últimos 25 años fueron unos 50 los que se fueron de la Fórmula 1, o vinieron y se fueron, o vinieron, a veces como actores principales muchas veces como comparsas. Para casi todos ellos se convirtió el luminoso mundo de los Grandes Premios en cementerio de ilusiones y tragaperras: sólo en la astronáutica y en la bolsa se puede gastar más dinero en menos tiempo.

Ejemplo British Racing Motors: profundamente enraizada desde 1951 en el fecundo suelo del nacionalismo inglés, la BRM trajo consigo desde los años sesenta sobre todo el herrumbroso renombre del Campeonato Mundial de 1962 de Graham Hill. En 1971, el equipo perdió, en el lapso de trens meses, a sus corredores Pedro Rodríguez y Jo Siffert, muertos las carreras. En 1972 se malgastó —espoleados por una ayuda al desarrollo por parte de Marlboro por valor de dos millones de francos suizos— en una armada de cinco coches, pero el piloto de BRM Jean-Pierre Beltoise ganó también el Gran Premio de Mónaco bajo una lluvia descomunal. Pero después comenzó la tortuosa agonía de los doce cilindros de la soñolienta ciudad de Bourne que se prolongó hasta 1977. Cuando el *boss* de la BRM «Big» Louis Stanley paseaba, a fines de 1977, con su esposa Jean por el pasaje *boxes*, ambos semejaban monumentos de otra época, lo mismo que sus coches de carreras —primeramente redondeados, luego de diseño simplemente grotesco— que hoy se han destinado a la Tom Wheatcrofts Donington Collection.

Ejemplo March: bautizado en abril de 1969, con Max Mosley, Alan Rees, Graham Coaker y Robin Herd como orgullosos padrinos, silenciosamente rezagado al final de la temporada de 1992, triunfarion tres veces en el Gran Premio. El aparentemente revolucionario 721X, en el que Herd había instalado la caja de cambios antes del eje trasero, trasladando así todo el peso a esta zona, resultó ser un tigre de papel que en la práctica no sacaba las garras. Un tres ejes con tracción en las cuatro ruedas traseras, como respuesta al P34 de Ken Tyrrell, hacía concienzudamente sus tareas a mediados de los setenta, pero, por suerte, no apareció nunca por el trabajo en las pistas de Grand Prix. Cuando en 1988 March, con un pequeño y compacto modelo 881 de Adrian Newey, volvió a ser aprovechable para los asientos de preferencia, el momento financiero ya estaba escrito. No obstante, la manufactura de *monoposto* con sede en el inglés Bicester había hecho méritos como mayorista de coches de carreras de todo tipo, desde el Formel Atlantic hasta el Indycar. ¿Qué se le ocurrirá al actual presidente de la FIA, Max Mosley, cuando rememora los años con March? Mucho trabajo, dice y sonríe, y el miedo de no poder pagar a los empleados a fin de mes.

Ejemplo Renault: tiempo de permanencia en el negocio del Grand Prix entre 1977 y 1985, o sea, de lleno en la era turbo; obra maestra a la vez, que, a pesar de las enjundiosas declaraciones de intenciones y de los recursos ilimitados del Régie Nationale francés, no puede alcanzar tan fácilmente todas las metas manifestadas: entre el primer triunfo de Jean-Pierre Jabouille en Dijon en 1979 y el último de Alain Prost en Zeltweg en 1983 se dieron el lujo de celebror otros 13 éxitos, y con ello, un triunfo-Renault en cada ocho carreras. Los conductores y constructores de Campeonatos Mundiales lo decidieron otros entre sí. Quizás se sufría bajo el síndroma Ferrari, demasiados caciques y pocos indios.

Ejemplo Alfa Romeo: el intento del milanés de continuar en 1979 en el punto en que el legendario Alfetta había terminado en 1951, maduró resultados catastrofales, y cuando la presidencia y los sindicatos se vieron sacudidos, en rara unanimidad, por la misma furia sobre los millones de liras perdidos, todos se dieron por satisfechos con el contrahecho *comeback*. El tranquilo austrocanadiense Walter Wolf había administrado sus escasos medios más económicamente: compró en 1976 al anteriormente empleado de la Lotus Peter Warr como *manager* de equipo, el economista de la Williams y doctor en Filosofía Harvey Postlethwaite como constructor, y a Jody Schecker, que ya había sido ligeramente ilustrado bajo la férula de Ken Tyrrell como conductor. En un tiempo record colocó el Wolf WR 1 sobre ruedas calzadas por Goodyear. Cuando éste ganó el Grand Prix de Argentina y más tarde otros dos más, Wolf se figuraba que la Fórmula 1 estaba a sus pies. Este no era precisamente el caso, de modo que, ya a finales de la temporada de 1979, el polifacético y arriesgado empresario estaba ya harto de su nuevo juguete. Incluso en el ostentoso mundo de los Grandes Premios dejó a su marcha una laguna, o mejor dicho dos, correspondientes a los lugares donde aparcaba su Lamborghini Countach privado y su caro helicóptero, ambos en los selectos azul y oro de sus coches de carreras.

Entretanto rondaba una persistente mala estrella sobre los intentos alemanes de probar suerte y casi siempre había un porqué. Sobre el Eifelland, un March 721 disfrazado del constructor milanés de caravanas Hennerici, volcó el poeta del diseño Luigi Colani en 1972 una cornucopia de ideas a medio cocer que no daban la talla ante las inflexibles exigencias de la realidad. Los equipos de carreras del fabricante de llantas palatino Günter Schmid —ATS entre 1977 y 1984, Rial entre 1988 y 1989— eran víctimas de querellas personales, jefes de equipo y la mitad del personal eran constantemente relevados. Zakowski, por el contrario, quería demasiado de golpe, un Ferrari Eifel sin los medios para ser un mito. Dos puntos en Imola 1987: parecía que la luz brillaba al final del túnel para el equipo Zakspeed (1985 - 1989). Sus restantes 26 Grand Prix abatían entretanto al pequeño pero aliñado reclutamiento de Zakowski como una orden permanente de lo insoportable en ritmo de dos semanas. Pero todos ellos se convirtieron en víctimas de la leyenda Mercedes, en la que está escrito que hay que llegar, ver y vencer. Al prometedor equipo del confederado Peter Sauber le toca hoy por suerte el patrocinio y el dinero del consorcio de Stuttgart. Quizá sea aceptado un día en la familia, como las flechas de plata de Sauber en el grupo C. De momento, Sauber ha llegado y ha visto, pero todavía no ha vencido...

DESIGN

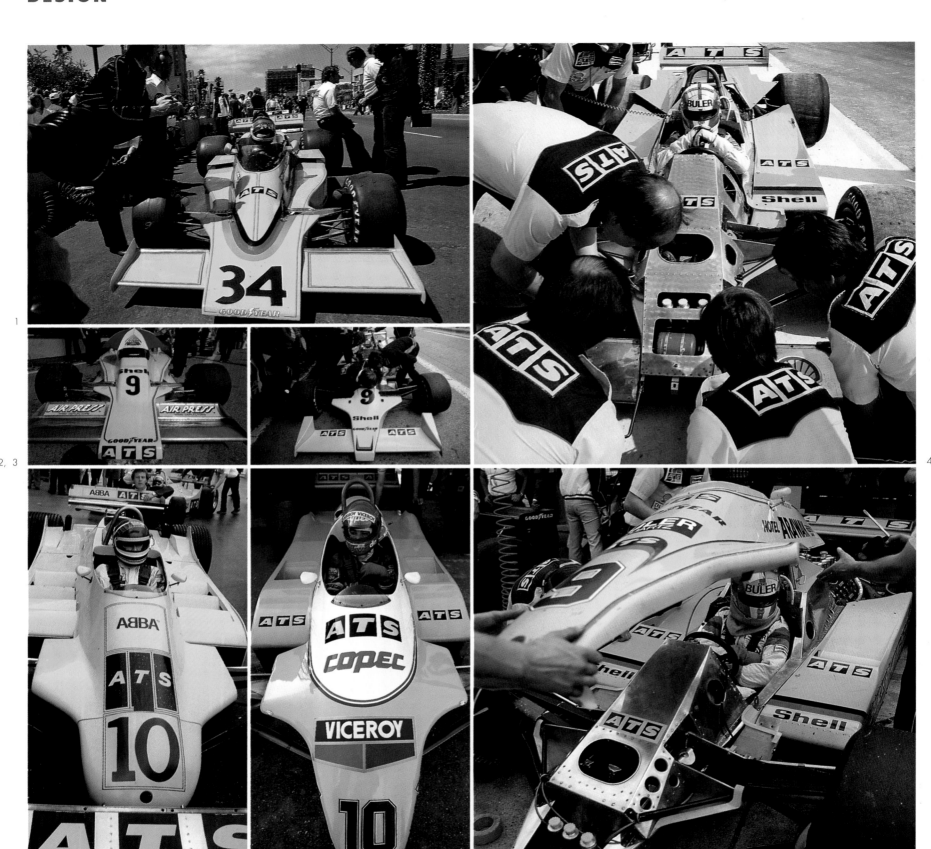

1 ATS Penske PC 4 Ford
   Jean - Pierre Jarier (F)
   Long Beach (USA) 1977

2 ATS HS 1 Ford
   Jochen Mass (D)
   Jarama (E) 1978

3 ATS D 2 Ford
   Hans - Joachim Stuck (D)
   Jarama (E) 1979

4 ATS D4 Ford
   Marc Surer (CH)
   Imola (RSM) 1980

5 ATS A38 Ford
   Slim Borgudd (S)
   Imola (RSM) 1981

6 ATS D5 Ford
   Eliseo Salazar (CHILE)
   Dijon - Prenois (F) 1982

7 ATS D4 Ford
   Marc Surer (CH)
   Hockenheim (D) 1980

8 *Teamwork ATS*
 Hockenheim (D) 1980

9 ATS D6 BMW Turbo
 Manfred Winkelhock (D)
 Long Beach (USA) 1983

10 ATS D6 BMW Turbo
  Manfred Winkelhock (D)
  Zandvoort (NL) 1983

11 ATS D6 BMW Turbo
  Silverstone (GB) 1983

12 ATS D7 BMW Turbo
  Manfred Winkelhock (D)
  Monaco 1984

1   Rial ARC 01 Ford
    Monaco 1988

2   Rial ARC 01 Ford
    Andrea de Cesaris (I)
    Spa - Francorchamps (B) 1988

3 Rial ARC 01 Ford
   Andrea de Cesaris (I)
   Monaco 1988

4 Rial ARC 02 Ford
   Christian Danner (D)
   Monaco 1989

5 Rial ARC 02 Ford
   Christian Danner (D)
   Hockenheim (D) 1989

DESIGN

1, 2, 3

4

5

6

7

8

9

10

1   Zakspeed 841
    Jonathan Palmer (GB)
    Brands Hatch (GB) 1986

2   Zakspeed 871
    Bernd Schneider (D)
    Silverstone (GB) 1988

3   Zakspeed 891 Yamaha
    Aguri Suzuki (J)
    Imola (RSM) 1989

4   *Formel 1 - Transporter / Formula 1 car
    transporter / camion de transport de voiture
    Formule 1 / camión de transporte de
    vehículos de fórmula 1*
    Zakspeed
    Monza (I) 1987

5   West Zakspeed Yamaha
    *Kopfhörer / headphones /
    casque / audífonos*

6   Zakspeed 841, Jonathan Palmer (GB)
    Monaco 1985

7   Zakspeed 861
    Jonathan Palmer (GB)
    Monaco 1986

8   Zakspeed 871
    Martin Brundle (GB)
    Monaco 1987

9   Zakspeed 871 B
    Piercarlo Ghinzani (I)
    Monaco 1988

10 Zakspeed 891 Yamaha
    Bernd Schneider (D)
    Monaco 1989

1, 12

13

14

15

11 Bernd Schneider (D)
Helmut Barth (D)
Chefingenieur/ chief engineer /
ingénieur chef / ingeniero jefe

Erich Zakowski (D)
Teamchef / team boss / directeur
d'équipe / director de equipo

Zakspeed

Hockenheim (D) 1988

12 Imola (RSM) 1988

13 Piercarlo Ghinzani (I)
Zakspeed
Imola (RSM) 1988

14 Bernd Schneider (D)
Zakspeed Yamaha
Jerez (E) 1989

15 Zakspeed
Christian Danner (D)
Hungaroring (H) 1987

1   Warsteiner Arrows A2 Ford
    Jochen Mass (D)
    Dijon - Prenois (F) 1979

2   Warsteiner Arrows A2 Ford
    Jochen Mass (D)
    Hockenheim (D)

3   Warsteiner Arrows A2 Ford
    Riccardo Patrese (I)
    Hockenheim (D) 1979

4   Warsteiner Arrows A2 Ford
    Riccardo Patrese (I)
    Dijon - Prenois (F) 1979

5   Warsteiner Arrows A2 Ford
    Hockenheim (D) 1979

6   Warsteiner Arrows A3 Ford
    Jochen Mass (D)
    Long Beach (USA) 1980

7, 8

9, 10

11

13

14

7 Ragno Arrows A3 B Ford V-8
   Siegfried Stohr (D/I)
   Long Beach (USA) 1981

8 Barclay Arrows A7
   BMW M Turbo
   Marc Surer (CH)
   Brands Hatch (GB) 1984

9 Barclay Arrows A8
   BMW Turbo
   Thierry Boutsen (B)
   Monaco 1985

10 Barclay Arrows A8
   BMW Turbo
   Thierry Boutsen (B)
   Hockenheim (D) 1986

11 Arrows A 11 B Ford V-8
   Bernd Schneider (D)
   Jerez (E) 1990

12 Footwork FA 12 C Ford V-8
   Michele Alboreto (I)
   Monza (I) 1991

13 Footwork FA 12 C Ford V-8
   Monaco 1991

14 Footwork FA 13 / Mugen Honda V-10
   Aguri Suzuki (J)
   Mexiko 1992

1 Minardi M 185 Motori Moderni V-6 Turbo
Estoril (P) 1985

2 Minardi M 192 Lamborghini V-12
Gianni Morbidelli (I)
Imola (RSM) 1992

3 Minardi M 189 Ford V-8
Pierluigi Martini (I)
Jerez (E) 1989

4 Minardi M 193 Ford V-8
Kyalami (ZA) 1993

5 BMS Dallara 188 Ford V-8
Alex Caffi (I)
Monaco 1988

6 BMS Dallara 189 Ford V-8
Alex Caffi (I)
Monaco 1989

7 BMS Dallara 190 Ford V-8
Andrea de Cesaris (I)
Monaco 1990

8 BMS Dallara 191 Judd V-10
   JJ. Letho (SF)
   Monaco 1991

9 BMS Dallara 192 Ferrari V-12
   JJ. Letho (SF)
   Monaco 1992

10 Lola - BMS T 93/30 Ferrari V-12
    Luca Badoer (I)
    Monaco 1993

11 Lola - BMS T 93/30 Ferrari V-12
    Michele Alboreto (I)
    Kyalami (ZA) 1993

12 Lola - BMS T 93/30 Ferrari V-12
    Michele Alboreto (I)
    Kyalami (ZA) 1993

13 Lola - BMS T 93/30 Ferrari V-12
    Interlagos (BR) 1993

14 Lola - BMS T 93/30 Ferrari V-12
    Kyalami (ZA) 1993

1 Renault RS 01 R Turbo
   Jean - Pierre Jabouille (F)
   Silverstone (GB) 1977

2 Renault RE 20 R Turbo
   Hockenheim (D) 1980

3 Renault RE 30 Turbo
   Patrick Tambay (F)
   Monaco 1984

4 Renault RE 40 Turbo
   Alain Prost (F)
   Long Beach (USA) 1983

5 Renault RE 60/60 B Turbo
   Patrick Tambay (F)
   Monaco 1985

6 Renault RE 60/60 B Turbo
   Derek Warwick (GB)
   Imola (RSM) 1985

7

9, 10

11

8

12

7 Ligier JS 5 Matra
   Jacques Laffite (F)
   Le Castellet (F) 1976

8 Talbot Ligier JS 17 Matra
   Patrick Tambay (F)
   Dijon - Prenois (F) 1981

9 Ligier JS 9 Matra
   Jacques Laffite (F)
   Monaco 1978

10 Ligier JS 7 Matra
   Jacques Laffite (F)
   Monaco 1978

11 Ligier JS 37 Renault
   Thierry Boutsen (B)
   Le Castellet (F) 1992

12 Ligier JS 39 Renault
   Monaco 1993

2, 3

4, 5

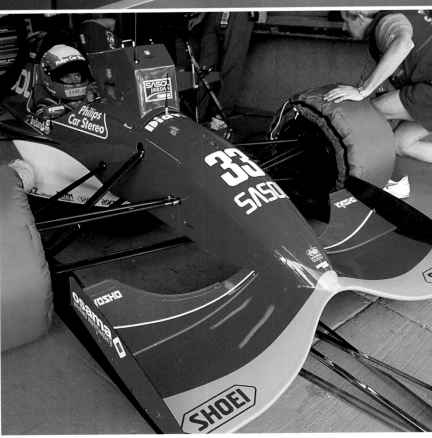

1

6

7

1 Jordan 191 Ford V-8
  Spa - Francorchamps (B) 1991

2 Jordan 191 Ford V-8
  Bertrand Gachot (F)
  Imola (RSM) 1991

3 Jordan 191 Ford V-8
  Montreal (CDN) 1991

4 Jordan 191 Ford V-8
  Bertrand Gachot (F)
  Monaco 1991

5 Jordan 191 Ford V-8
  Bertrand Gachot (F)
  Monaco 1991

6 Jordan 192 Yamaha V-12
  Mauricio Gugelmin (BR)
  Mexiko 1992

7 Jordan 193 Hart 1035 V-10
  Rubens Barrichello (BR)
  Monaco 1993

8   Sauber C 12 Ilmor V-10
    Karl Wendlinger (A)
    Interlagos (BR) 1993

9   Sauber C 12 Ilmor V-10
    Kyalami (ZA) 1993

10 Sauber C 12 Ilmor V-10
    Barcelona (E) 1993

11 Sauber C 12 Ilmor V-10
    Karl Wendlinger (A)
    Barcelona (E) 1993

12 Sauber C 12 Ilmor V-10
    Monaco 1993

13 Sauber C 12 Ilmor V-10
    JJ. Letho (SF)
    Monaco 1993

TECHNIK

In die Rezeptur für den Grand Prix-Sieg gehörte 1991, was der zuständige Shell-Direktor Roger Lindsay Designerbenzin oder, fast zärtlich, seine Grand Crus nannte, gereift und gekeltert in den Labors der großen Spritlieferanten der Formel 1. Ein Tank voll kostete den Gegenwert eines kleineren Mittelklassewagens. Seitdem diese Elixiere des Teufels im Bannstrahl der Motorsportbehörde FISA verpufft sind, bedarf es einer ausgeklügelten Elektronik, will man als erster über die Ziellinie fahren, auch sie von dubiosem sportlichen, dafür aber von deftigem materiellen Wert.

Unberührt von dergleichen kostspieligen Zeitmoden erhielten sich die drei Säulen, mit denen der Erfolg in diesem Sport steht oder fällt: Reifen, Chassis und Motor. Die Geschichte der vergangenen 25 Jahre im Grand Prix-Geschäft ist auch die Geschichte des DFV, für Double Four Valves (zweimal vier Ventile). 1966 ein Auftragswerk von Ford England für die kleine, aber feine Motorenschmiede Cosworth im Norden von London, war der Cosworth DFV ein Stück Politik, stand er doch werbewirksam für die viel schlichter ausgelegten Serien-Acht-zylinder des amerikanischen Mutterkonzerns. Er stellte überdies ein pragmatisches Kabinettstückchen dar, denn in ihm fanden sich praktisch zwei FVA-Triebwerke für die Formel 2 zu einem kompakten und leichten V8 zusammen – ein Artikel, den Erstkunde Colin Chapman dringend benötigte, um seine Lotus-Leichtbauphilosophie zu instrumentieren. Und er war preiswert: Nicht mehr als die vereinbarten 100.000 Pfund Sterling standen auf dem Scheck, unter den Ford-Boß Stanley Gillen seine Unterschrift setzte. Als Lebenserwartung rechnete man das Übliche hoch: drei bis vier Jahre. Dann aber setzte ein, was Cosworth-Chef Keith Duckworth, in Personalunion beides, den Triumph des Entwicklers über den Designer nennt. Er kostete ihn weidlich aus: 153 weitere DFV-Siege lagen zwischen dem ersten durch Jim Clark in Zandvoort 1967 auf dem Lotus 49 und dem letzten durch Michele Alboreto 1983 in Detroit mit dem Tyrrell. Da hieß der Ford V8 bereits DFY und war ein Kurzhuber, über 520 PS stark und nur 133 Kilo schwer, wo der Ur-DFV 162 Kilo auf die Waage und 405 PS auf die Bremse gebracht hatte. Zweimal wurde er von existentiellen Krisen gebeutelt – mit der ersten konnte er leben, der zweiten erlag er.

Die Bedrohung durch die Zwölfzylinder, stets latent, wurde in den siebziger Jahren konkret. Die V12 von BRM, Matra, Tecno, Alfa und anfänglich noch Maserati mochten schön aussehen und schön klingen, aber echte Gefahr ging von ihnen nicht aus. Die jedoch konnte man förmlich festmachen an der Marke Ferrari und dem Mann Niki Lauda und an der Koalition zwischen beiden. Drei Championate mußten die Ford-Fahrer in alternierendem Rhythmus an Piloten der roten Renner aus Maranello abgeben: 1975 und 1977 an Lauda, 1979 an Scheckter. Zwischen 1980 und 1982 bestätigte sich, was sich mit der vernichtenden Lotus-Dominanz 1978 angedeutet hatte: Der DFV harmonierte perfekt mit dem Flügel-Prinzip, das nach schmalen Fahrzeugkörpern verlangte.

Dann jedoch, nach sechs Lehrjahren, begannen die sechs Herrenjahre der Turbos, wurde die Formel 1 zum Erbhof des BMW-Vierzylinders und der V6 von Porsche und Honda. 1985 wankte mit Ken Tyrrell der Treueste der Treuen mitten in der Saison und wurde nach dem Grand Prix der USA Ost aus der Cosworth-Abonnentenliste gestrichen. Da leisteten die Top-Turbos bereits 1100 PS im Training und 900 im Rennen. Für die Wiederkunft der Saugmotoren ab 1987 reichte die Bausubstanz des DFY nicht mehr aus. Ein paar Zitate entlehnte man ihm bei der Konzeption des 3,5 Liter Cosworth DFR und des HB mit pneumatischen Ventilen, aber mehr noch vom V6 Turbo aus dem gleichen Hause. Nur: Gegen die Zehn- und Zwölfzylinder von Honda und den Renault-V10 hatten die V8 von Ford bisher einen schweren Stand. Vielleicht hat die ideale Maschine für die 3,5 Liter-Formel ja weniger als zwölf, aber mehr als acht Zylinder...

Wurde bei der Aufbereitung der Triebwerke schon seit einiger Zeit mit Edelmetallen, Keramik und Kunststoff gearbeitet, so gab es bei den Chassis schon längst keine Alternative mehr zu hochwertigem Chemie-Gebäck aus dem Ofen. Anfang der achtziger Jahre waren die konventionellen Aluminium-Monocoques den irrsinnigen Kräften, die an ihnen rüttelten, zerrten und drehten, einfach nicht mehr gewachsen. Das Rückgrat von Gordon Murrays Brabham BT 49 von 1980 bestand größtenteils aus Kohlefaser. 1981 sattelten Lotus und McLaren drauf mit kompletten Monocoques aus Kohlefaserlaminaten und Kevlar, verstärkt mit Honigwaben aus Nomex. 1983 wies Gustav Brunner mit seinem geschlossenen Kohlefasermonocoque für den ATS D7 den Weg in die Zukunft. Es wog 18 Kilo, halb soviel wie die leichtesten Alusandwichchassis einer Vergangenheit, die bis zum Lotus 25 von 1962 zurückreichte. Ein Triumph des Entwicklers über den Designer, gewiß. Nur: Colin Chapman war ein Leonardo seiner Kunst, ein Erfinder alten Schlages. In so einem Fall brauchen die Evolutionäre halt ein bißchen länger für ihre Erfolgserlebnisse.

TECHNOLOGY

In 1991 combined into the package for winning a Grand Prix was what Shell director Roger Lindsay called designer fuel or, almost tenderly, his Grand Crus, concocted in the laboratories of the big petrol suppliers. A tankful cost the equivalent of a small middle-class car. Since those elixirs of the devil evaporated in the wrath of FISA, the prerequisite for winning a Grand Prix ever since has been the use and command of sophisticated electronic devices, which are of dubious sporting, but considerable material value, too.

Apart from those expensive vogues of the day the three columns on which all success in this sport is based have remained stable: tyres, chassis, and engine. The history of the last quarter of a century in the Grand Prix business is also the history of the DFV (for Double Four Valves). An order placed with the small but noble engine tuner Cosworth in the north of London by the British Ford branch in 1966, the Cosworth DFV was also a political item, on the grounds that it symbolically stood for the much simpler off-the-peg V8s of the American parent company. Moreover, it was the epitome of pragmatic thinking combining a couple of DFA Formula Two engines into a light and compact V8, an article urgently needed by its first customer, Lotus impresario Colin Chapman, to orchestrate his lightweight construction philosophy. And it was also cheap, since Ford boss Stanley Gillen only had to set his signature to the 100,000-pound cheque that had originally been agreed upon. The life expectancy of the engine would be about three or four years, as usual. But then began what Cosworth supremo Keith Duckworth calls the triumph of development over design. The DFV just kept on winning: 153 further Grand Prix victories lay between Jim Clark's first at Zandvoort in 1967 with the Lotus 49 and Michele Alboreto's last at Detroit in 1983 on a Tyrrell. Then the Ford V8 was already called DFY, having become a short-stroke engine. It weighed 133 kilos, its output over 520 horsepower, compared to the 162 kilos and 405 horsepower of the original DFV. Twice it had to face severe crises. It could live with the first, but had to succumb to the second.

In the seventies the twelve cylinders, always a latent peril, became a real threat. The V12s from BRM, Matra, Tecno, Alfa and initially even Maserati looked and sounded gorgeous, but were comparatively harmless. Concrete danger did, however, emanate from the Ferrari marque and the man Niki Lauda and the coalition of the two. Hence the Ford pilots had to concede three world championships to the red cars from Maranello, in alternating rhythm: to Niki Lauda in 1975 and 1977, to Jody Scheckter in 1979. Between 1980 and 1982 it became obvious what the crushing Lotus predominance of 1978 had already foreshadowed: the DFV harmonized perfectly with the wing car principle, which asked for slender cars.

Then, however, after six years of apprenticeship, ensued the supremacy of the turbos for another six years. Formula One became the domain of the BMW four cylinder and, later, the V6s from Porsche and Honda. In 1985 even Cosworth stalwart Ken Tyrrell faltered and was struck off the customer list after Detroit. At that time the output of the top turbos had risen to a monstrous 1100 horsepower in practice and 900 in race trim. For the resurrection of the normally aspirated engines from 1987 on the DFY was no longer suited. A couple of quotations were made when the new 3,5 litre Cosworth was being conceived, but even more came from the V6 Cosworth Engineering had grudgingly built as its contribution to the turbo craze. But the new Ford V8 has had to face the tough opposition of the ten and twelve cylinders from Honda and the Renault V10, the latter engine configuration most likely being the way to go.

For a long time exotic metals, ceramics, and synthetic materials have been part and parcel of the modern Formula One engine. In chassis building high-quality chemical products have become indispensable altogether. At the beginning of the eighties conventional aluminium monocoques could no longer cope with the enormous forces they were exposed to. That is why the backbone of Gordon Murray's 1980 Brabham BT 49 largely consisted of carbon fibre laminates. In 1981 Lotus and McLaren went one step further building complete monocoques of carbon fibre and Kevlar, reinforced by honeycomb structures made of Nomex. How rigid these chassis were was spectacularly demonstrated by McLaren number two driver Andrea de Cesaris, who acquired his nom de guerre de Crasheris shunting countless cars without ever injuring himself. In 1983 Gustav Brunner's ATS D7 broke new ground with its full carbon fibre chassis, which was to show the way into the future. It weighed 18 kilos, half as much as the lightest aluminium sandwich construction of a past reaching back to the Lotus 25 of 1962. Of course this was another triumph of development over design. As Colin Chapman was an inventor of the old school, a Leonardo of his art, as it were, it had only taken a bit longer.

TECHNOLOGIE

Dans la recette qui mène à la victoire du Grand Prix, il y avait en 1991 ce que Roger Lindsay, directeur compétent de chez Shell, appelait l'essence des designers ou presque tendrement, ses grands crus, mûris et pressés dans les laboratoires des grands livreurs d'essence de la Formule 1. Un réservoir plein coûtait l'équivalent d'une petite voiture de classe moyenne. Depuis que ces élixirs du diable se sont perdus en fumée, car ils ont été excommuniés par l'autorité du sport automobile FISA, on a besoin de moyens électroniques performants si on veut passer le premier la ligne d'arrivée, et ils sont eux aussi d'une valeur sportive douteuse, mais pour cela d'une valeur matérielle exorbitante.

Trois piliers sont restés intacts au milieu de ces modes passagères et coûteuses et servent toujours dans ce sport à apporter le succès ou à l'empocher: pneus, châssis et moteur. L'histoire des 25 années passées dans le Grand Prix est aussi celle de la DFV, pour Double Four Valves (deux fois quatre soupapes). En 1966, une commande a été envoyée par Ford England à la petite mais bonne usine de moteurs Cosworth au nord de Londres et il était pour Cosworth intéressant d'être là, de se faire de la publicité et de mettre en valeur les séries de huit cylindres bien plus simplement bâtis de la maison mère américaine. En plus, ce moteur représentait une petite pièce de choix, car on avait pratiquement rassemblé en lui deux moteurs FVA de Formule 2 en un V8 compact et léger, un article dont avait absolument besoin Colin Chapman pour étayer sa philosophie de construction légère Lotus. Et il était bon marché. Le chèque qu'a signé Stanley Gillen, le boss de chez Ford, était bien du montant dont on avait convenu: 100.000 livres Sterling. Comme espérance de vie, on a calculé très large, comme à l'habitude: trois à quatre ans. Puis il arriva ce que le chef de Cosworth, Keith Duckworth, appelle le triomphe du chercheur sur le designer. Il profita de lui copieusement: on compte 153 autres victoires de la DFV entre la première de Jim Clark à Zandvoort en 1967 sur la Lotus 49 et la dernière par Michele Alboreto en 1983 à Détroit avec la Tyrrell. Là, la Ford V8 s'appelait déjà DFY. Elle avait un moteur à faible course de 520 CV et ne pesait que 133 kilos alors que la première DFV avait fait 162 kilos sur la balance et possédait 405 CV. Elle a été secouée deux fois de crises existentielles. Elle a pu vivre avec la première, elle est morte de la seconde.

La menace, toujours latente des douze cylindres, s'est concrétisée dans les années 70. Les V12 de BRM, Matra, Tecno, Alfa et au début encore de Maserati, pouvaient peut-être être belles et bien sonner, mais elles n'étaient pas dangereuses. Le danger venait sans aucun doute de la marque Ferrari, de l'homme Niki Lauda et de la coalition des deux. Les pilotes de chez Ford ont dû laisser trois championnats aux pilotes des voitures de course rouges de chez Maranello dans un rythme d'alternance: 1975 et 1977 à Lauda, 1979 à Scheckter. Entre 1980 et 1982, s'est trouvé confirmé ce qui s'était dessiné avec la domination accablante de Lotus en 1978: La DFV était en harmonie parfaite avec le principe des ailes, qui exigeait des corps de châssis étroits.

Pourtant, ensuite, après six ans d'apprentissage, on est passé aux six ans de domination des turbos et la Formule 1 devint le domaine de la quatre cylindres BMW et de la V6 de Porsche et Honda. En 1985, Ken Tyrrell, le fidèle des fidèles vacilla, au beau milieu de la saison et fut rayé de la liste des abonnés de Cosworth après le Grand Prix des USA Est. A ce moment-là, les top-turbos donnaient déjà 1100 CV aux essais et 900 en course. Pour le retour des moteurs à aspiration, à partir de 1987, la substance de construction de la DFY ne suffisait plus. On lui a emprunté quelques citations dans la conception de la DFR Cosworth 3,5 litres et dans celle de la HB avec des soupapes pneumatiques mais encore plus de la V6 turbo de la même maison. Seulement les V8 de Ford avaient la vie dure jusque-là par rapport aux dix et douze cylindres de Honda et aux V10 de Renault. Peut-être que la machine idéale pour la formule de 3,5 litres a bien moins de 12 cylindres mais plus de huit...

Si cela faisait déjà un moment que l'on travaillait avec des métaux précieux, de la céramique et des matières plastiques pour construire les propulseurs, il y avait longtemps qu'il n'y avait plus d'autre alternative dans le domaine des châssis. Au début des années 80, les monocoques en aluminium conventionnelles ne faisaient tout simplement plus face aux forces incroyables qui les secouaient, tiraillaient et faisaient tourner. La structure de la Brabham BT 49 de Gordon Murray de 1980 était constituée en grande partie de fibre de carbone. En 1981, Lotus et McLaren en firent autant avec des monocoques complets de laminés de fibre de carbone et de kevlar, renforcé par des alvéoles de Nomex. En 1983, Gustav Brunner a ouvert la voie avec son monocoque fermé de fibre de carbone pour la ATS D7. Elle pesait 18 kilos, moitié moins que le plus léger des châssis en aluminium qui remontait à la Lotus 25 de 1962. Un triomphe du chercheur sur le designer, certes. Seulement: Colin Chapman a été une sorte Léonard De Vinci, un inventeur de la vieille trempe. Dans un cas comme celui-ci, les évolutionnistes ont bien besoin d'un peu plus de temps pour voir

TECNOLOGÍA

En la preparación de recetas para la victoria del Grand Prix de 1991, había que poner lo que el director de la Shell Roger Lindsay llamaba gasolina de diseño o, con más dulzura, su Grand Crus, madurado y prensado en los laboratorios de los grandes proveedores de *sprit* para la Fórmula 1. Llenar el tanque costaba tanto como un pequeño turismo de clase media. Desde que estos endiablados elixeres han detonado en el anatema de la administración del deporte motorizado, FISA, hay que echar mano de una sofisticada electrónica si se quiere llegar primero a la línea de meta; electrónica dudosamente deportiva, pero, eso sí, de elevado valor económico.

Estas costosas modas de temporada no afectaron a los tres pilares sobre los que se asienta el éxito —o el fracaso— en este deporte: neumáticos, chasis y motor. La historia de los últimos 25 años en el negocio del Grand Prix es también la historia del DFV, Double Four Valves (dos veces cuatro válvulas). Un encargo que la Ford hizo en 1966 al pequeño pero selecto yunque del motor Cosworth, en el norte de Inglaterra, fue el Cosworth DFV, al mismo tiempo un ítem político, pues respaldaba publicitariamente a los mucho más simples 8 cilindros en serie del consorcio americano. Representaba además una pequeña obra maestra, pues en él concurrían prácticamente dos motores FVA de Fórmula 2, formando un compacto y ligero V8. Un artículo que el primer cliente, Colin Chapman, necesitaba urgentemente para orquestar su filosofía de peso ligero para el Lotus. Y era barato: en el cheque, adornado con la firma del *boss* de la Ford Stanley Gillen, no figuraban más que las 100000 libras esterlinas acordadas. La esperanza de vida de estos motores era la normal, de tres a cuatro años. Pero entonces comenzó lo que el jefe de la Cosworth, Keith Duckworth —hombre y empresa eran todo uno— definió como el triunfo del desarrollo sobre el diseño. De él disfrutó como es debido: entre la primera victoria en Zandvoort 1967 con Jim Clark al mando del Lotus 49, y la última en Detroit 1983 con Michele Alboreto en su Tyrrell, hay otras 153 victorias DFV. El V8 Ford ya se llamaba DFY y era un motor de émbolo corto, de más de 520 CV de potencia y sólo 133 kilos de peso, mientras que el abuelo DFV arrojaba 162 kilos en la báscula y disponía de una potencia de 405 CV. Dos veces había sido asolado por crisis existenciales; la primera la superó, la segunda acabó con él.

La amenaza de los doce cilindros, siempre latente, se hizo concreta en los años setenta. Los V12 de BRM, Matra, Tecno, Alfa y al principio también Maserati, tenían buena planta y buen sonido, pero muy peligrosos no eran. Eso sí, se podían relacionar con la marca Ferrari y el hombre Niki Lauda y la coalición de ambos, que sí era peligrosa. Los corredores de la Ford tuvieron que ceder por tres veces en ritmo alternante el Campeonato Mundial a pilotos de los coches rojos de Maranello: en 1975 y 1977 a Lauda, en 1979 a Scheckter. Entre 1980 y 1982 se confirmó lo que en 1978 se había manifestado tímidamente con el destructor dominio Lotus: el DFV armonizaba perfectamente con el principio de alerones, que exigía una delgada silueta a los coches.

Pero después de seis años de aprendizaje comenzaron los seis años de supremacía de los turbos. Y la Fórmula 1 pasó a ser dominio del cuatrocilindros de BMW y del V6 de Porsche y Honda. Junto con Ken Tyrrell, titubeó en 1985 el más fiel de los fieles en plena temporada y, tras el Grand Prix de la USA Este, fue borrado de la lista de suscriptores de la Cosworth. Los *top-turbos* daban ya entonces un rendimiento de 1100 CV en entrenamiento y 900 en carrera. Para la resurrección de los motores de aspersión a partir de 1987 ya se quedaba corto el DFY. Se le citó un par de veces en la concepción del Cosworth DFR de 3,5 litros y en la del HB con ventiladores neumáticos, si bien más aportaciones rindió el V6 turbo de la misma casa. Sólo que: contra los diez y doce cilindros de Honda y del Renault V10, los V8 de la Ford tenían que mantener una reñida lucha. Tal vez el motor ideal para una fórmula de 3,5 litros tenga efectivamente menos de doce cilindros, pero más de ocho…

Si en la ejecución de los motores de Fórmula 1 se experimenta ya desde hace tiempo con metales preciosos, cerámica y materiales sintéticos, para el chasis no hay otra alternativa que productos químicos de alta calidad. Los convencionales *monocoques* de aluminio no estaban, ya a principios de los ochenta, en condiciones de soportar las dementes fuerzas que los sacudían, arrastraban y hacían girar. La columna vertebral del Brabham BT 49 de 1980 de Gordon Murray estaba constituida, en su mayor parte, por fibra de carbono. Lotus y McLaren dieron un paso más adelante en 1981, construyendo los *monocoques* sólo con laminado de fibra de carbono y Kevlar, reforzado con panale de Nomex. Con su *monocoque* cerrado de fibra de carbono d 1983, Gustav Brunner abrió el nuevo camino a recorrer en el futuro por el ATS D7. Pesaba 18 kilos, la mitad de lo que pesaba el más ligero chasis *sandwich* de aluminio de un pasado que alcanzaba hasta el Lotus 25 de 1962. Un triunfo del desarrollo sobre el diseño, de seguro. Sólo que: Colin Chapman era un Leonardo de su arte, un descubridor de la vieja escuela. En casos así, se necesita un poco más de tiempo para llegar a resultados favorables.

Vorherige Seite / Previous page /
Page précédente / Página anterior:

Penske PC 4 Ford V-8
John Watson (GB)
Sieger am / winner at /
vainqueur de / triunfador de
Österreichring (A) 1976

1 McLaren M5A - BRM V-12
   Monaco 1967

2 Gurney - Weslake V-12
   Monaco 1967

3 Tyrrell Ford - DFV - V-8
   Long Beach (USA) 1980

4 Lamborghini Chrysler V-12
Monaco 1989

5 Renault R55 V-10
Monaco 1993

6 Porsche V-12
Footwork Porsche
Monaco 1991

1   Gilles Villeneuve (CDN)
    Ferrari 312 T4
    Monza (I) 1979

2   Emerson Fittipaldi (BR)
    SKOL Fittipaldi Ford
    Zandvoort (NL) 1980

3   Alan Jones (AUS)
    Saudia Williams FW 07B Ford
    Zeltweg (A) 1980

4   Jean - Pierre Jarier (F)
    ATS Penske PC4 Ford
    Zolder (B) 1977

5

6, 7

8

5   Niki Lauda (A)
    Marlboro Mclaren MP4/1C Ford V-8
    TAG Porsche Turbo
    Silverstone (GB) 1983

6   Elio de Angelis (I)
    JPS Lotus 97T Renault Turbo
    Monaco 1985

7   Alain Prost (F)
    Renault Elf Turbo
    Zandvoort (NL), 1983

8   Gerhard Berger (A)
    Marlboro McLaren MP4/6 Honda
    Jerez (E) 1990

1   Yardley McLaren Ford
    Clermont - Ferrand (F) 1972

2

2   Ayrton Senna (BR)
    Marlboro McLaren Ford
    Barcelona (E) 1993

1   Tyrrell March - Ford 701
    Jackie Stewart (GB)
    Spa - Francorchamps (B) 1970

2   Ferrari 312 B
    Jacky Ickx (B)
    Spa - Francorchamps (B) 1970

3   Tyrrell 019 Ford DFR V-8
    Satoru Nakajima (J)
    Jean Alesi (F)

    Monaco 1990

4   Marlboro McLaren TAG Porsche Turbo
    Niki Lauda (A)
    Alain Prost (F)

    Monza (I) 1984

1

1 *12 · Zylinder Honda von / The 12 · cylinder Honda of / Le moteur 12 cylindres Honda de / El vehículo Honda de 12 cilindros de*

Richie Ginther (USA)
Monza (I) 1966

2   Renault - V-6, Lotus,
    Brands Hatch (GB) 1986

3   Renault - V-6, Ligier,
    Brands Hatch (GB) 1986

4   Honda - V-6, Williams,
    Paul Ricard (F) 1986

5   TAG - Porsche - V-6, McLaren,
    Brands Hatch (GB) 1986

6   Ferrari - V-6
    Monza (I)

7   Ford - V-6, Lola,
    Brands Hatch (GB) 1986

8   Nelson Piquet (BR), Brabham BMW Turbo,
    Estoril (P) 1985

9   BMW 4 - Zylinder / BMW 4 - cylinder /
    Le 4 cylindres BMW / BMW de 4
    cilindros
    Benetton
    Imola (RSM) 1986

10 BMW 4 - Zylinder / BMW 4 - cylinder /
    le 4 cylindres BMW / BMW de 4
    cilindros
    Arrows
    Imola (RSM) 1986

11 BMW - 4 - Zylinder / BMW 4 - cylinder /
    le 4 cylindres BMW / BMW de 4
    cilindros
    Brabham
    Imola (RSM) 1986

12 Zakspeed 4 - Zylinder / Zakspeed 4 -
    cylinder / le 4 cylindres Zakspeed /
    Zakspeed de 4 cilindros
    Imola (RSM) 1986

13 Motori Moderni - V-6, Minardi,
    Imola (RSM) 1986

14 Alfa Romeo - V-8, Osella,
    Brands Hatch (GB) 1986

1

2, 3, 4

1 Ferrari
Imola (RSM) 1984

2 JPS Lotus Ford
Dijon - Prenois (F) 1981

3 Marlboro McLaren Ford
Hockenheim (D) 1978

4 ATS - Team, nachdem M. Winkelhock (D)
bereits ausgefallen ist / The ATS team after
M. Winkelhock (D) was already out of
the race / L'équipe ATS après le hors course
de M. Winkelhock (D) / El equipo ATS
despuès de que M. Winkelhock (D) había
salido de la carrera

Long Beach (USA) 1983

5 Renault Elf Turbo
Long Beach (USA) 1980

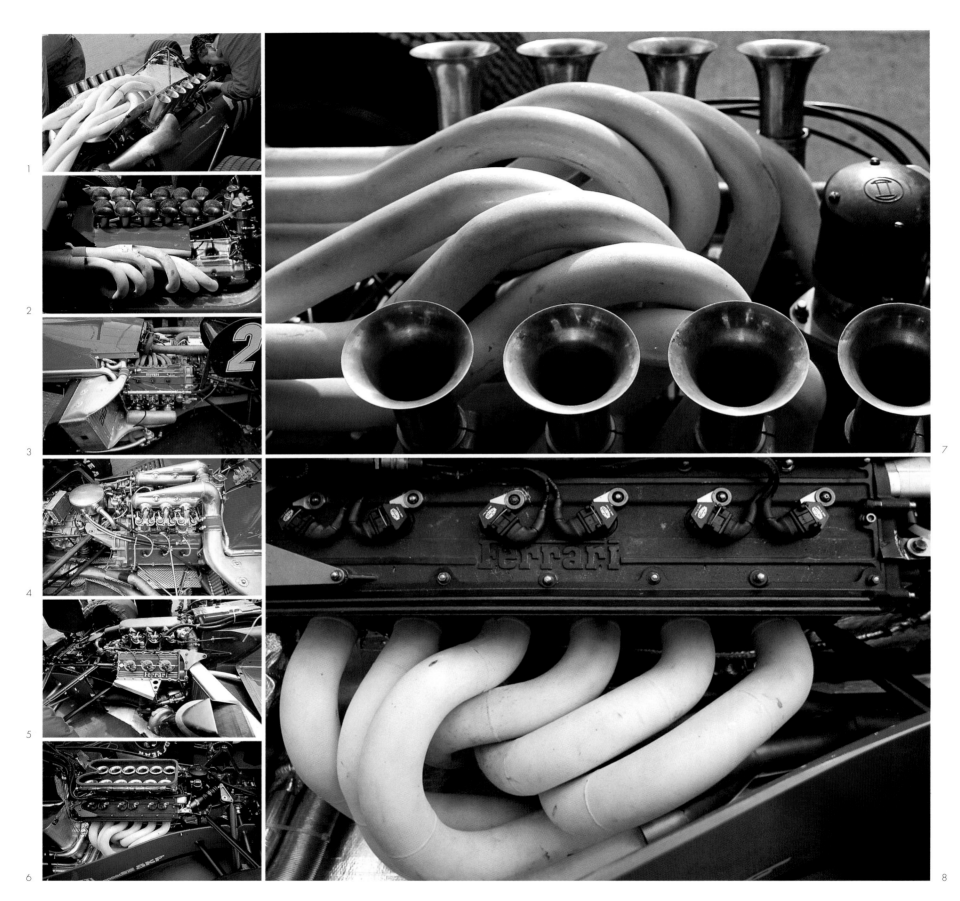

1   Ferrari 312, V-12
    Monaco 1967

2   Ferrari 312 F1 V-12
    Clermont - Ferrand (F) 1969

3   Ferrari 126 C4, V-6 Turbo
    Monza (I) 1984

4   Ferrari 126 C V-6 Turbo
    Monaco 1985

5   Ferrari 126 C, F1, V-6 Turbo
    Imola (RSM) 1987

6   Ferrari 3500, F1, V-12
    Monaco 1989

7   Ferrari 312, V-12
    Monaco 1967

8   Ferrari 3500, F1, V-12
    Monaco 1989

9, 10

11, 12

13

4, 15

16, 17

9 Ferrari 312, V-12
   Monza (I) 1967

10 Ferrari 312 B, V-12
   Monza (I) 1971

11 Ferrari 312 T3, V-12
   Jarama (E) 1978

12 Ferrari 126 C, V-6 Turbo
   Estoril (P) 1985

13 Ferrari 312 B, V-12
   Monaco 1971

14 Ferrari 312 T2, V-12
   Brands Hatch (GB) 1976

15 Ferrari 126 C, V-6 Turbo
   Long Beach (USA) 1983

16 Ferrari 126 C, F1, V-6 Turbo
   Imola (RSM) 1987

17 Ferrari 126 C, F1, V-6 Turbo
   Imola (RSM) 1987

1 Vorbereitung für das Training
Preparations for the practice
Preparations pour les essais
Preparativos para el fogueo

2 Computer Check
Vérification par ordinateur
Revisión con ordenador

3 Getriebe - Montage
Assembling the gearbox
Assemblage de la boîte de vitesse
Montaje de la caja de transmisiones

4 Cockpit

5 Doppelter Heckflügel
  Twin rear spoiler
  Aileron arrière double
  Alerón trasero doble

6 An der Box
  In the pit
  Dans le stand
  En la jaula

  Ferrari 642, V-12

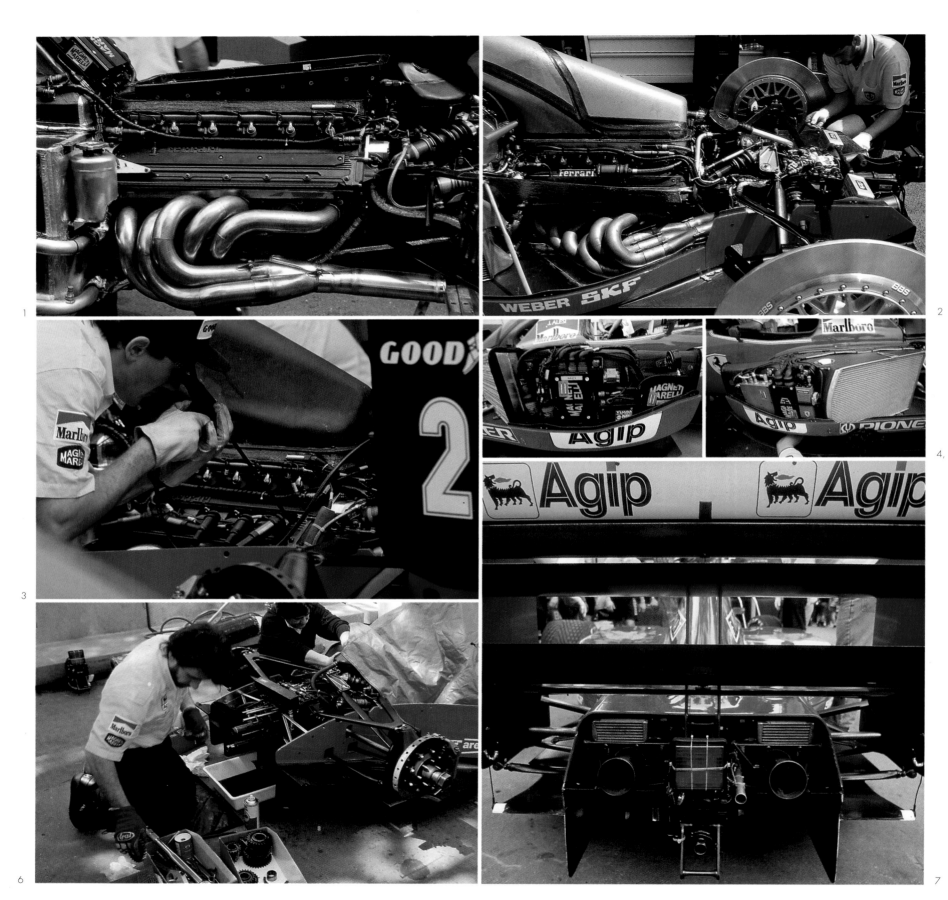

1   Ferrari F1 91, V-12
    Monaco 1991

2   Ferrari F 92 A, V-12
    Monaco 1992

3   Ferrari F1 91, V-12
    Monaco 1991

4   Ferrari F 92 A, V-12
    Monaco 1992

5   Ferrari F 92 A, V-12
    Monaco 1992

6   Ferrari F1 91, V-12
    Monaco 1991

7   Ferrari F 92 A, V-12
    Monaco 1992

8

9

10

8 - 10 Ferrari F 93 A, V-12

1 McLaren M 5 A - BRM V-12
   Monaco 1967

2, 3 BRM P 138, V-12
      John Surtees (GB)

      Jacky Oliver (GB)

      Monza (I) 1969

4 Pedro Rodríguez (MEX)
   Yardley BRM P 153, V-12
   Zandvoort (NL) 1970

5 Marlboro BRM P 160 E, V-12
   Zolder (B) 1973

6 Clay Regazzoni (I)
   Marlboro BRM P 160 E, V-12
   Montjuich (E) 1973

7   Jim Clark (GB)
     Lotus 49 Ford Cosworth DFV V-8
     Zandvoort (NL) 1967

8 - 11 Jo Siffert (CH)
        Walker Lotus 49 B Ford V-8
        Monza (I)

12   Gold Leaf Lotus 49 Ford V-8
     Jochen Rindt (A)
     Graham Hill (GB)

     Monza (I) 1969

13 - 14 Gold Leaf Lotus 72 Ford V-8
         Zandvoort (NL) 1971

15   Ford Cosworth V-8
     Clermont - Ferrand (F) 1972

16   Emerson Fittipaldi (BR)
     Colin Chapman (GB)
     Team boss
     JPS Lotus Ford V-8
     Zolder (B) 1973

1 - 4 Lotus 56 B, Pratt & Whitney gas turbine
       Emerson Fittipaldi (BR)
       Monza (I) 1971

5 - 6 Lotus 102 D Ford HB V-8
       Monaco 1992

7 Lotus 107 B Ford HB V-8
   Interlagos (BR) 1993

8, 9 Lotus 107 B Ford HB V-8
      Monaco 1993

10 Warsteiner Arrows A2 Ford V-8
    Jochen Mass (D)
    Dijon - Prenois (F) 1979

11 Arrows A8 BMW M 12/13, 4 cyl. Turbo
    Thierry Boutsen (B)
    Dijon - Prenois (F) 1985

12 Arrows A10 Megatron M 12/13
    4 cyl. Turbo
    Monaco 1987

13 Arrows A10 B Megatron M12/13
    4 cyl. Turbo
    Eddie Cheever (USA)
    Hockenheim (D) 1988

14 Footwork FA 12 Porsche V-8
    Monaco 1991

15 Footwork FA 12 Porsche V-8
    Imola (RSM) 1991

16 Footwork FA 14 Mugen Honda V-10
    Monaco 1993

17 Footwork FA 14 Mugen Honda V-10
    Monaco 1993

1, 2   Tyrrell 003 Ford Cosworth DFV V-8
        Jackie Stewart (GB)
        Zandvoort (NL) 1971

   3   Tyrrell 005 Ford Cosworth DFV V-8
        François Cevert (F)
        Nivelles (B) 1972

   4   Tyrrell 005 Ford Cosworth DFV V-8
        Jackie Stewart (GB)
        Monza (I) 1972

   5   Tyrrell P 34 Ford Cosworth DFV V-8
        Patrick Depailler (F)
        Long Beach (USA) 1977

   6   Tyrrell P 34 Ford Cosworth DFV V-8
        Patrick Depailler (F)
        Hockenheim (D) 1977

7   Tyrrell 007 Ford Cosworth DFV V-8
    Patrick Depailler (F)
    Anderstorp (S) 1974

8   Tyrrell 014 Ford Cosworth DFV V-8
    Stefan Bellof (D)
    Le Castellet (F) 1985

9   Tyrrell 018 Ford Cosworth DFR V-8
    Jonathan Palmer (GB)
    Monaco 1987

10 Tyrrell 016 Ford Cosworth DFZ V-8
    Jonathan Palmer (GB)
    Monaco 1987

11 Tyrrell 020 Honda V-10
    Monaco 1991

12 Tyrrell 020 - 021 Ilmor V-10
    Kyalami (ZA) 1992

13 Tyrrell 020 C Yamaha 0X10A V-10
    Monaco 1993

1, 2 Matra MS 120, V-12
Henri Pescarolo (F)
Zandvoort (NL) 1970

3 UOP Shadow Matra V-12
Österreichring (A) 1975

4 Ligier JS 11/15 Cosworth DFV V-8
Österreichring (A) 1980

5 Talbot - Ligier JS 17 Matra MS 81 V-12
Patrick Tambay (F)
Long Beach (USA) 1981

6 Talbot - Ligier JS 17 Matra MS 81 V-12
Patrick Tambay (F)
Hockenheim (D) 1981

7 Talbot Ligier JS 17 B Matra MS 81 V-12
Long Beach (USA) 1982

8 Toleman TG 181 Hart 415 T 4 cyl. Turbo
Dijon - Prenois (F) 1981

9 RAM 03 Hart 415 T 4 cyl. Turbo
Zolder (B) 1985

10 · Brabham BT 50 BMW M 12/13
4 cyl. Turbo
Monaco 1982

11 Brabham BT 52 BMW M 12/13
4 cyl. Turbo
Long Beach (USA) 1983

12 Brabham BT 54 BMW M 12/13
4 cyl. Turbo
Monaco 1985

13, 14 Brabham BT 53 BMW M 12/13
4 cyl. Turbo
Brands Hatch (GB) 1984

15 Brabham BT 54 BMW M 12/13
4 cyl. Turbo
Nelson Piquet (BR)
Zandvoort (NL) 1985

16 Brabham BT 56 BMW M 12/13
4 cyl. Turbo
Hungaroring (H) 1987

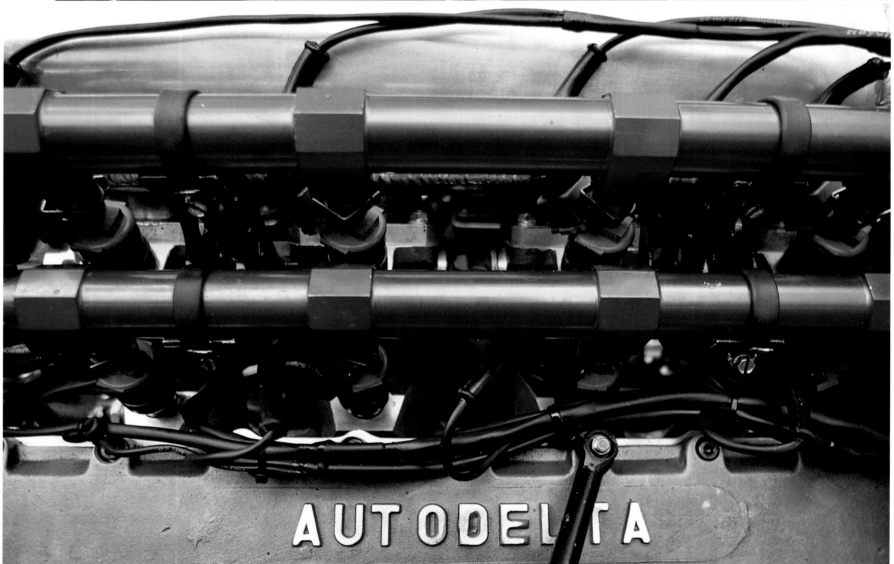

1   Brabham BT 45 Alfa Romeo 115 V-12
    Jarama (E) 1976

2   Marlboro Alfa Romeo 179 C V-12
    Monaco 1981

3   Marlboro Alfa Romeo 179 C V-12
    Hockenheim (D) 1983

4, 5   Osella FA 1E Alfa Romeo V-12
       Silverstone (GB) 1983

6   Benetton Alfa Romeo 890T V-8 Turbo
    Monaco 1985

7

7   Benetton Alfa Romeo 890T V-8 Turbo
    Hockenheim (D) 1984

1 Renault RE 20
   Renault - Gordini EF 1 V-6 Turbo
   Hockenheim (D) 1980

2 Renault RE 20
   Renault - Gordini EF 1 V-6 Turbo
   Long Beach (USA) 1980

3 Renault RE 20 B
   Renault - Gordini EF 1 V-6 Turbo
   Long Beach (USA) 1981

4 Lotus 94 T
   Renault EF 1 V-6 Turbo
   Zandvoort (NL) 1983

5 Lotus 95 T
   Renault EF 4 V-6 Turbo
   Brands Hatch (GB) 1984

6 Lotus 97 T
   Renault EF 4B V-6 Turbo
   Monaco 1985

7 - 9   Spirit 201 C Honda B7 LE V-6 Turbo
         Silverstone (GB) 1983

10   Lotus T 100 Honda RA 168 E V-6 Turbo
         Hungaroring (H) 1988

11 - 13   Lotus T 99 Honda RA 167 E V-6 Turbo
              Monza (I) 1987

1, 2

3

8

4

5

9

1 Zakspeed 814 4cyl. Turbo
Le Castellet (F) 1985

2 Zakspeed ZK 871 B 4cyl. Turbo
Monaco 1988

3 Zakspeed 891,
Yamaha OX 88 V-8
Jacarepagua (BR) 1989

4 Lola Haas Ford V-6 Turbo
Patrick Tambay (F)
Hungaroring (H) 1986

5 Rial ARC 01 Ford V-8
Monaco 1988

6 Life Racing F 490 Life F 35 W 12
Monaco 1990

7 Subaru Coloni Racing MM 12 cyl.
Phoenix (USA) 1990

8 Minardi 185 Motori Moderni V-6 Turbo
Imola (RSM) 1988

9 Minardi M 189 Ford V-8
Zolder (B) 1989

10 Minardi M 191 Ferrari V-12
    Phoenix (USA) 1991

11 Dallara BMS 191 Judd V-10
    Monaco 1991

12 Dallara BMS 192 Ferrari V-12
    Monaco 1992

13 Lola BMS T 93/30 Ferrari V-12
    Monaco 1993

14 Larrousse Lamborghini Lola 90 V-12
    Monaco 1990

15 Lola LC 89 Lamborghini V-12
    Monaco 1989

16 Lamborghini 291 V-12
    Nicola Larini (I)
    Imola (RSM) 91

17 Lamborghini 291 V-12
    Eric van de Poele (B)
    Montreal (CDN) 1991

18 Larrousse Lamborghini V-12
    Monaco 1993

1 McLaren M23 Ford Cosworth DFV V-8
 Montjuich (E) 1973

2 McLaren M23 Ford Cosworth DFV V-8
 Zolder (B) 1975

3 McLaren M28 Ford Cosworth DFV V-8
 Patrick Tambay (F)
 Hockenheim (D) 1979

4 McLaren M26 Ford Cosworth DFV V-8
 Nürburgring (D) 1976

5 McLaren M23 Ford Cosworth DFV V-8
 Long Beach (USA) 1977

6 McLaren M29 Ford Cosworth DFV V-8
 John Watson (GB)
 Zandvoort (NL) 1980

7, 8

9, 10

— 11

2, 13

14, 15

7 McLaren MP 4/2, Cockpit
Brands Hatch (GB) 1984

8 McLaren MP 4/2, Cockpit
Niki Lauda (A)
Österreichring (A) 1984

9 McLaren MP 4/2
TAG Porsche TTE - P01 V-6
Zolder (B) 1984

10 McLaren MP 4/2
TAG Porsche TTE - P01 V-6
Imola (RSM) 1984

11 McLaren MP 4/2
TAG Porsche TTE - P01 V-6
*Porsche Engineer /Porsche engineer /
Ingénieur chez Porsche / ingeniero de
Porsche*
Hans Mezger (D)
Monza (I) 1984

12 McLaren MP 4/1 E
TAG Porsche TTE - P01 V-6
Zandvoort (NL) 1983

13 McLaren MP 4/1 E
TAG Porsche TTE - P01 V-6
Zandvoort (NL) 1983

14 McLaren MP 4/2 B
TAG Porsche TTE - P01 V-6
Keke Rosberg (SF)
Brands Hatch (GB) 1986

15 McLaren MP 4/2 B
TAG Porsche TTE - P01 V-6
Brands Hatch (GB) 1986

TECHNOLOGY

1, 2

3, 4

5

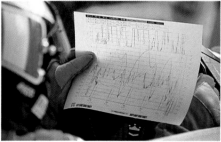

6, 7

8, 9

1   McLaren MP 4/4
    Honda RA 168 E V-6 Turbo
    Monaco 1988

2   McLaren MP 4/4
    Honda RA 168 E V-6 Turbo
    Monaco 1988

3   McLaren MP 4/5
    Bord - Camera / on - board camera /
    caméra de bord / cámara de a bordo
    Jerez (E) 1989

4   McLaren MP 4/5
    High tech / high - tech /
    technologie de pointe / tecnología punta
    Jerez (E) 1989

5   McLaren MP 4/4
    Honda RA 168 E V-6 Turbo
    Monaco 1988

6   McLaren MP 4/5
    Computerzentrale / computer centre /
    centre d'ordinateur / central de ordenadores
    Jerez (E) 1989

7   McLaren MP 4/6
    Computer Ergebnisse / computer results /
    résultats par ordinateur de / resultados de
    ordenador de
    Gerhard Berger (A)
    Magny - Cours (F) 1991

8   McLaren MP 4/5 B
    Honda RA 110 E, V-10
    Gerhard Berger (A)
    Jerez (E) 1989

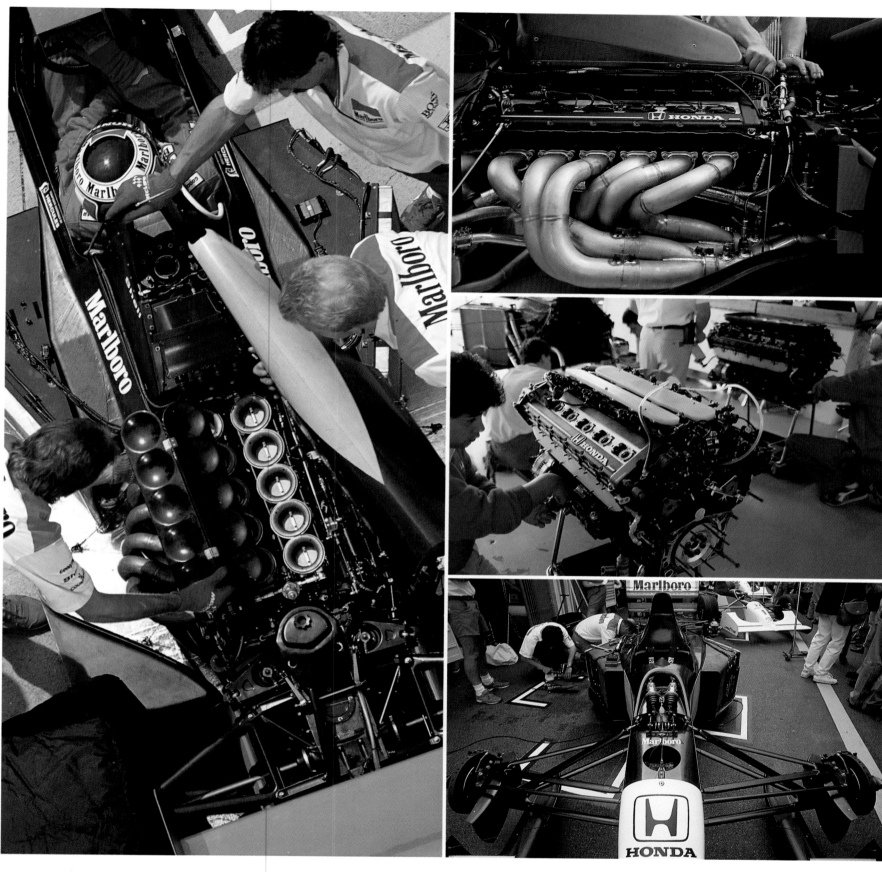

9   McLaren MP 4/6
    Monaco 1991

10 McLaren MP 4/5 B
    Honda RA 110 E V-10
    Gerhard Berger (A)
    Hungaroring (H) 1990

11 McLaren MP 4/6
    Honda RA 121 E V-12
    Monaco 1991

12 McLaren MP 4/6
    Honda RA 121 E V-12
    Silverstone (GB) 1991

13 McLaren MP 4/7 A
    Honda RA 122 E V-12
    Monaco 1992

1 Mclaren Box / Mclaren pit / Le stand
Mclaren / La jaula Mclaren

Elektronische Ausrüstung für Senna (BR) und
Andretti (USA) / Electronic Equipment for
Senna (BR) and Andretti (USA) /
équipment électronique pour Senna (BR) et
Andretti (USA) / equipo electrónico para
Senna (BR) y Andretti (USA)

Interlagos (BR) 1993

2 Mclaren MP 4/8, Ford HB V-8
Injection system
Monaco 1993

3 Mclaren MP 4/8, Ford HB V-8
Monaco 1993

4 Mclaren MP 4/8, Ford HB V-8
Front actuator
Monaco 1993

5 Mclaren MP 4/8, Ford HB V-8
Monaco 1993

6 Mclaren MP 4/8, Ford HB V-8
Suspension actuator
Monaco 1993

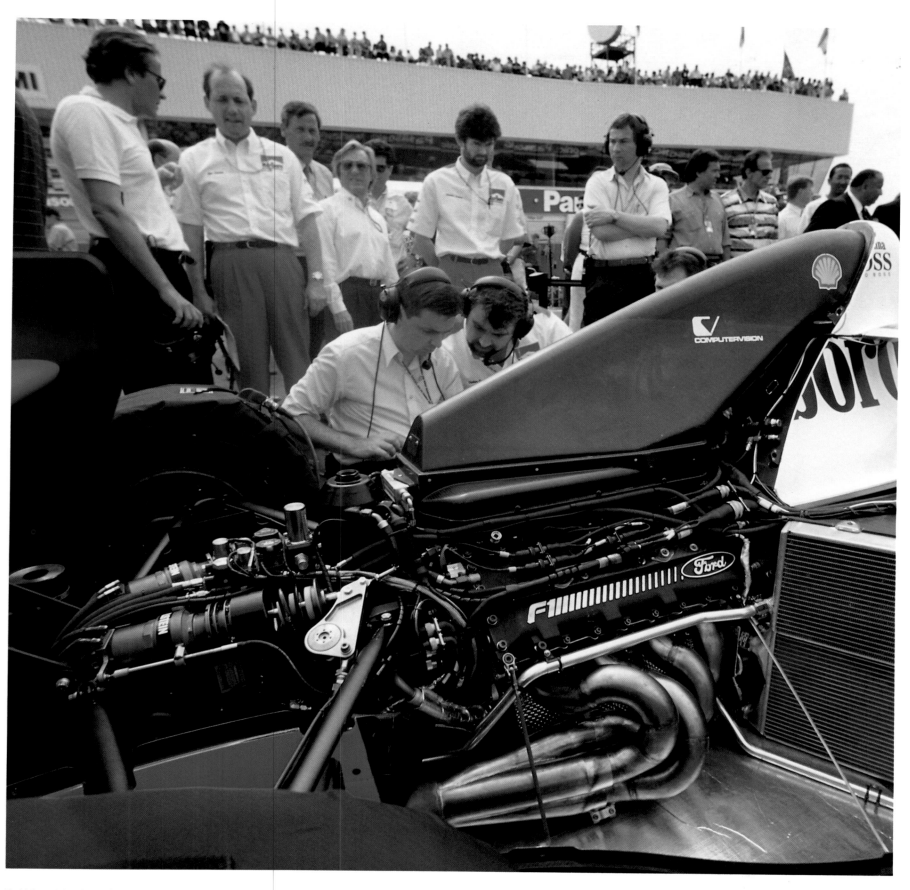

7 McLaren MP 4/8, Ford HB V-8
Kyalami (ZA) 1993

1 Williams FW 05, Cosworth DFV V-8
Long Beach 1976 (USA)

2 Williams FW 07 C, Cosworth DFV V-8
Monza (I) 1982

3 Williams FW 09/09, Cockpit
Brands Hatch (GB) 1984

4 Williams FW 09/09 B, Honda RA 163-E,
V-6 Turbo
Monaco 1984

5 Williams FW 09/09 B, Honda RA 163-E,
V-6 Turbo
Brands Hatch (GB) 1984

6 Williams FW 09/09 B, Honda RA 163-E,
V-6 Turbo
Jacques Laffite (F)
Hockenheim (D) 1984

7 Williams FV 10/FV 10 B, Honda RA 166-E,
V-6 Turbo
Estoril (P) 1985

8 Williams FW 011 B, Honda RA 167-E,
V-6 Turbo
Monza (I) 1987

9 Williams FW 011 B, Honda RA 167-E,
V-6 Turbo
Nelson Piquet (BR)
Hungaroring (H) 1987

10 Williams FV 112 B, Judd CV, V-8 SM
Jacarepagua (BR) 1985

11, 12

13, 14

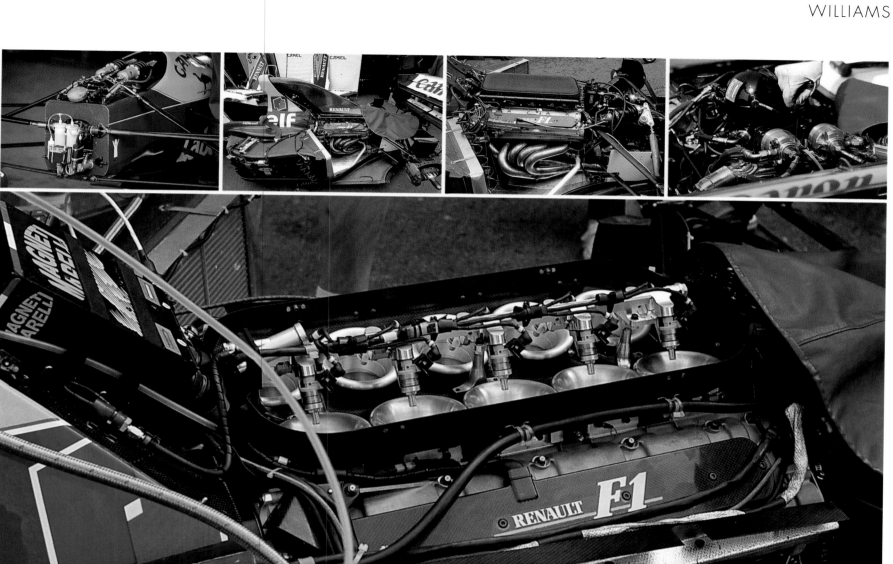

15

5, 17

18, 19

11 Williams FW 14, Renault V-10
    Interlagos (BR) 1991

12 Williams FW 14 B, Renault V-10
    Monaco 1992

13 Williams FW 14, Renault V-10
    Monaco 1991

14 Williams FW 14 B, Renault V-10
    Hungaroring (H) 1992

15 *Engine with fuel rail and injectors*
    Williams FW 15 C, Renault RS5, V-10
    Monaco 1993

Monaco 1993:

16 *Front actuators*
17 *Covered system*
18 *Suspension actuator*
19 *Fuel station*

1, 2

3, 4

5

6, 7

8, 9

1 Tyrrell Benetton Ford
   Silverstone (GB) 1983

2 - 3 Tyrrell Benetton Ford
   Zandvoort (NL) 1983

4 Benetton Alfa Romeo 890T V-8 Turbo
   Silverstone (GB) 1985

5 Benetton B186 BMW M12/13 4 cyl. Turbo
   Hungaroring (H) 1986

6 - 9 Benetton BMW M12/13 4 cyl. Turbo
   Test / test / pruebo
   Silverstone (GB) 1986

10, 11

12, 13

14

5, 16

17, 18

10   Benetton B187 Ford TEC F1 V-6 Turbo
     Le Castellet (F) 1987

11   Benetton B187 Ford TEC F1 V-6 Turbo
     Imola (RSM) 1987

12   Benetton B188 Ford DFR (V-8 5M)
     Zolder (B) 1988

13   Benetton B188 Ford DFR (V-8 5M)
     Jacarepagua (BR) 1988

14   Camel Benetton B 193 B Ford HB V-8
     Barcelona (E) 1993

15   Camel Benetton B 189 Ford V-8
     Monaco 1989

16   Benetton B191 Ford V-8
     Monaco 1991

17 - 18   Camel Benetton B 193 B Ford HB V-8
          Monaco 1993

1. March 711 Ford V-8
   Ronnie Peterson (S)
   Silverstone (GB) 1971

2. March 721 Ford V-8
   Ronnie Peterson (S)
   Clermont - Ferrand (F) 1972

3. March 711 Alfa Romeo 33/3 V-8
   Ronnie Peterson (S)
   Le Castellet (F) 1971

4. March 711 Ford V-8
   Le Castellet (F) 1971

5. March CG 911 B / Ilmor V-10
   Karl Wendlinger (A)
   Mexico 1992

6. March CG 911 B / Ilmor V-10
   Monaco 1992

7. Leyton House CG 911 Ilmor V-10
   Monaco 1991

8. March CG 911 B / Ilmor V-10
   Barcelona (E) 1992

9   Sauber C12 Ilmor V-10
    Monaco 1993

10 Sauber C12 Ilmor V-10
    Imola (RSM) 1993

11 Sauber C12 Ilmor V-10
    Kyalami (ZA) 1993

12 Sauber C12 Ilmor V-10
    Monaco 1993

13 - 14 Sauber C12 Ilmor V-10
         Kyalami (ZA) 1993

REIFEN

Wenn man die Poeten in der Branche beim Wort nimmt, haben die Schwarz-Künstler in den Labors der großen Pneuproduzenten den Stein der Weisen gefunden: Sie sublimieren Triviales wie Kautschuk, Öl, Rußpartikel und Chemikalien zu schwarzem Gold. Zumindest sind moderne Rennreifen nicht mit Gold aufzuwiegen: An den vier Stellen, wo sie den Kontakt zwischen Wagen und Straße herstellen, werden sie von brachialen Gewalten längs und quer geschunden. Zur Zeit der Flügel-Autos widersetzten sie sich Zentrifugalkräften bis zum Vierfachen der Erdbeschleunigung, vermittelten später die Wucht des Vortriebs, zu dem an die 1200 Turbo-PS fähig waren, und übertragen seit den frühen Achtzigern die buchstäblich atemberaubenden Verzögerungen, mit denen Bremsscheiben aus Kohlenstoff Fahrer und Gefährt beim Schlafittchen packen. Kein Wunder, daß sie im Laufe der Zeit in die Breite wucherten, bis zu einer Schuhgröße von über einem halben Meter. Als man den Argentinier Carlos Reutemann einmal fragte, was denn sein beherrschender Eindruck beim Start sei, antwortete er spontan: „Räder, überall Räder!" Von der Saison 1993 an setzte die FISA dem Walzen-Wachstum die neue Grenze von 38,1 Zentimetern, ein Gesetzes-Akt, der vom Alleinlieferanten Goodyear mit Ingrimm zur Kenntnis genommen wurde, denn nun taugten alle Schablonen nichts mehr, die noch für dralle 45,7 Zentimeter geschmiedet waren.

Seit 1971 sind die Trockenreifen der Formel 1 kahl wie die Glatze des Kommissars Kojak, zäh-pappig und schmiegsam nach dem Vorbild ihrer Pendants an Dragster und Go-Kart. Immer dünner wurde die Lauffläche, immer schmaler der Grat zwischen Haltbarkeit und Effizienz. Beim Großen Preis von Deutschland 1975 gab es im Training 26 Reifenpannen, im Rennen 12. Mit Renault kam 1977 Michelin in die Formel 1, mit Michelin das Radial-Prinzip, nach dem auch die Pneus von Pirelli aufgebaut waren, 1981 eine Mitgift für den Toleman-Rennstall. Goodyear zog 1984 nach – da gehörte der Diagonalreifen zum Sperrmüll der Rennhistorie. Durch diese zieht sich auch die Radierspur der Reifenkriege. Treu wie sein schwarzes Gold, selbst unbeschadet einiger heftiger Verstimmungen, blieb der Formel 1 der amerikanische Gigant Goodyear. Auch nachdem Dunlop am Ende der Saison 1969 aus den Kampfhandlungen ausgestiegen war, hatte man sich auseinanderzusetzen, bis 1974 mit Firestone, zwischen 1977 und 84 mit Michelin, von 1981 bis 86 sowie 1990 und 91 auch mit Pirelli, während Avon 1981 und 82 wenig Kopfzerbrechen bereitete. Ein Auswuchs des Gummi-Haders, seit 1972 im Arsenal der Kombattanten: Qualifikations-Slicks, extrem haftend, wenig haltbar, damals auf einer Strecke wie Brands Hatch vielleicht 15 Kilometer. Häufig, wie 1978, wurde ihr Besitz zum Privileg. 1991 schrumpfte die Lebenserwartung dieser Pole Position-Pneus auf knapp über anderthalb Minuten: Nicht einmal für eine komplette Runde hätten sie gereicht, beschwerte sich Ferrari-Pilot Alain Prost in Spa. Ein Jahr später schulterte Goodyear wieder die Bürde des Monopols, wie schon Mitte der siebziger Jahre. Das erleichtert das Leben, gewiß, aber es ist auch ein teurer Spaß: Für Monaco zum Beispiel hatte man 1992 nicht weniger als 1900 Reifen im Gepäck.

TYRES

If you take the poets in the business by the word, the sorcerers in the laboratories of the big tyre manufacturers have found the philosophers' stone, sublimating trash and trivia such as caoutchouc, soot, oil, and chemicals into black gold. Modern racing tyres are invaluable: at the four points where they establish the contact between the car and the road they are maltreated by brutal forces. During the period of the wing cars already they had to resist centrifugal forces approaching 4g, later they transmitted the acceleration 1200 turbo horsepower were capable of, and since the early eighties they have had to cope with the virtually breathtaking deceleration carbon fibre brake disks permit. No wonder that, in the course of time, they grew exuberantly reaching widths of more than half a metre. When Argentinian Carlos Reutemann was asked what his overriding impression during a start was he said: "Wheels, wheels all over the place." From the 1993 season on FISA reduced tyre breadth to 15 inches, to the annoyance of sole supplier Goodyear on the grounds that they had to scrap existing tools built for producing 18-inch rear tyres.

Since 1971 Formula One dry tyres have been bald, sticky, and supple like their equivalents in karting and dragster racing. The thinner their tread became, the smaller was the edge between their durability and efficiency. The 1975 German Grand Prix was marred by 26 punctures during practice and 12 in the race. When Renault came into Formula One in 1977 they brought Michelin, whose tyres were built along the radial ply principle like those of their Italian competitor Pirelli, introduced into the highest motor racing echelon in 1981 by the Toleman team. When Goodyear followed suit in 1984 cross ply tyres were history, which has been full of the so-called tyre wars. In spite of the odd irritation, the American giant has always remained faithful to Formula One. Even after Dunlop had withdrawn at the end of the 1969 season, Goodyear had to face stiff opposition, from Firestone until 1974, from Michelin between 1977 and 1984, from Pirelli between 1981 and 1986 as well as in 1990 and 1991, whereas the Avon interlude in 1981 and 1982 caused no headache at all. Since 1972, a typical making of the perpetual battle for pole position between the tyre suppliers has been the existence of qualifiers, even more sticky, even less durable, good for about ten miles at Brands Hatch, for instance. Frequently, as in 1978, having them was a privilege, the have-nots coining the term "wooden tyres" for what they had to content themselves with. In 1991 the life expectancy of qualifiers dwindled to a minute and a half in the heat of the battle. At Spa Alain Prost pointed out that they had not even lasted out a complete lap. A year later Goodyear again shouldered the burden of having the monopoly, as in the mid-seventies. That may make life easier but it is also costly: In 1992, an arsenal of 1900 tyres had to be taken to Monaco alone.

LES PNEUS

Si l'on en croit les poètes de ce secteur, les artistes noirs travaillant dans les laboratoires des grands producteurs de pneus ont trouvé la pierre philosophale. Ils font une sublimation du trivial que sont le caoutchouc, l'huile, le noir de fumée et les produits chimiques pour en faire de l'or noir. Du moins, les pneus modernes destinés aux courses sont inestimables. Aux quatre endroits où ils créent le contact entre la voiture et la route, ils sont maltraités en long et en large par des forces brutales. A l'époque des voitures à ailes, ils devaient résister à des forces centrifuges atteignant près de quatre fois l'accélération due à la gravité et ont transmis plus tard la pulsion vers l'avant dont étaient capables près de 1200 CV turbo, et ils transfèrent depuis le début des années 80 les décélérations à vous couper littéralement le souffle provoquées par les disques de frein carbone, qui prennent au collet le pilote et le véhicule. Ce n'est donc pas étonnant, qu'au cours de l'évolution, ils se soient élargis jusqu'à atteindre plus de cinquante centimètres. Le jour où on a demandé à l'Argentin Carlos Reutemann ce qui l'impressionnait le plus au départ, il a répondu spontanément: «Des roues, rien que des roues partout!» A partir de la saison 1993, la FISA a fixé à 38,1 centimètres la largeur des pneus, une loi dont le livreur exclusif Goodyear prit connaissance avec une rage contenue, car alors, tous les plans que l'on avait conçus pour des pneus de 45,7 centimètres ne valaient plus rien.

Depuis 1971, les pneus lisses de la Formule 1 sont aussi chauves que la tête du commissaire Kojak, coriaces, et flexibles d'après le modèle de leurs parallèles sur dragster et go-karts. La surface de roulement est devenue de plus en plus mince, l'arête de plus en plus étroite entre la résistance et la capacité de rendement. Au Grand Prix d'Allemagne en 1975, il y a eu 26 pannes de pneus aux essais et 12 en course. Michelin entra dans la Formule 1 en 1977 avec Renault. Michelin a apporté le principe radial d'après lequel les pneus de Pirelli ont été élaborés, eux aussi, en 1981, une dot pour l'écurie Toleman. Goodyear s'y est mis en 1984. Ce pneu diagonal s'est alors retrouvé à la poubelle de l'histoire de la course. Tout au long de celle-ci, on peut voir la trace des guerres de pneus. Le géant américain Goodyear est resté fidèle comme son or noir à la Formule 1, sortie indemne de quelques vives contrariétés. Même après le départ de Dunlop, à la fin de la saison de 1969, on a dû s'arranger jusqu'en 1974 avec Firestone, entre 1977 et 84 avec Michelin, de 1981 à 86 ainsi qu'en 1990 et 1991 avec Pirelli aussi, tandis qu'Avon n'a pas trop été un casse-tête en 1981 et 1982. Un argument de plus dans la discorde concernant le caoutchouc depuis 1972: les pneus lisses de qualification, qui adhèrent de façon extrême, mais peu résistants, à l'époque sur un parcours comme le Brands Hatch, de 15 kilomètres peut-être. En 1991, l'espérance de vie de ces pneus de Pole Position s'est réduite à une minute et demie à peine, dans la chaleur intense du combat. Ils n'auraient même pas suffi à faire un tour complet si l'on en croit les plaintes du pilote de chez Ferrari, Alain Prost à Spa. Un an plus tard, Goodyear s'est remis seul à la tâche, comme il l'avait fait déjà au milieu des années 70.

NEUMÁTICOS

Si interpretamos a los poetas del ramo al pie de la letra, los artistas negros de los laboratorios de los grandes productores de neumáticos son quienes han dado con la piedra de la sabiduría: ellos subliman trivialidades como caucho, aceite, partículas de hollín y productos químicos, convirtiéndolos en oro negro. Al menos los modernos neumáticos de carreras no tienen comparación con el oro: en los cuatro puntos en que se produce el contacto entre coche y carretera, son maltratados por fuerzas brutales. En la época de los coches de ala, los neumáticos tenían que oponerse a fuerzas centrífugas de hasta cuatro veces la aceleración de la tierra, más tarde transmitían el ímpetu de propulsión de que eran capaces —hasta 1200 CV turbo— y, desde los años ochenta, transmiten las impresionantes declaraciones con que los discos de freno de fibra de carbono agarran por el cogote al conductor y al vehículo. No es de extrañar que fueran expandiéndose a lo ancho en el curso del tiempo hasta llegar a calzar una anchura de más de medio metro. Al preguntar en una ocasión al argentino Carlos Reutemann cuál era la impresión dominante a la salida, contestó espontáneamente: «Ruedas, ruedas y ruedas por todas partes.» A partir de la temporada de 1993, la FISA puso al de la cilindrada el nuevo límite de 38,1 centímetros, un acto de justicia del que sólo el proveedor Goodyear tomó nota con ira contenida, pues ahora podía tirar a la basura todos los moldes fundidos para rechonchos neumáticos de 45,7 centímetros.

Desde 1971, los neumáticos de cámara de la Fórmula 1 son lisos como la calva de Kojak, correosos, acartonados y flexibles, siguiendo el modelo de sus equivalentes en carreras de *dragster* y *karting*. Cuanto más se estrechaba la superficie de rodamiento, más se acortaba el filo entre su duración y su eficiencia. Con Renault vino Michelin a la Fórmula 1 en 1977; con Michelin, el principio radial, base también de los neumáticos de Pirelli —la dote que el equipo Toleman trajo en 1981 a las carreras—. Goodyear siguió el ejemplo en 1984. Por entonces, el neumático diagonal se encontraba ya en el basurero de la historia de las carreras, una historia llena de las llamadas guerras de neumáticos. A pesar de las fuertes desavenencias, el gigante americano Goodyear permaneció tan fiel a la Fórmula 1 como su oro negro. Aún después de que, al final de la temporada de 1969, Dunlop había abandonado tras duros combates, había que continuar con los enfrentamientos: hasta 1974 con Firestone, entre 1977 y 84 con Michelin, de 1981 a 86, así como en 1990 y 91, también con Pirelli, mientras que Avon en 1981 y 82 dio menos dolores de cabeza. Un tumor de los litigios de las gomas, desde 1972 en el arsenal de los combatientes: mañas de cualificación, extrema capacidad de adherencia, corta duración. En 1991 se redujo la esperanza de vida de estos neumáticos de *pole position* en lo más recio del combate a poco más de minuto y medio: no hubieran alcanzado ni para una vuelta completa, se quejaba el piloto de Ferrari Alain Prost en Spa. Un año más tarde volvió Goodyear a terciar al hombro el fardo del monopolio, como ya hiciera a mediados de los setenta.

TYRES

1 Brands Hatch (GB) 1984

2 Monaco 1983

3 Benetton Ford
   Monza (I) 1992

4 Marlboro McLaren Ford
   Monaco 1981

5 Silverstone (GB) 1983

6 *Reifeninspektorin von Goodyear bei der
   Arbeit / Goodyear tyre inspector at work /
   Inspecteur de pneu de Goodyear au travail /
   Inspectora de neumáticos de Goodyear
   trabajando*

   Interlagos (BR) 1993

7 *Warten auf den Boxenstop / Waiting for the
   pit stop / Attente de l'arrêt de stand /
   Esperando en la parada de jaula*

   Marlboro McLaren Ford
   Interlagos (BR) 1993

8 Zandvoort (NL) 1984

9 *Goodyear - Reifen - Service
   Goodyear - Tyres - Service
   Goodyear - Pneus - Service
   Servicio de neumáticos de Goodyear*

   Spa - Francorchamps (B) 1991

10 Ferrari
Monaco 1980

11 *Nach einem Ausflug in den Kies:*
After running into the gravel :
Après une excursion dans le gravier :
Después de una excursión en la grava:

Ferrari
Le Castellet (F) 1983

TYRES

1 Regenreifen
   Wet - weather tyres
   Pneus pluie
   Neumáticos para lluvia

   Alain Prost (F)
   Marlboro McLaren
   Dijon - Prenois (F) 1984

2 Alfa Romeo - Mechaniker kühlt Reifen /
   Alfa Romeo - mechanics cooling the tyres /
   Mécanicien Alfa Romeo réfroidissant les
   pneus /
   Mecánico de Alfa Romeo enfriando
   neumáticos

   Paul Ricard (F) 1980

3 Gummi - Abrieb
   Rubber wear
   Usure du caoutchouc
   Desgaste de la goma

   Dijon - Prenois (F) 1984

4 Temperatur - Prüfung
   Temperature check
   Contrôle de température
   Control de temperature

   Brands Hatch (GB) 1978

5 Mario Andretti (USA)
   JPS Lotus Ford
   Brands Hatch (GB) 1978

6   Slicks
    Michael Schumacher (D)
    Benetton Ford
    Estoril (P) 1992

7   Reifen - Vorheizung
    Preheating the tyres
    Echauffement des pneus
    Precalentamiento de neumáticos

    Williams Renault
    Monaco 1992

8   Reifen als Schutzwall
    Tyres as a protective barrier
    Les pneus comme barrière de protection
    Barrera de protección de neumáticos

    Phoenix (USA) 1990

GESICHTER / HELME

Das Antlitz, sagt man, sei der Spiegel der Seele. Früher gewährten Helme so viel Einblick in dieses Schaufenster des Ego, daß man darin lesen konnte. 1968 jedoch führte Sicherheits-Fetischist Jackie Stewart den Integralhelm ein. Seitdem wird die Persönlichkeit des Rennfahrers durch diesen Teil seiner Berufskleidung gefiltert und stilisiert. Der Helm wurde zum Medium der Ich-Aussage, das mitteilt, was der Mensch dahinter will – oder muß. Der schottische Patriot Stewart zeigte durch ein umlaufendes Tartanband in Halbglatzenhöhe, ihm liege dieser Teil des Vereinigten Königreichs besonders am Herzen. Damon Hill betreibt auf seinem Helm die gleiche Schwarzweißmalerei wie einst sein Vater Graham, der via Farbe und Design seine Treue zu seinem Ruderclub bekundete. Ein ähnliches Clanbewußtsein durchdringt die weitverzweigte Familie Andretti, die sich durch Rot und Blau auf Silber zu erkennen gibt. Andere bekennen sich zum toten Idol: Jean Alesi ließ seinen Helm zum Gedächtnis an Elio de Angelis gestalten. Wo gut bezahlt wird, ist natürlich Corporate Identity gefragt: Lauda-Logos von Römerquelle über Parmalat bis hin zu Marlboro erzeugten das Verlangen nach kompletten Menüs mit anschließender Zigarettenpause, während die Helm-Devise „Jesus Saves" des kleinen Brasilianers Alex Ribeiro gratis, aber zuversichtlich metaphysisches Heil verhieß. Ein nach oben gerichteter Pfeil unterstrich diese Aufwärts-Tendenz, sonst gerne horizontal als Symbol für reine Dynamik verwendet, bei Derek Daly zum Beispiel oder bei Carlos Pace. Häufig belegt Top-Dekor einfach die Lust an der eigenen Identität, ein gut leserliches Jody etwa auf dem Helm des bärigen Südafrikaners Scheckter, der Nachname Cevert, der die Trikolore auf dem Kopfschutz des gutaussehenden Parisers säumte. Von einem ungebrochenen Verhältnis zum Ich zeugt auch, wenn Männer wie Hans Stuck, Danny Sullivan oder Michael Schumacher, heraldisch gesehen, zu den Sternen greifen, wogegen sich die stolze Formel 1-Praktikantin Desiré Wilson gar eine Krone auf den Helm sprühen ließ. Nur: Da war ihr die Ambition wohl zu sehr zu Kopfe gestiegen.

BOSSE

Selbst dem unbefangenen Betrachter im Fernsehliegesessel wird bald klar, daß ein Grand Prix kaum Ähnlichkeit mit einer Tagung des Christlichen Vereins Junger Männer hat. Nur der Fitteste überlebt – dieser Grundsatz evolutionären Wildwuchses gilt bis hinab in den Troß der schnellen Truppe. Skeptiker behaupten gar, die Ellbogenwelt der Großen Preise sei ein chemisch reiner Extrakt menschlichen Zusammenlebens überhaupt. Natürlich bilden die Bosse da keine Ausnahme, im Gegenteil. So legt Frank Williams gerne ein grantiges Bekenntnis zur Niedertracht ab: Für Mister Nice Guy, den netten Kerl, sei kein Platz in diesem Handwerk. In der Tat: Nach dem Grand Prix von Belgien 1991 luchste Benetton-Manager Flavio Briatore dem smarten Iren Eddie Jordan das knospende Supertalent Michael Schumacher ab, in einem Procedere, das man im Eishockey als Powerplay bezeichnen würde — gelinde ausgedrückt. Das warf

Fragen auf, die sich an altmodische Begriffe wie Moral und Vertragstreue anlagerten. Indes: Das sei nicht elegant gewesen, gewiß, hatte Briatore dazu zu sagen. Aber manchmal müsse man einfach Dinge tun, die sonst ungetan blieben.

Im Spannungsfeld der Verpflichtungen wird denn auch gelegentlich das journalistische Gegenüber jäh zur Zielscheibe: Ron Dennis zum Beispiel macht häufig mal einen überraschenden kleinen Ausfall gegen den allzu Wißbegierigen: „In der Stunde, die ich jetzt mit Ihnen verbringe, hätte ich vielleicht an den Autos irgendein Defizit entdeckt und wäre so meinem Ziel, der Weltmeisterschaft, ein Stück nähergekommen." Und auch Formel 1-Impresario Bernie Ecclestone, der sich von der Reinlichkeit der Bedürfnisanstalten bis hin zur Entfernung unerwünschter Personen um wirklich alles höchstselbst kümmert, hat in solchen Stunden der Wahrheit wenig Ermutigendes zu sagen: „Ihr Pressefritzen seid meistens zu faul oder zu vorsichtig, als daß ihr hinter die Kulissen sehen wolltet."

Eine Armee von Einzelkämpfern: Er sei sehr einsam und sehr arrogant. Seine Fahrer behandle er als notwendiges Übel, beklagte sich bereits Phil Hill, Weltmeister von 1961, über den enigmatischen Enzo Ferrari. Daß überall Eiskristalle glitzern auf dem Zwischenmenschlichen, bedauert auch François Guiter, selber ein Boß, der 1967 den französischen Treibstoffkonzern ELF in die Formel 1 brachte. Er sucht und findet Zuflucht und Trost in der guten alten Zeit, als zum Beispiel Jackie Stewart zum Lunch auf einem Haufen Reifen ein Butterbrot verzehrt habe und für jedermann anzusprechen gewesen sei. Gleichwohl, sagt Guiter, gebe es viele charmante Leute in der Formel 1. Man müsse sie nur näher kennenlernen, sogar einige, die als notorisch schwierig gälten wie Senna oder Ron Dennis. Dabei hat es Mister McLaren der Zweite manchmal nicht einfach gehabt im Leben: Project Four hieß sein eigenes Unternehmen, das er 1980 kurz vor dem italienischen Grand Prix mit dem maroden Team McLaren zur Renommier-Marke McLaren International verschmolz. Mit den ersten drei Projekten hatte er keineswegs immer eine glückliche Hand gehabt, zum Beispiel, als er 1971 mit einem Budget von 2000 Pfund die Formel 2-Equipe Rondel Racing aus der Taufe hob und sich bald in einer Armada von fünf Wagen verzettelte. Überhaupt – eine geradezu stupende Beharrlichkeit gehört unbedingt ins Rüstzeug des Formel 1-Bosses. Frank Williams mußte sich zehn Jahre gedulden bis zu seinem ersten Grand Prix-Sieg, Ken Tyrrell, inzwischen zerzaust und verwittert wie eine alte Eiche, wartet seit zehn Jahren auf seinen nächsten, während sich bei Ferrari die Zuständigkeiten und damit der Frust über Erfolgs-Flauten häufig in anonymen Führungs-Kollektiven verlieren. Der schlitzäugige und schlitzohrige Teddy Yip indes, steinreicher Entrepreneur aus Hongkong und Rennsport-Mäzen aus Leidenschaft, der eine Menge Pfunde in den Ensign-Rennstall (1973-1982) des kahlköpfigen Briten Mo Nunn pumpte, sah das alles ganz locker: Als das Spielzeug Formel 1 keinen Spaß mehr machte, warf er es einfach weg.

The face, they say, is the mirror of the soul. In earlier times helmets granted much insight into this shop-window of the ego. In 1968, however, safety-conscious Jackie Stewart introduced the integral helmet. Since then the driver's personality has been reduced to what he discloses through this part of his work clothes, the helmet changed into the medium of an I-message that tells us what the man behind it wants or is expected to make known. Scottish patriot Stewart showed by means of a tartan band that he held his native part of the United Kingdom in high esteem whereas Jo Siffert and Clay Regazzoni were crusaders in the Land of Grand Prix Promise sporting the Swiss cross on their helmets. Damon Hill carries on the family tradition once begun by his father Graham, who manifested his sympathy for his rowing club using the black and white colours as well as the design of his helmet. The widely ramified Andretti clan can be recognized by red and blue on a silver foil while others display the colours of their dead idols, Jean Alesi making use of a design reminding of the late Elio de Angelis'. When you are being well paid, you inevitably have to show corporate identity. Niki Lauda's logos from Römerquelle via Parmalat to Marlboro invited the reader to indulge in square meals plus a stop for a smoke whereas the message "Jesus Saves" on the helmet of diminutive Brazilian Alex Ribeiro promised salvation in the next world, confidently but, of course, free of charge as well. That upward tendency was endorsed by a vertical arrow, its horizontal counterpart standing for sheer dynamics, as on Derek Daly's and Carlos Pace's helmets. Frequently the design betrays the delight a driver takes in his own identity, fat initials for example as on Mike Thackwell's and Mark Blundell's helmets, a well legible Jody on "Baby Bear" Scheckter's one, the surname Cevert bordering the tricolor on the good-looking French-man's headgear. When men like Hans Stuck, Danny Sullivan or Michael Schumacher reach for the stars, heraldically speaking, it shows that they value themselves quite highly. Formula One apprentice Desiré Wilson, however, certainly went one step too far having a crown sprayed on her helmet, her ambition virtually gone to her head....

BOSSES

Even a naïve armchair enthusiast will soon recognize that there are few parallels between a Grand Prix and a YMCA meeting. The fittest survive – this maxim of the evolutionary jungle goes for the camp-followers of the Grand Prix circus, too. Sceptics maintain that the competitive world of motor racing epitomizes human coexistence altogether. Of course bosses are no exceptions, on the contrary. Frank Williams will point out that there is no room for Mister Nice Guy in this business. Indeed: The way Benetton manager Flavio Briatore wrestled budding superstar Michael Schumacher out of Eddie Jordan's embrace after the 1991 Belgian Grand Prix was hardly cricket, to say the least, as it also entailed the sacking of thunderstruck Brazilian Roberto Moreno from the Benetton team. Questions arose from this focusing on old-fashioned notions like loyalty or morals. Briatore, however, was not tormented at all by pangs of conscience: Certainly, he admitted, his proceeding had not been very elegant. But sometimes things had to be done which otherwise would have remained undone.

Where millions are at stake even the journalistic vis-à-vis will suddenly be reduced to a target butt. Ron Dennis, for instance, tends to make rapid lunges at the questioner: "In the hour I am spending here with you I might perhaps have discovered something that is wrong with my cars, coming a bit closer to my aim, the world championship." And what Formula One impresario Bernie Ecclestone, who looks after everything from the cleanness of toilets to the expulsion of gate-crashers, has to say in such moments of truth is also hardly encouraging: "You press people are either a bit too lazy or a bit too cautious about trying to find out the real facts."

Seen from this angle, Formula One people appear to be an army of solitary fighters: He was very lonesome and very arrogant, treating his drivers as a necessary evil, the 1961 world champion, Phil Hill, already complained about enigmatic Enzo Ferrari. The noticeable chilling affecting human relations in the bel étage of racing is also regretted by François Guiter, every inch a boss himself, who brought the French fuel company ELF into Formula One in 1967. Occasionally he resorts to his memories of the good old days when Jackie Stewart was sitting on a stack of wheels having a sandwich for lunch, friendly and accessible to everybody. For all that, says Guiter, there are lots of amiable and charming people in the Grand Prix business. You must only know them more intimately, even characters universally considered as difficult like Senna or Ron Dennis, whose off-hand speeches and dry sense of humour he appreciates. Mister McLaren the Second has had to weather hard times, after all. His own enterprise, which he amalgamated with the ailing Team McLaren into McLaren International shortly before the 1980 Italian Grand Prix, was called Project Four. The first three had sometimes been rough going, in 1971 for example, when Dennis ran his Formula Two team Rondel Racing on the shoestring budget of 2000 pounds, dissipating his activities into five cars. You have to be stupendously tenacious anyway so as to be a Formula One boss. Frank Williams had to bide his time for ten years until Clay Regazzoni scored the first victory for him. Ken Tyrrell, weather-worn like an old Kentish oak, has been waiting for a decade for his next illustrating Ernest Hemingway's dictum that a man can be destroyed but not defeated. Ferrari lows have been easier to endure because they were due to collectives rather than individuals, with responsibilities shifting frequently. Teddy Yip, however, an immensely rich Hong Kong and Macao entrepreneur and sponsor imbued with a life-long motor racing obsession, favoured a light-hearted approach nevertheless. He did invest a small fortune in bald-headed Briton Mo Nunn's Ensign team (1973 - 1982), for instance. But when he did not enjoy the toy Formula One any longer, he threw it away.

VISAGES / CASQUES

On dit que le visage est le miroir de l'âme. Autrefois, les casques en laissaient voir assez dans cette vitrine de l'ego pour qu'on puisse y lire. En 1968, le fétichiste de la sécurité, Jackie Stewart, introduisit le casque intégral. Depuis, la personnalité du pilote de course est filtrée et stylisée à l'aide de cette partie du vêtement professionnel. Le casque est devenu un moyen d'expression du moi qui fait part de ce que l'homme qui se cache derrière veut ou doit. Stewart, le patriote écossais, montrait par une bande de tartan qu'il portait une haute estime à cette partie du Royaume Uni. Damon Hill fait la même peinture en noir et blanc sur son casque, que son père autrefois, Grabham qui, par la couleur et le design, exprimait sa fidélité à son club d'aviron. Une conscience de clan analogue est imprégnée dans la famille Andretti très ramifiée que l'on reconnaît par du rouge et du bleu sur fond argent. D'autres s'orientent à l'idole décédée: Jean Alesi fit dessiner son casque à la mémoire d'Elio de Angelis. Et là où on paie bien, on demande la Corporate Identity: les logos de Lauda, qui allaient de Römerquelle à Marlboro en passant par Parmalat, ont engendré l'exigence de menus complets avec une pause cigarettes à la fin, tandis que la devise du casque «Jesus Saves» du petit Brésilien Alex Ribeiro promet le salut gratuitement et avec une confiance métaphysique. Souvent, le décor veut montrer simplement l'envie d'une propre identité un Jody bien lisible sur le casque de Scheckter, le Sud-Africain à la stature d'ours, le nom de Cevert qui se trouvait au bord du drapeau tricolore sur le casque du beau Parisien.Cela témoigne d'un rapport ininterrompu avec leur Moi quand des hommes comme Hans Stuck, Danny Sullivan ou Michael Schumacher, vus héraldiquement, veulent saisir les étoiles tandis que la fière débutante de Formule 1, Désiré Wilson, s'était même fait vaporiser une couronne sur le casque. Seulement: là, l'ambition lui était vraiment montée à la tête.

BOSSES

Il y a trois choses qui deviennent vite très claires, même pour le profane assis devant la télévision: Un Grand Prix ne ressemble pas tellement à un séminaire de l'association de Jeunes chrétiens. Il n'y a que celui qui est le plus en forme qui survit, ce principe de croissance sauvage évolutionniste est même valable jusqu'en bas de l'échelle. Les gens sceptiques affirment que le monde dans lequel on arrive en jouant des coudes, celui des Grands Prix, ne serait qu'un extrait chimiquement pur de la vie sociale, et c'est ce qui fait sûrement une partie de sa fascination. Naturellement, les bosses ne font pas exception, au contraire. C'est ainsi que Frank Williams aime bien se montrer object. Il n'y a pas de place dans ce métier pour Mister Nice Guy, le gentil gars. On n'a qu'à regarder toute cette clique, ils sont tous méchants, sans égards et égocentriques. En effet: après le Grand Prix de Belgique en 1991, le manager de Benetton, Flavio Briatore, a dérobé le supertalent qui allait éclore, Michael Schumacher, à l'Irlandais élégant, Eddie Jordan, dans une procédure que l'on qualifierait en hockey sur glace de jeu de pouvoir – ce qui serait un euphémisme.

Amsi s'est-on posé des questions qui étaient reliées aux vieux concepts de morale et de fidélité au contrat.

Dans le champ de tension des obligations, occasionnellement, le journaliste devient brusquement une cible: Ron Dennis par exemple, endurci dans des milliers d'interviews et avec la viligance d'une vieille fouine, fait souvent une petite remarque désagréable et surprenante à l'encontre de celui qui veut en savoir trop. «En ce moment, moi qui vous parle, j'aurais peut-être pu découvrir certains déficits à mes voitures et me serais rapproché un peu plus de mon but qui est d'arriver au championnat du monde.» De même, Bernie Ecclestone, imprésario de la Formule 1, qui s'occupe absolument de tout, que cela soit de la propreté des toilettes ou de l'éloignement de personnes indésirables, n'a que très peu de choses encourageantes à dire dans ces heures de vérité: «Vous, les types de la presse, la plupart du temps vous êtes bien trop paresseux ou trop prudents pour vouloir regarder ce qui se passe derrière les coulisses.»

Une armée de cavaliers seuls: il doit être très seul et très arrogant. Il traite ses pilotes comme un mal obligatoire, se plaignait déjà Phil Hill, champion du monde de 1961 à propos de l'énigmatique Enzo Ferrari. Des cristaux de glace scintillent partout dans le contact relationnel, et François Guiter le regrette bien, qui a fait lui-même entrer le groupe pétrolier français Elf dans la Formule I en 1967. Il cherche et trouve un refuge et une consolation dans la formule 3000 où cela se passe encore bien entre les gens. Et comme au bon vieux temps, quand Jackie Stewart par exemple mangeait un sandwich le midi, assis sur un tas de pneus et que tout le monde pouvait lui adresser la parole. N'importe, dit Guiter, il y a beaucoup de gens charmants dans la Formule I. Il faut simplement faire plus ample connaissance, et même de ceux qui passent pour être notoirement difficiles comme Senna ou Ron Dennis. Pourtant, Mister McLaren II n'a pas eu toujours une vie facile: sa propre entreprise s'appelait Project Four qu'il fit associer en 1980, peu avant le Grand Prix italien, avec l'équipe fatiguée de chez McLaren pour en faire la marque renommée de McLaren International. Il n'avait pas toujours eu la main heureuse avec ses trois premiers projets, quand, par exemple, il a fait naître l'équipe Rondel Racing de Formule 2 avec un budget de 2.000 livres et qu'il s'est bientôt éparpillé dans une armada de cinq voitures. De toute façon, il faut être extrêmement tenace quand on veut être boss de Formule I. Frank Williams a dû attendre dix ans avant sa première victoire de Grand Prix. Ken Tyrrell, maintenant échevelé et décomposé comme un vieux chêne, attend la prochaine depuis dix ans déjà, tandis que chez Ferrari, les responsabilités et, en même temps, la frustration des fluctuations de succès se perdent souvemt dans des collectifs de direction anonymes. Cependant, Teddy Yip, l'homme aux yeux bridés et malins, le richissime entrepreneur de Hong Kong et mécène du sport automobile par passion, qui a injecté force de livres dans l'écurie Ensign (1973-1982) de Mo Nunn, le Britannique chauve, a vu tout cela de façon très cool: quand la Formule I ne l'a plus amusé, il l'a jetée, tout simplement.

ROSTROS / CASCOS

Se dice que el rostro es el espejo del alma. En otros tiempos los cascos garantizaban una vista tan buena en este escaparate del alma que se podía leer en él. En 1968 introdujo el fetichista de la seguridad Jackie Stewart el casco integral. Desde entonces la personalidad de los pilotos es filtrada y estilizada por esta pieza de su vestido profesional. El casco se convirtió en el medio transmisor del yo, el mensaje que la persona tiene oculto detrás y quiere o debe transmitir. El patriota escocés Stewart demostraba, mediante una cinta tartán enmarcando su media calva, que tenía en gran estima esta parte del Reino Unido. Damon Hill decora su casco con pintura en blanco y negro, continuando la tradición de su padre Graham, quien manifestaba fidelidad a su club de remo mediante el color y el diseño. Una semejante conciencia de clan prevalece en la ampliamente ramificada familia Andretti, que se da a conocer con los colores rojo y negro. Otros glorifican a sus ídolos muertos: Jean Alesi hizo diseñar su casco en recuerdo a Elio de Angelis. Donde se paga bien, se exige también *corporate identity*: los logotipos de Lauda, de Römerquelle a Marlboro pasando por Parmalat, invitaban al lector a menús completos con pausa para fumar incluida, mientras la divisa «Jesus saves» del casco del pequeño brasileño Alex Ribeiro prometía salvación en el otro mundo, con toda confianza, pero, eso sí, gratis. La decoración del tocado da a menudo testimonio del gusto por la propia identidad: gordas iniciales, por ejemplo, caracterizan los cascos de Mike Thackwell o de Mark Blundell; un bien visible Jody en el del osito sudafricano Scheckter; el apellido Cevert rodeando la tricolor en el casco del bienparecido parisiense. Cuando hombres como Hans Stuck, Danny Sullivan o Michael Schumacher coleccionan estrellas, desde el punto de vista heráldico, documentan que se tienen a sí mismos en alta esti-ma. En cambio cuando la orgullosa aprendiz de Fórmula 1 Desiré Wilson manda pintar una corona en su casco da muestras de que la ambición se le había subido un poco a la cabeza.

BOSSES

Incluso el despreocupado televidente sentado en su sillón se dará cuenta de que un Grand Prix tiene poco en común con una reunión de jóvenes cristianos. Sólo el mejor sobrevive: este principio de la jungla evolutiva es válida incluso para el séquito de la tropa rápida, ya se trate solamente de lograr que un responsable de la FISA desembuche un pase especial. Los escépticos aseguran que el mundo de codazos de los Grandes Premios no es más que un puro estrato químico de la convivencia humana, lo que seguramente constituye una parte de su fascinación. Por supuesto que los *bosses* no son ninguna excepción, todo lo contrario. Frank Williams no tiene el menor problema en descalificar a Mister Nice Guy, un hombre amable, para ocupar un puesto en este negocio. En efecto: tras el Grand Prix de Bélgica en 1991, el *manager* de Benetton Flavio Briatore timó al elegante irlandés Eddie Jordan robándole al tierno supertalento Michael Schumacher con un procedimiento que en tenis se llamaría *powerplay*

—una expresión aún demasiado indulgente—. Al mismo tiempo, el patrón de Benetton ponía de patitas en la calle al consternado Roberto Moreno. Esto dio lugar a cuestiones enfocadas en conceptos pasados de moda como moral y legalidad.

En el tenso campo de los compromisos ocurre de vez en cuando que lo periodístico es reducido a tiro al blanco: Ron Dennis, por ejemplo, un hombre endurecido con miles de entrevistas, espabilado y astuto como una vieja garduña, tiende a sorprender a sus entrevistadores con pequeñas arremetidas: «En la hora que estoy pasando con usted, podría haber descubierto alguna deficiencia en los coches, acercándome así un poco más al propósito de mi meta, el Campeonato Mundial». También el empresario de la Fórmula 1, Bernie Ecclestone, que se ocupaba personalmente de todo, desde la limpieza de los servicios hasta la expulsión de personas no gratas, y lo que solía decir en tales momentos no es precisamente alentador: «vosotros, periodistas de pacotilla, sois o demasiado vagos o demasiado cautelosos para descubrir lo que se oculta trasero.»

Un ejército de luchadores solitarios: él sería demasiado solitario y muy arrogante. Trata a sus corredores como un mal necesario, se quejaba Phil Hill, Campeón Mundial en 1961, sobre el enigmático Enzo Ferrari. Sobre los cristales de hielo que brillan en las relaciones humanas se quejaba también François Guiter, el patrón que en 1967 trajo a la compañía francesa de combustible ELF a la Fórmula 1. Este hombre busca y encuentra refugio en los buenos tiempos, cuando Jackie Stewart, por ejemplo, se zampaba por almuerzo un bocadillo sobre un montón de neumáticos, amistoso y asequible a todo el mundo. Al mismo tiempo, dice Guiter, habría mucha gente encantadora en la Fórmula 1. Sólo habría que conocerlos más de cerca, incluso caracteres con fama de difíciles, como Senna o Ron Dennis, a quien era un placer escuchar cuando tenía uno de sus raptos de humor. Al fin y al cabo, Mister McLaren II no siempre lo tenía fácil en la vida: su propia empresa, que él amalgamó en 1980 con el fatigado equipo McLaren poco después del Grand Prix italiano, se convirtió en la marca McLaren, de renombre internacional. No siempre había tenido buena suerte con los tres primeros proyectos, como cuando en 1971, con un presupuesto de 2000 libras, se metió a la Fórmula 2 con el equipo Rondel Racing, disipando una flotilla de cinco coches. Entre las armas de un patrón de Fórmula 1 no puede faltar una buena dosis de tenacidad. Frank Williams tuvo que esperar durante diez años hasta conseguir su primera victoria Grand Prix; Ken Tyrrell, entretanto desgreñado apergaminado como un viejo roble, espera desde hace diez años por el siguiente, mientras que en Ferrari se dispersan las responsabilidades en colectivos anónimos y con ello también la frustración sobre triunfos estancados. Sin embargo, el taimado Teddy Yip, empresario riquísimo de Hong Kong y apasionado mecenas del automovilismo, se lo tomaba todo con mucha filosofía. Invirtió una pequeña fortuna en el equipo Ensign (1973-1982) del calvo británico Mo Nunn, cuando el juguete Fórmula 1 dejó de interesarle, simplemente lo tiró a la basura.

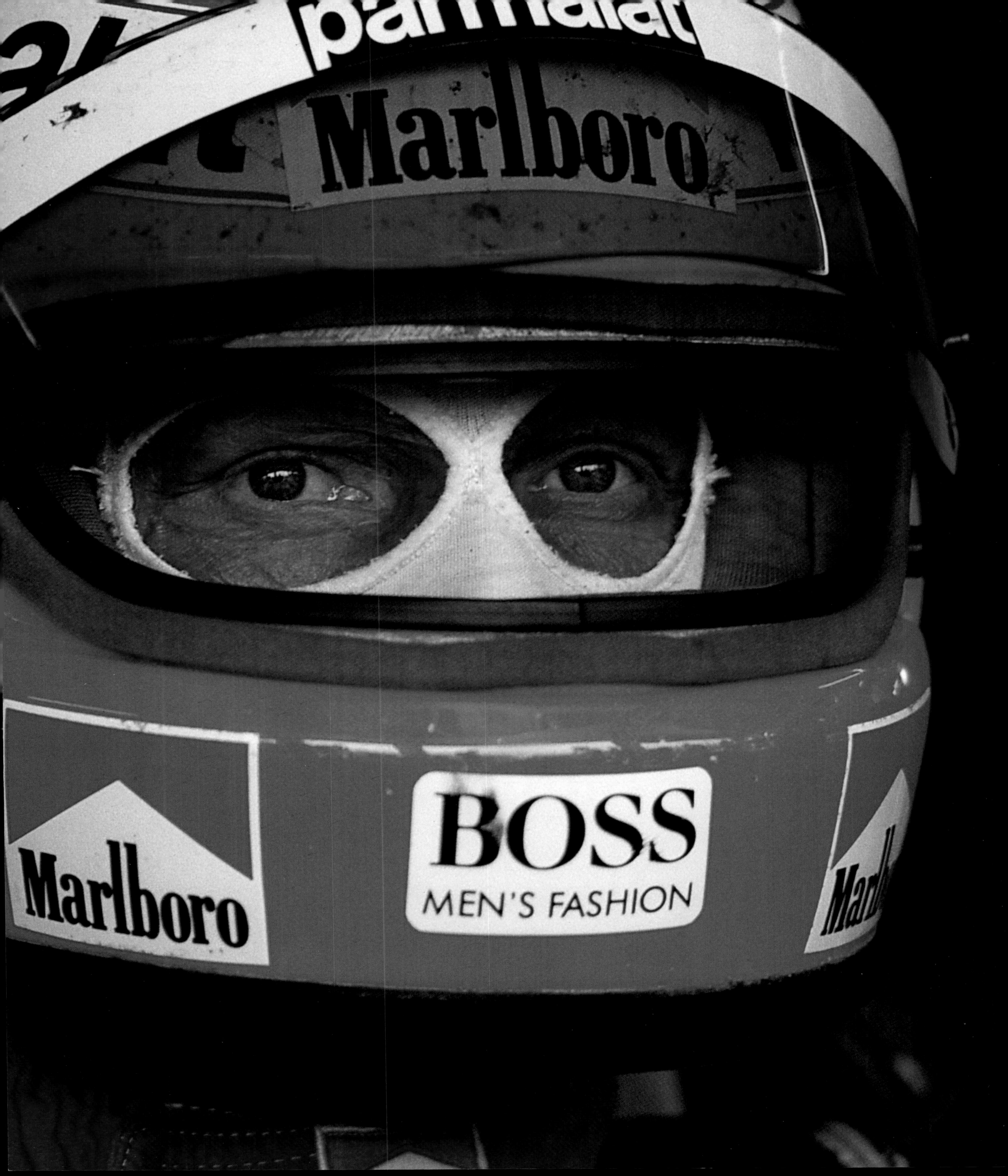
parmalat
Marlboro
Marlboro
BOSS
MEN'S FASHION

FACES/HELMETS

1, 2

3, 4

5, 6, 7

8 Niki Lauda (A)
Ferrari
Nürburgring (D) 1976

Einen Tag vor seinem Unfall
One day before his accident
Un jour avant son accident
Un día antes de su accidente

1   Jackie Stewart (GB)
    Elf Tyrrell Ford
    Zandvoort (NL) 1971

2   Jackie Stewart (GB)
    Elf Tyrrell Ford
    Monza (I) 1972

3   Ignazio Giunti (I)
    Ferrari
    Spa - Francorchamps (B) 1970

4   James Hunt (GB)
    Marlboro McLaren Ford
    Brand Hatch (GB) 1978

5   Emerson Fittipaldi (BR)
    JPS Lotus Ford
    Zolder (B) 1973

6   Jacky Ickx (B)
    Ligier Gitanes Ford
    Hockenheim (D) 1979

1 Stefan Bellof (D)
   Tyrrell Ford
   Monaco 1984

2   Michele Alboreto (I)
Ferrari
Hockenheim (D) 1984

3   Clay Regazzoni (CH)
Ferrari
Le Castellet (F) 1971

4 - 7   Nelson Piquet (BR)
Brabham Olivetti BMW Turbo
Le Castellet (F) 1985

8   Emerson Fittipaldi (BR)
Marlboro Texaco McLaren Ford
Le Castellet (F) 1975

9   Nelson Piquet (BR)
Brabham Parmalat BMW Turbo
Hockenheim (D) 1984

10   John Watson (GB)
Martini Brabham Alfa
Dijon - Prenois (F) 1977

11   Hans Stuck (D)
ATS Ford
Hockenheim (D) 1979

1 Michael Schumacher (D)
   Benetton Ford
   Hungaroring (H) 1992

2 Michael Schumacher (D)
   Benetton Ford
   Hockenheim (D) 1992

3 Jean Alesi (F)
   Ferrari
   Estoril (P) 1990

4 Michael Schumacher (D)
   Benetton Ford
   Hungaroring (H)

5 Satoru Nakajima (J)
   Tyrrell Honda
   Adelaide (AUS) 1991

6 Johnny Herbert (GB)
   Lotus Ford
   Montreal (CDN) 1992

7 Luis Perez Sala (E)
   Minardi Ford
   Jerez (E) 1989

8 Yannik Dalmas (F)
   AGS Ford
   Hungaroring (H) 1990

9 Alessandro Nannini (I)
Benetton Ford
Estoril (P) 1990

10 Nelson Piquet (BR)
Benetton Ford
Montreal (CDN) 1990

11 Mark Blundell (GB)
Brabham Yamaha
Barcelona (E) 1991

12, 13 Riccardo Patrese (I)
Benetton Ford
Kyalami (ZA) 1993

Nigel Mansell (GB):

1   Williams Renault, Hungaroring (H) 1991

2   Williams Judd, Silverstone (GB) 1988

3   Ferrari, Imola (RSM) 1989

4   Williams Judd, Hockenheim (D) 1988

5   Bernd Schneider (D), Zakspeed
    Aguri Suzuki (J), Zakspeed
    Jerez (E) 1989

6   Gerhard Berger (A)
    Ferrari
    Monza (I) 1988

7   Stefan Johansson (S)
    Ligier Judd
    Paul Ricard (F) 1988

8   Bertrand Gachot (F)
    Onyx Ford
    Silverstone (GB) 1989

9   Roberto Moreno (BR)
    Benetton Ford
    Phoenix (USA) 1991

10 Derek Warwick (GB)
    Lotus Lamborghini
    Estoril (P) 1990

11 Thierry Boutsen (B)
    Barclay Arrows BMW
    Spa - Francorchamps (B) 1985

12 Nelson Piquet (BR)
    Lotus Judd
    Imola (RSM) 1989

13 Alain Prost (F)
    Ferrari
    Phoenix (USA) 1991

14 Alain Prost (F)
    Marlboro McLaren Honda
    Hungaroring (H) 1988

15 Alain Prost (F)
    Ferrari
    Montreal (CDN) 1991

16 Alain Prost (F)
    Camel Williams Renault
    Kyalami (ZA) 1993

1

2, 3

4

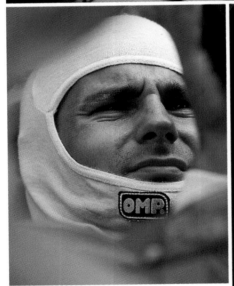

5

6

1 Michael Andretti (USA)
   Marlboro McLaren Ford
   Kyalami (ZA) 1993

2 Mario Andretti (USA)
   Martini - Lotus Ford
   Dijon - Prenois (F) 1979

3 Mario Andretti (USA)
   Martini Lotus Ford
   Hockenheim (D) 1979

4 Gerhard Berger (A)
   Ferrari
   Hockenheim (D) 1988

5 Gerhard Berger (A)
   Ferrari
   Jerez (E) 1989

6 Gerhard Berger (A)
   Marlboro McLaren Honda
   Spa - Francorchamps (B) 1990

7, 8

9, 10

11

7   Ayrton Senna (BR)
    Lotus Honda
    Imola (RSM) 1987

8   Ayrton Senna (BR)
    Marlboro McLaren Honda
    Hockenheim (D) 1992

9   Ayrton Senna (BR)
    Marlboro McLaren Honda
    Inetrlagos (BR) 1991

10 Ayrton Senna (BR)
    Marlboro McLaren Honda
    Magny Cours (F) 1991

11 Ayrton Senna (BR)
    Marlboro McLaren Honda
    Hockenheim (D) 1992

1   Enzo Ferrari
Monza (I) 1967

2   Colin Chapman (GB)
Martini Lotus
Hockenheim (D) 1979

3   Frank Williams (GB)
Saudia Williams
Monza (I) 1979

4, 5

6, 7

8

9

10

4   Luca di Montezemolo (I)
     Mauro Forghieri (I)
     Ferrari

     Brands Hatch (GB) 1974

5   Lord Hesketh (GB)
     Hesketh
     Paul Ricard (F) 1975

6   David Thieme (MC)
     Essex Lotus
     Hockenheim (D) 1980

7   Teddy Yip (Hongkong)
     Ensign
     Imola (RSM) 1980

8   Ken Tyrrell (GB)
     Elf Tyrrell
     Dijon - Prenois (F) 1974

9   Teddy Mayer (GB), Team
     Marlboro McLaren
     Jarama (E) 1978

10   Bernie Ecclestone (GB), Brabham Parmalat
     Teddy Mayer (GB), Marlboro McLaren

     Monaco 1980

BOSSES

1, 2

3, 4

5

6, 7

9

8

10, 1

1 Bernie Ecclestone (GB), Brabham Parmalat
  Max Mosley (GB)

  Jarama (E) 1979

2 J. - M. Balestre
  FISA President
  Hockenheim (D) 1981

3 Bernie Ecclestone (GB)
  Nelson Piquet (BR)
  Team Brabham Parmalat
  Jarama (E) 1979

4 Bernie Ecclestone (GB)
  Nelson Piquet (BR)
  Brabham Olivetti

  Zeltweg (A) 1984

5 Paul Rosche (D)
  BMW
  Zeltweg (A) 1982

6 Paul Rosche (D)
  BMW
  Nürburgring (D) 1984

7 Paul Rosche (D)
  BMW
  Monaco 1985

8 Bernie Ecclestone (GB)
  Brabham Parmalat
  Zeltweg (A) 1981

9 Hans Mezger (D)
  Porsche
  Dijon - Prenois (F) 1984

10 Hans Mezger (D)
  Porsche
  Monza (I) 1984

11 Hans Mezger (D), Porsche
  Niki Lauda (A), McLaren TAG

  Zeltweg (A) 1984

12, 13

15

8, 19

14

16, 17

20

12 Jean Sage (F)
    Renault
    Zeltweg (A) 1981

13 Guy Ligier (F)
    Ligier Gitanes
    Long Beach (USA) 1983

14 Erich Zakowski (D)
    Helmut Barth
    Zakspeed
    Jerez (E) 1986

15 Frank Williams (GB)
    Patrick Head (GB)
    Saudia Williams
    Paul Ricard (F) 1983

16 Günter Schmid (D)
    ATS
    Monaco 1984

17 Günter Schmid (D), RIAL
    Steffi Graf, Peter Graf (D)
    Hockenheim (D) 1988

18 Gérard Ducarouge (F)
    Lotus Renault
    Monza (I) 1986

19 Gérard Larrousse (F)
    Renault Elf
    Monza (I) 1980

20 Roland Bruynseraede
    FISA Renn - Direktor
    FISA race director
    FISA directeur de course
    FISA director de carreras
    Silverstone (GB) 1989

BOSSES

1   Cal Lindt (USA)
    Leo Mehl (USA)
    Goodyear

    Monza (I) 1992

2   François Guiter (F), Elf
    Bernard Cahier
    Journalist, IRPA - President

    Hockenheim (D) 1990

3   Heini Mader (CH)
    Engineer
    Jacarepagua (BR) 1989

4   Ken Tyrrell (GB)
    Braun Tyrrell
    Imola (RSM) 1991

5   John Barnard (GB), *Designer*
    Ferrari
    Jerez (E) 1989

6   Tony Rudd (GB)
    Lotus Lamborghini
    Interlagos (BR) 1990

7   J. - P. van Rossem (B)
    Onyx
    Jerez (E) 1989

8   Mauro Forghieri (I), *Engineer*
    Lamborghini
    Phoenix (USA) 1990

9   Max Mosley (GB),
    FISA president
    Emerson Fittipaldi,
    Indycar driver,
    Formula 1 World Champion 1972, 1974

    Estoril (P) 1992

14, 15

16

17

18

19

20

21

Gustav Brunner, *Engineer:*

10 Rial, Silverstone (GB) 1988

11 Zakspeed, Monza (I) 1988

12 March, Hungaroring (H) 1990

13 Minardi, Kyalami (ZA) 1993

14 Ron Dennis (GB), Alain Prost, Niki Lauda
Marlboro McLaren
Estoril (P) 1984

15 Ron Dennis (GB)
Gordon Murray, *Designer*
Marlboro McLaren
Jerez (E) 1987

16 Ron Dennis (GB), Marlboro McLaren
Mansour Ojjeh, McLaren - TAG *(McLaren
Mitinhaber / McLaren co - owner / co -
propriétaire de McLaren / copropietario de
McLaren)*
Phoenix (USA) 1990

17 Ron Dennis (GB)
Marlboro McLaren Teamboss
Monza (I) 1991

18 Harvey Postlethwaite (GB)
Ferrari designer
Barcelona (E) 1993

19 Luca di Montezemolo (I), *Ferrari president*
Barcelona (E) 1992

20 Niki Lauda (A), *(Ex - Ferrari - Pilot und
Ferrari Berater / ex - Ferrari driver and
Ferrari adviser / ex - pilote Ferrari et
conseiller Ferrari / ex - piloto de Ferrari y
asesor de Ferrari)*
Magny - Cours (F) 1992

21 Jean Todt (F), *Ferrari Team manager*
Silverstone (GB) 1993

BOSSES

1   Wataro Ohashi (J)
    Jackie Oliver (GB)
    Footwork Arrows

    Phoenix (USA) 1990

2   Alan Jenkins (GB)
    Footwork Arrows
    Imola (RSM) 1991

3   Michael Kranefuß (D, USA), Ford
    Eddie Jordan (IRL), Jordan Ford

    Imola (RSM) 1991

4   Tom Walkinshaw (GB)
    Engineering director
    Benetton Ford
    Imola (RSM) 1992

5   Flavio Briatore (I)
    Team boss
    Benetton Ford
    Montreal (CDN) 1993

6   Aleardo Buzzi
    President Philip Morris
    Monza (I) 1990

7   Osamu Goto (J)
    Engineer
    Honda
    Phoenix (USA) 1990

8   Bernie Ecclestone (GB), FOCA - president

    Cyril Ramaposa (ZA)
    Minister

    Ayrton Senna (BR)
    Marlboro McLaren

    Kyalami (ZA) 1993

9   Peter Sauber (CH), *Team boss*
    Mario Illien, Ilmor Engineering

    Imola (RSM) 1993

10 Frank Williams (GB)
   Nigel Mansell (GB)
   Williams Honda

   Imola (RSM) 1987

11 Frank Williams (GB)
   Nigel Mansell (GB)
   Williams Renault

   Montreal (CDN) 1992

12 Alain Prost (F), Williams Renault
   Christian Contzen
   *und sein Renault Team / and his Renault
   team / et son équipe Renault / y su
   equipo Renault*

   Kyalami (ZA) 1993

13 Frank Williams (GB)
   Team Williams Renault
   Estoril (P) 1992

14 Frank Williams (GB)
   Alain Prost (F)
   Williams Renault

   Kyalami (ZA) 1993

15 Frank Williams (GB)
   Williams Renault
   Interlagos (BR) 1990

WERBUNG / FRAUEN / FANS / SCHNAPPSCHÜSSE

Inmitten des wimmelnden und wuselnden Chaos der Ferrari-Box, das sich bei näherer Betrachtung als höhere Form der Ordnung entpuppt, strahlt ein gepflegter Greis jene unaufgeregte Würde aus, die nur eine erfüllte Fan-Vergangenheit von 70 Jahren schenkt. Das ist Silvio Ferri, 85, von Beruf Grand Prix-Besucher. Begünstigt von der Teilidentität seines Namens mit dem Kultwort Ferrari, gehört er seit 25 Jahren zum lebenden Inventar der Scuderia, von Jacky Ickx bis Jean Alesi als Maskottchen akzeptiert und ruhender Pol in Triumph und Tragödie. Ferri hat geschafft, wovon andere jenseits des Hochsicherheitstrakts Pit und Paddock mit seinen Schutzleuten und Schäferhunden nur träumen: Er siedelt im Herzen des Mythos. Dabei hat sich die Fan-Kultur beispielsweise von Monza in dieser Zeit grundlegend gewandelt. Im Vergleich mit ihren tosenden Vorfahren auf deren wankenden Eigenbau-Tribünen wirken die tifosi von heute wie Scala-Publikum neben Hooligans in einem Beatschuppen. Schuld daran: ins Phantastische gestiegene Eintrittspreise und flügellahme Ferrari. Der Hexenkessel 1993 ist eine relativ neue japanische Errungenschaft, nur daß der fernöstliche Formel 1-Freak auf mehr erpicht ist als nur die physische Nähe zum Idol: Er will strategisch wichtige Kleidungsstücke oder, besser noch, den ganzen Mann, wie etwa Nigel Mansell 1991 in Suzuka schmerzlich erfahren mußte. Der deutsche Fanatiker führt sich da weitaus gesitteter auf, organisiert sich vereinsmeiernd in Interessenverbänden wie dem Zakspeed Fan-Club und dem Michael Schumacher Fan-Club und begnügt sich notfalls gar mit Streicheleinheiten per Post.

Fan zu sein – das erleichtert auch den Damen das Leben, die in das Gravitationsfeld des schwarzen Lochs Grand Prix geraten. Frank Williams' Gattin Ginny ist keiner: In ihrer Auto-Biographie „A Different Kind of Life" berichtet sie bittersüß von der Unmöglichkeit, einen Mann mit der Formel 1 zu teilen. Norah Tyrrell hingegen läßt gerne durchblicken, noch nie ein Rennen des Teams ausgelassen zu haben. Allerdings zeichnet sich selbst für sie Langeweile am Horizont ab, seitdem Frauenarbeitslosigkeit die Boxengasse heimgesucht hat: Früher, da habe man noch zu etwas getaugt, habe die Zeiten genommen und Rundentabellen geführt. Das erledige heute alles die Elektronik. Ehefrau Joann stand Bleifuß-Mozart Gilles Villeneuve gar bereits im zarten Alter von 16 Jahren in Treue fest zur Seite, mehr abgestoßen als angezogen von seinem Gewerbe: „Ich muß mich damit abfinden, aber es macht mir auch Angst." Im übrigen ist das Umfeld der Grand Prix kein guter Nährboden für die christliche Ehe – zu groß sind die Versuchungen des Vagabundendaseins, zuviel geht von der Faszination dieses Sports über auf die, die ihn betreiben. So richteten sich Mike Hailwoods amouröse Neigungen eher auf die Gattung Frau als solche, ähnlich denen von Max Frischs Bühnenheld Don Juan, der ziellos bekennt: „Ich liebe – aber wen?" Als ihm Fotografin Jutta Fausel einmal ein Bild von seiner Begleiterin des vorigen Wochenendes zeigte, fragte sie Mike the Bike ratlos, wer das sei. Und nachdem Nelson Piquet, auch kein Freund von Armut, Keuschheit und Gehorsam, von zwei verschiedenen jungen Damen synchron mit Nachwuchs beglückt worden war, raunte die Branche verstohlen – respektvoll vom

Doppel-Decker. Mag das zeitlos Zwischenmenschliche auch keinen konjunkturellen Schwankungen unterworfen sein, beklagen doch alle, das Klima sei kälter geworden in der Formel 1, seitdem sie nach den ehernen Grundgesetzen von Show und Big Business ablaufe. Ihren Charme hat das kaum beschädigt: Wer viel ausstrahlt, zieht auch viele an. John Hogan, seit fast 20 Jahren Werbe-Manager bei Marlboro und selbst bekennender Fan, zitiert in diesem Zusammenhang mit Vorliebe ein kluges Wort von Jack Brabham: „Auf dieser Seite der Boxenmauer mag es ein Geschäft sein, auf der anderen bleibt es Sport." In den Rennwagen verquickt sich gleichwohl beides, wenn etwa das High Tech-Gerät McLaren seit über zwei Jahrzehnten in rasendem Tempo Marlboro-Werbung transportiert, bis hin zur Schein-Identität von Sponsor und Gesponsertem. Da kann aus dem Dreizack Farbe, Form und Schrift ruhig schon einmal ein Zinken herausbrechen, der Schriftzug Marlboro zum Beispiel in Ländern, deren Recht Zigarettenwerbung verbietet – das markant komponierte Rotweiß der Marke erreicht den Raucher allemale. Schon paradox: wie Designer aus einem Minimum von Fläche ein Maximum von Effekt herausholen, dazu eingezwängt von streng vorgegebenen Strukturen. Skurril auch: wie der winzige Jan Lammers 1979 seinen Shadow im Löwen-Look seines Mäzens Samson durch die Straßenschluchten von Long Beach hetzte. Ironie eines Rennfahrer-Schicksals schließlich: daß Revlon-Erbe Peter Revson 1972 und 1973 einen McLaren chauffierte, der in den Farben des Konkurrenzfabrikats Yardley lackiert war – gänzlich ungepeinigt von Gewissensqualen.

Eines indessen ist der Formel 1 zweifellos ein bißchen abhanden gekommen in diesen Jahren – der Humor. In den siebziger Jahren wurde er schwerpunktmäßig im Umfeld des Großen Preises von Südafrika praktiziert, und zwar in der Nobel-Herberge Kyalami Ranch bei Johannisburg. Es war ein kerniger Humor mit einem entschiedenen Macho-Touch, und Männer wie Hans-Joachim Stuck schwelgten darin. Abends, plaudert er aus dem Schmäh-Körbchen, habe immer die Jagd auf die Stewardessen stattgefunden, die in der Ranch nächtigten. Einmal habe Ronnie Peterson einen Superhasen von der Alitalia erwischt. Beim Frühstück fehlte der Schwede, und durch das Fenster seines Bungalows machten Stuck und Gunnar Nilsson aus, daß dort ein Schäferstündchen in die finale Phase getreten war. Indes: „Zufällig lag da der Gartenschlauch." Stuck zielte, Nilsson drehte den Hahn auf. Erst sehr viel später sei Peterson aufgekreuzt, der das Humorige dieser lustfeindlichen Intervention nicht nachzuvollziehen vermochte, betreten, wortkarg und mit hochrotem Kopf. Von einem feineren und durchaus bedenkenswerten Sinn für Komik zeugt eine andere Episode, die sich 1976 ereignete, im Jahr des James Hunt. Inmitten des üblichen Jahrmarkts der Eitelkeiten gab es in einer der Boxen des Circuit Paul Ricard einen improvisierten Schnellimbiß. Irgendjemand hatte das Angebot an Brötchen, Bier und Baguettes von der Tafel gewischt, auf der es feilgeboten wurde, und diagonal mit Kreide darübergeschrieben: „But it`s only a sport" – aber es ist doch nur ein Sport....

ADVERTISING / WOMEN / FANS / SNAPSHOTS

Amidst the teeming chaos of the Ferrari pit, which turns out to be a higher form of order on second examination, a well-groomed octogenarian radiates the unruffled dignity rooted in the 70 years of an accomplished fan past. That is Silvio Ferri, 85, a Grand Prix visitor by profession. For 25 years he has been a familiar face in the livestock of the Scuderia, accepted as a mascot by Jacky Ickx as well as Jean Alesi and a source of tranquility in triumph and in tragedy. Ferri has achieved what others outside the confines of pit and paddock with their barbed wire fences and Alsatian dogs are dreaming of: He has settled in the centre of the myth. The fan behaviour at Monza, for instance, has fundamentally changed in that period. In comparison with their hysterical forbears on their swaying homemade stands today's tifosi resemble the upper middle class audience of a Glyndebourne opera performance, lame Ferraris and horrendous entrance fees having their fair share in that development. Crowds do, however, go berserk in Japan, only that the Far Eastern freak wants more than just being physically close to his idol: he is keen on carrying away as a trophy important parts of his apparel or, preferably, the man as a whole, as painfully experienced by Nigel Mansell at Suzuka in 1991. By way of contrast, German fans used to be utterly well-behaved quietly joining the Zakspeed Fan Club and waiting patiently for their heroes' autographs to arrive by mail. But then Michael Schumacher arrived on the scene stirring up a whirlpool of national emotions in the Hockenheim stadium, German flags brandished all over the place in 1993.

To be a fan definitely makes life easier for the ladies who happen to be absorbed by the gravitational field of the Grand Prix. Frank Williams' wife Ginny is none. Her autobiography "A Different Kind of Life" is a bittersweet account of the impossibility of sharing a husband with Formula One. Norah Tyrrell, on the other hand, likes to point out that she has never omitted a race of the team. But boredom has been looming ever since ladies' unemployment has visited the pitlane. In former times, she laments, the female entourage was busy timing the drivers or keeping lapcharts until the arrival of the electronic equipment that carried the day. Gilles Villeneuve's wife Joann firmly stood by her husband at the tender age of sixteen already. But she was repelled rather than attracted by what he was doing: "I have to put up with it somehow, but it also frightens me," she imparted to friends in 1979. The Villeneuves were an exception in that obviously Formula One is no ideal breeding ground for Christian marriage. Too strong are the temptations of vagrancy, too much of the fascination of this sport passes over to its protagonists. Mike Hailwood's amorous inclinations, for instance, were definitely directed at the species woman as such, reminding one of Max Frisch's stage character Don Juan, who aimlessly confesses: "I'm in love - but with who?" When German photographer Jutta Fausel once showed him a picture of last weekend's playmate Mike the Bike asked, nonchalalantly: "Who's she?" And Nelson Piquet surprised even callous observers of the scene fathering the babies of two young ladies at the same time. Obviously timeless human relations have not been subject to change although everybody keeps complaining that the average temperature in Formula One has gone down so much since the sport has been organized along the iron laws of show and big business. Fortunately, its spell has not suffered at all: he who radiates a lot will attract many. John Hogan, who has been in charge of sponsorship for Marlboro for twenty years, likes to quote a wise word of Jack Brabham's: "It may be a business on this side of the pit wall, but on the other side it's bloody well a sport." The cars, of course, combine both aspects, with the high-tech medium McLaren, for instance, carrying Marlboro advertising at racing speeds, having done so for two decades, achieving partial identity of sponsor and sponsored one. Even if the Marlboro logo is missing in countries that ban cigarette advertising, the unmistakable combination of red and white remains untouched reaching the smokers anyway. The way designers make the most of a minimum of space, strait-jacketed in structures dictated by necessity, borders on the paradox. What an odd sight when tiny Dutchman Jan Lammers raced through the streets of Long Beach in 1979, his Shadow sporting the enormous lion of the tobacco brand Samson! What an irony of fate that Revlon heir Peter Revson in 1972 and 1973 drove a McLaren painted in the colours of archrival Yardley, without ever being haunted by compunction!

One of life's essentials, however, has almost gone lost in Formula One in these 25 years – unadulterated fun. In the seventies the South African Grand Prix used to be the setting of a lot of humorous action, the posh Kyalami Ranch being a hotbed in particular. The fun in question had a decisive macho touch about it, and men like Hans-Joachim Stuck wallowed in it. In the evenings, he narrates, there was the inevitable hunt for the stewardesses who also stayed at the Ranch. Once Ronnie Peterson had got hold of a super bird from Alitalia. When everybody else was having breakfast the Swede was missing, and through the open window of his bungalow Stuck and Gunnar Nilsson made out that an amorous encounter had entered into its final phase. However: "The garden hose happened to be lying there." Stuck aimed, Nilsson turned on the tap. Only late did Peterson show up, unable to appreciate the comicality of that intervention, taken aback, monosyllabic, and with a red face. A much more refined and rather thoughtful sense of humour is epitomized by another episode that happened in 1976, the year of James Hunt's world championship. Surrounded by the usual hubbub and vanity fair there was an impromptu quick-lunch counter at the pitlane of the Ricard circuit. Somebody, presumably a McLaren mechanic from the adjoining pit, had wiped out part of the price list with all its baguettes, beers and mineral waters, and chalked diagonally across the board: "But it's only a sport...."

PUBLICITE / FEMMES / FANS / INSTANTANES

Au milieu du chaos grouillant et pullulant du box de chez Ferrari qui s'avère être une forme supérieure de l'ordre quand on y regarde de plus près, se trouve un vieillard très soigné dont il émane une dignité sereine qui ne peut être offerte que par un passé bien rempli de fan pendant 70 ans. C'est Silvio Ferri, 85 ans, profession, spectateur de Grand Prix. Favorisé par l'identité partielle de son nom avec le mot de culte Ferrari, il fait partie depuis vingt-cinq ans de l'inventaire vivant de la Scuderia, de Jacky Ickx à Jean Alesi, accepté comme une mascotte et pôle tranquille dans le triomphe et la tragédie. Ferri a réussi ce dont rêvent d'autres au-delà du complexe de haute sécurité des circuits et des paddocks avec leurs gardes du corps et leurs bergers allemands: il est installé au cœur du mythe. Le comportement des fans à Monza, par exemple, a changé fondamentalement à cette époque. Comparés à leurs ancêtres délirants sur les tribunes archaïques et branlantes, les tifosi d'aujourd'hui ont plutôt l'air d'un public de la Scala. Quelle en est la raison? Les prix d'entrée qui ont augmenté de façon fantastique et les Ferrari sans entrain. Le chaudron aux sorcières de 1993 est une acquisition japonaise relativement récente, la seule différence est que le fan de Formule 1 d'Extrême-Orient recherche plus que la proximité physique de l'idole. Il veut des vêtements importants au niveau stratégique ou, mieux encore, l'homme tout entier, comme Nigel Mansell en a fait douloureusement l'expérience par exemple en 1991 à Susuka. Le fanatique allemand se comporte là avec bien plus de contenance, s'organise en association d'intérêt commun, comme le fan-club de Zakspeed et le fan-club de Michael Schumacher, et se contente à la rigueur d'autographes qu'il reçoit par la poste.

Etre fan, cela facilite aussi la vie des dames qui se retrouvent dans le champ de gravitation du trou noir du Grand Prix. L'épouse de Frank Williams, Ginny, n'en est pas une: dans son autobiographie «A Different Kind of Life», elle rapporte de façon douce amère comment il est impossible de partager un homme avec la Formule 1. Norah Tyrrell, par contre, aime faire entrevoir qu'elle n'a jamais manqué une course de l'équipe. Il est vrai que même pour elle, l'ennui règne depuis que le chômage des femmes sévit dans les boxes. Autrefois, on servait encore à quelque chose, on prenait son temps pour remplir les tableaux de marquage. Aujourd'hui, tout est exécuté par l'électronique. Dès l'âge tendre de seize ans, l'épouse Joann est toujours restée fidèle au côté du Mozart au pied de plomb, Gilles Villeneuve, plus dégoûtée qu'attirée par son métier: «Je dois m'y faire, mais cela me fait peur.» Du reste, tout ce qui se trouve autour du Grand Prix n'est pas un terrain très favorable à l'union chrétienne; les tentations sont trop grandes de vagabonder à droite et à gauche. La fascination de ce sport se transmet bien trop à ceux qui l'exercent. C'est ainsi que Mike Hailwood a plutôt des inclinations qui vont vers l'espèce féminine, comme celles du héros de Max Frisch, Don Juan, qui reconnaît sans but: «J'aime – mais qui?» Alors qu'une fois, la photographe Jutta Fausel lui montrait une photo de sa compagne datant du week-end précédent, Mike lui demanda perplexe qui c'était. Et après que Nelson Piquet, qui n'était pas non plus un ami de la pauvreté, de la chasteté et de

l'obéissance, ait été rendu heureux papa par deux fois et au même moment, par deux jeunes dames différentes, il y eut des murmures furtifs qui parlaient respectueusement de biplan. Le rapport entre les gens n'est peut-être pas soumis aux fluctuations conjoncturelles mais est plutôt hors du temps; cependant, tous se plaignent de ce que le climat soit devenu plus froid depuis que la Formule 1 est devenue Show et Big Business. Mais cela a à peine endommagé son charme. Celui dont il émane beaucoup, attire aussi beaucoup de monde. John Hogan, manager publicitaire depuis près de 20 ans chez Marlboro et fan, aime citer à ce propos un mot intelligent de Jack Brabham: «De ce côté du mur des boxes, c'est peut-être un négoce, mais de l'autre côté, cela reste un sport.» Dans la voiture de course, les deux se confondent quand par exemple, l'appareil High-tech de McLaren transporte à une allure folle depuis deux décennies la publicité de Marlboro; ceci fait penser à une identité fictive du sponsor et de celui qui se fait sponsoriser. Il est alors très possible qu'une dent puisse tomber du trident couleur, forme et écriture du mot Marlboro par exemple, dans les pays où la publicité des cigarettes est interdite pour que de toutes façons, le rouge et blanc suggestifs de la marque, parviennent à rejoindre le fumeur. Vraiment paradoxal: la façon dont les designers retirent un maximum d'effets d'un minimum de surface, et en plus, à l'intérieur de structures sévèrement imposées. Bizarre aussi: comment le minuscule Jan Lammers en 1979 faisait traverser à toute allure la Shadow au look de lion de son mécène Samson dans les goulets de Long Beach. Finalement, l'ironie d'un destin de coureur automobile. L'héritier de Revlon, Peter Revson conduisait en 1972 et 1973 une McLaren peinte aux couleurs d'une marque concurrente Yardley et n'était pas du tout tourmenté par sa conscience.

Il y a pourtant une chose qui s'est un peu perdue au cours de ces dernières années et c'est l'humour. Il était très pratiqué autour du Grand Prix d'Afrique du Sud, dans la noble demeure du Kyalami Ranch près de Johannisburg. C'était un humour vigoureux, un brin macho et des hommes comme Hans-Joachim Stuck s'en enivraient. Le soir, on bavardait et on racontait des histoires d'un goût douteux, et on faisait toujours la chasse aux hôtesses de l'air qui passaient la nuit dans le ranch. Une fois, Ronnie Peterson avait levé un super lapin de la compagnie Alitalia. Le Suédois manquait au petit déjeuner et au travers de la fenêtre de son bungalow, Stuck et Gunnar Nilsson se rendirent compte qu'une rencontre amoureuse arrivait là à sa phase finale. «Le tuyau d'arrosage était là, par hasard.» Stuck visa, Nilsson ouvrit le robinet. Ce n'est que bien plus tard que Peterson resurgit, bien incapable de comprendre l'humour de cette intervention, gêné, avare de paroles et tout rouge. Un autre épisode, qui se passa en 1976, témoigne d'un sens du comique plus raffiné et tout à fait bien réfléchi, l'année du championnat de James Hunt. Au milieu du marché habituel des vanités, il y avait dans l'un des boxes du circuit Paul Ricard un buffet improvisé. Quelqu'un avait balayé tout ce qu'il y avait sur la table: petits pains, bière et baguettes et on avait écrit en diagonale à la craie: «But it's only a sport» – mais ce n'est qu'un sport.

PUBLICIDAD / MUJERES / FANS / INSTANTÁNEAS

En medio del pululante y abundante caos del *box* de Ferrari, que de cerca resulta ser una forma más elevada del orden, un cuidado anciano irradia la tranquila dignidad que sólo un pasado de 70 años de aficionado satisfecho hace posible. Se trata de Silvio Ferri, 85, de profesión asiduo espectador de la Fórmula 1. Favorecido en parte por la identidad de su nombre con la palabra mágica Ferrari, desde hace 25 años forma parte del inventario vivo de la escudería, y es aceptado por todos, desde Jacky Ickx hasta Jean Alesi, como mascota y polo de tranquilidad en el triunfo y en la tragedia. Ferri ha conseguido lo que para otros, fuera de los confines del *box* y el *paddock* con sus protectores y sus perros de guardia, sólo es un sueño: vivir en el corazón del mito. Sin embargo, la cultura del aficionado en Monza, por ejemplo, ha cambiado decisivamente en esta época. Comparados con sus atronadores antepasados en sus tambaleantes tribunas de manufactura casera, los *tifosi* de hoy parecen un distinguido público del Scala. El culpable: los astronómicos precios de las entradas y los lisiados Ferraris. El atolladero de 1993 es una adquisición relativamente nueva de los japoneses, sólo que el aficionado de Fórmula 1 del Lejano Oriente está obstinado con algo más que la cercanía al ídolo: quiere piezas estratégicas importamtes de su indumentaria o, mejor aún, al hombre entero, como dolorosamente tuvo que experimentar Nigel Mansell en 1991 en Suzuka. El fanático alemán se comporta mucho más civilizadamente, se organiza en clubes de interesados, como el Zakspeed Fan-Club, y espera pacientemente que el autógrafo de su héroe llegue por correo.

La vida se hace más fácil a las damas que son atraídas al campo gravitatorio del agujero negro Grand Prix. La esposa de Frank Williams, Ginny, no es una de ellas: en su autobiografía sobre coches «A Different Kind of Life», da cuenta con dulce amargura de la imposibilidad de compartir un hombre con la Fórmula 1. Norah Tyrrell, por el contrario, gusta de destacar que no ha pasado por alto ninguna carrera del equipo. Por otra parte, incluso para ellas se asoma el aburrimiento en el horizonte desde que el paro se ha introducido en los *boxes*: antes aún valían para hacer algo, medir tiempos y llevar los marcadores de vueltas. Ahora, todo lo hace la electrónica. La esposa de Gilles Villeneuve incluso ya le acompañaba fielmente a la tierna edad de 16 años, pero aborreció lo que hacía más de lo que la atraía: «tengo que aceptarlo, pero me da miedo». Por lo demás, el Grand Prix no es el mejor terreno para un matrimonio cristiano —las tentaciones del vagabundo son demasiado grandes y demasiada la fascinación que este deporte ejerce sobre los que lo practican—. Así, las inclinaciones amorosas de Mike Hailwood se dirigían a la clase de mujer en forma parecida al del héroe teatral Don Juan de Max Frisch, que reconoce indeciso: «Yo amo, ¿pero a quién?». Cuando la fotógrafa Jutta Fausel le enseñaba a Mike the Bike una foto con su acompañante de la semana anterior, éste se preguntaba desconcertado quién era la mujer. Y Nelson Piquet, enemigo de la pobreza, la castidad y la obediencia, sorprendió al ramo con una paternidad doble y sincrónizada. Si bien las relaciones humanas no están sujetas a cambios coyunturales, todo el mundo se queja de que el clima en la Fórmula 1 se ha vuelto más frío desde que ésta funciona según los férreos principios del *show* y el *big business*. Por fortuna, su encanto no ha sufrido mucho: quien irradia mucho atrae también a muchos. A John Hogan, desde hace casi 20 años *manager* publicitario de Marlboro y aficionado declarado, le encanta citar a este repecto un sabio dicho de Jack Brabham: «En este lado de los muros de los *boxes* puede que sea un negocio, al otro lado es un deporte.» No obstante, en el coche de carreras se entrevera todo, cuando el aparato *high-tech* McLaren, por ejemplo, Marlboro transporta publicidad a toda velocidad desde hace más de dos decenios hasta alcanzar una identificación parcial entre patrocinador y patrocinado. Aún cuando el logotipo Marlboro tenga que ocultarse en países que prohíben la publicidad del tabaco, la característica composición de los colores blanco y rojo alcanza a los fumadores de todas formas. Y es paradójico como los diseñadores obtienen el máximo efecto en un mínimo de superficie, para colmo, constreñida por medio de rígidas estructuras. Y es grotesco como el diminuto Jan Lammers atizaba en 1979 a su *Shadow* con el *look* de león de su mecenas Samson, productor de tabaco, a través de las quebradas calles de Long Beach. Y una ironía del destino de un corredor: el heredero de Revlon Peter Revson rodaba en 1972 y 1973 un McLaren laqueado con los colores de la competencia, los del fabricante Yardley, y ello sin atormentadores remordimientos de conciencia.

Pero es indiscutible que la Fórmula 1 ha perdido una cosa en los últimos años: el humor. En los años setenta, el humor era el centro gravitatorio en el Gran Premio de Sudáfrica, en el noble albergue Kyalami Ranch, cerca de Johannisburg. Era un humor vigoroso con un decisivo toque de machismo y hombres como Hans-Joachim Stuck lo saboreaban a tope. Por las noches, cuenta, tenía lugar la inevitable caza de azafatas que pasaban la noche en el Ranch. Ronnie Peterson dio alcance en una ocasión a un superbombón de Alitalia. El sueco faltaba en la mesa del desayuno y Stuck y Gunnar Nilsson comprobaron a través de la ventana de su *bungalow* que el encuentro amoroso estaba tocando a su fase final. Pero: «Por casualidad, allí estaba la manguera del jardín.» Stuck apuntó, Nilsson abrió el grifo. Peterson tardó en dejarse ver, cortado, monosílabo y con la cabeza roja. No entendía la humorística intervención. Otro episodio que da muestras de un sentido de la comicidad digno de tener en cuenta sucedió en 1976, el año de James Hunt. En medio del normal carrusel de vanidades, en una de los *boxes* del *Circuit Paul Ricard* se improvisó un chiringuito. Alguien había borrado del pizarrín la oferta de bocadillos y cervezas y escrito por encima y en diagonal: «But it's only a sport» (Pero si no es más que un deporte)…

ADVERTISING

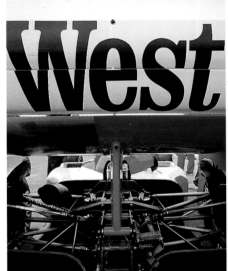

Vorherige Seite / Previous page /
Page précédente / Página anterior :

Imola (RSM) 1980

1 Zolder (B) 1982

2 *Menschliche Litfaßsäule*
human billboard
colonne d'affichage humaine
columna publicitaria humana

Manfred Winkelhock (D), ATS
Silverstone (GB) 1983

Werbung überall / adverts, adverts everywhere/
aucun endroit sans publicité / publicidad y más
publicidad (por todas partes):

3, 4 Estoril (P) 1985

5 Hungaroring (H) 1986

6 *Double für Michael Schumacher (D), Benetton /*
Benetton driver Michael Schumacher´s double /
Un sosie de Michael Schumacher (D),
Benetton /
un doble de Michael Schumacher (D),
Benetton

Estoril (P) 1991

7 Bescheidener Anfang im Formel 1 Geschäft
Modest beginnings in the Formula 1 business
Début modeste dans la Formule 1
el comienzo modesto en la fórmula 1

Imola (RSM) 1981

8 Der Renntransporter von Jordan
Jordan car transporter
Le camion de transport de Jordan
el camión de transporte de Jordan

Spa - Francorchamps (B) 1991

9 Die fahrende Dose
Drinks can on wheels
La boîte roulante
La lata rodante

Bertrand Gachot (F)
Jordan Ford
Monaco 1991

10 Michael Schumacher (D)
Benetton Ford

in den Werbeschluchten am
in the advertising gorge at the
dans les abîmes publicitaires du
en las cañadas publicitarias del

Hockenheimring (D)

ADVERTISING

1 Silverstone (GB) 1987

2 Imola (RSM) 1992
3 Magny - Cours (F) 1991
4 Barcelona (E) 1992
5 Jacarepagua (BR) 1988

6

7

6 Dijon - Prenois (F) 1981   7 Monza (I) 1992

1, 2 Imola (RSM) 1984

3 Monza (I) 1984

4 - 6 Ein neuer Sponsor für Prost (F) und Hill
(GB), Williams /
A new sponsor for Prost (F) and Hill (GB),
Williams /
Un nouveau sponsor pour Prost (F) et Hill
(GB), Williams /
un patrocinador nuevo para Prost (F) y
Hill (GB), Williams

Kyalami (ZA) 1993

WOMEN

1 Babro
Ronnie Petersons Freundin
Ronnie Peterson´s girlfriend
L´amie de Ronnie Peterson
La compañera de Ronnie Peterson

Hockenheim (D) 1970

2 Maria Helena Fittipaldi
Zeltweg (A) 1973

3 Pat Surtees
Monza (I) 1973

4 Maria Helena Fittipaldi
Babro Petersen

Le Castellet (F) 1973

5 Nina Rindt
Silverstone (GB) 1969

6 Helen Stewart
Zeltweg (A) 1973

7 Pamela Scheckter
Le Castellet (F) 1975

8 Betty Hill
Zandvoort (NL) 1970

9 *Harald Ertls zukünftige Frau Vera*
Harald Ertl's future wife Vera
La future femme de Harald Ertl, Vera
La futura esposa de Harald Ertl, Vera

Le Castellet (F) 1976

WOMEN

1   Long Beach (USA) 1981

2, 3   Long Beach (USA) 1983

4 - 7 *Strip vor dem Start / striptease before the start / striptease avant le départ / strip - tease antes de la salida*

Long Beach (USA) 1980

Linda Vaughn (USA):

8 - 11 Long Beach (USA)
        1976, 1977, 1982, 1983

12 Long Beach (USA) 1976

13 Zeltweg (A) 1984

14 Monza (I) 1969

15, 16 Zeltweg (A) 1984

17, 18 Monaco 1983

1, 2

3, 4

6

7

8

9

5

Flag marshals:

1, 2 Long Beach (USA) 1990

3 Estoril (P) 1992

4 Monza (I) 1992

5 Kyalami (ZA) 1992

6 Barcelona (E) 1991

7 Monaco 1992

8 Mexico 1992

9 Kyalami (ZA) 1992

11, 12

10

10 Moderne Geishas
Modern geishas
Geishas modernes
geishas modernas

Kyalami (ZA) 1993

13

11-13 Brigitte Nielsen im Fahrerlager und im
Wohnmobil bei Michael Schumacher.

Brigitte Nielsen in the paddock
and in the Benetton motorhome with
Michael Schumacher.

Brigitte Nielsen dans le paddock (camp des
pilotes) et dans le mobillhome Benetton avec
Michael Schumacher.

Brigitte Nielsen en el paddock (campamento de
los pilotos) y la casa rodante de Benetton con
Michael Schumacher.

Monza (I) 1992

WOMEN

1 Senna - Fan aus Japan / Senna fan from Japan / Fan japonaise de Senna / admiradora japonesa de Senna

Monza (I) 1988

2 Ostblockwerbung / Eastern Bloc advertising / publicité des pays de l'Est / publicidad de detrás de la cortina de hierro

Hungaroring (H) 1986

3 Verkäuferin von Zeitschriften / magazine seller / vendeuse de magazines / vendedora de revistas

Hockenheimring (D) 1990

Entdeckungen im Fahrerlager / Spotted in the paddock / Découvertes dans le paddock (camp des pilotes) / divisadas en el paddock (campamento de los pilotos):

4 Hungaroring (H) 1989

5, 6 Kyalami (ZA) 1993

7 Kyalami (ZA) 1992

8, 9

10, 11

13

14

15

12

8 *Ungarische Schönheit / Hungarian beauty*
   beauté hongroise / belleza húngara

   Hungaroring (H) 1986

9 *Noch ein Gast / another guest / encore une*
   invitée / otra invitada

   Hungaroring (H) 1987

Mrs Andretti:

10 Kyalami (ZA) 1993

11 Interlagos (BR) 1993

12, 13 *Brasilianisches Temperament*
        Brazilian temperament
        Tempérament brézilien
        temperamento brasileño

        Jacarepagua (BR) 1989

14 *Senna - Fan / Senna fan / fan de*
    Senna / admirador de Senna

    Phoenix (USA) 1990

15 *Arbeitspause / coffee break /*
    pause café / pausa durante el trabajo

    Kyalami (ZA) 1993

381

FANS

1

2

1 Nach dem Rennen stürmen die italienischen
Fans zur Siegerehrung von
Jacky Ickx (B), Ferrari

After the race, Italian fans dashing to the
victory ceremony for Jacky Ickx (B), Ferrari

Après la course, les fans italiens courent à la
remise des prix de Jacky Ickx (B), Ferrari

al finalizar la carrera, los aficiondos italianos
corren para asistir al homenaje por la
victoria de Jacky Ickx (B), Ferrari

Zeltweg (A) 1970

2 Englische Disziplin beim Pit - Walk in der
Boxenstraße

English discipline during the pit walk along
the pits

Discipline anglaise pendant le pit - walk dans
les stands

disciplina inglesa durante el pit - walk en la
línea de jaulas

Silverstone (GB) 1990

3　*Italienischer Einfallsreichtum*
A wealth of Italian ideas
Les bonnes idées italiennes
la ingeniosidad italiana

Monza (I) 1975

1 Monza (I) 1990

2 Monaco 1982

3 Silverstone (GB) 1983

4 Monaco 1982

5 Zeltweg (A) 1982

6 Monza (I) 1986

7 Monza (I) 1984

8 Zeltweg (A) 1982

9 Zeltweg (A) 1975

10 Long Beach (USA) 1981

11 Spa - Francorchamps (B) 1985

12 Imola (RSM) 1990

13 Silverstone (GB) 1985

14 Hockenheim (D) 1984

15 Hockenheim (D) 1980

16 Long Beach (USA) 1980

17 Long Beach (USA) 1981

18 Long Beach (USA) 1981

19 Long Beach (USA) 1980

20 Monza (I) 1984

21 Silverstone (GB) 1989

22 Zeltweg (A) 1983

23 Zeltweg (A) 1973

24 Zandvoort (NL) 1983

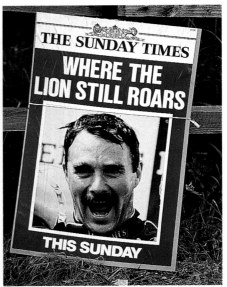

1, 2

3

4

1 Silverstone (GB) 1992

2 Flag marshals
   Silverstone (GB) 1989

3 Silverstone (GB) 1992

4 Ferrari - Flaggen in GB: Nigel Mansell (GB)
   fährt für Ferrari /
   Ferrari flags in Britain: Nigel Mansell (GB) is
   driving for Ferrari /
   Drapeaux Ferrari en Grande - Bretagne:
   Nigel Mansell (GB) est pour Ferrari au départ /
   banderas de Ferrari en Gran Bretaña: Nigel
   Mansell corre a nombre de Ferrari

   Silverstone (GB) 1990

5

6

7, 8

9

5 Silverstone (GB) 1991

6 Silverstone (GB) 1992

7 Nigel Mansell (GB)
   umringt von seinen Fans /
   surrounded by his fans /
   entouré de ses fans /
   rodeado por sus admiradores
   admiradores

   Silverstone (GB) 1987

8 Vor dem Start
   Before the start
   Avant le départ
   antes de la salida

   Hockenheim (D) 1990

9 Englische Fans
   British fans
   Fans anglais
   aficionados ingleses

   Silverstone (GB) 1992

1   Hockenheim (D) 1992

2   Monza (I) 1991

3   Hockenheim (D) 1991

4   Zeltweg (A) 1987

5   Silverstone (GB) 1988

6   Monaco 1992

7   Estoril (P) 1992

8   Estoril (P) 1991

9 - 11   Barcelona (E) 1991

SNAPSHOTS

1, 2

3, 4

5

6, 7

8, 9

10, 11

1 Nigel Mansell (GB)
   Lotus
   Hockenheim (D) 1983

2 René Arnoux (F)
   Ferrari
   Imola (RSM) 1984

3 Didier Pironi (F)
   Ferrari
   Long Beach (USA) 1982

4 Jochen Mass (D)
   Warsteiner Arrows
   Hockenheim (D) 1982

5 Keke Rosberg (SF)
   Williams Saudia TAG
   Monaco 1982

6 Alan Jones (AUS)
   Saudia Williams
   Zeltweg (A) 1979

7 Niki Lauda (A)
   Montreal (CDN) 1992

8 Nelson Piquet (BR)
   Brabham BMW
   Zeltweg (A) 1984

9 Jonathan Palmer (GB)
   West Zakspeed
   Monaco 1985

10 Alain Prost (F)
    Marlboro McLaren
    Estoril (P) 1985

11 Ayrton Senna (BR)
    Marlboro McLaren Honda
    Imola (RSM) 1992

12, 13

14, 1.

16

17

18, 19

20, 21

12 *Mechaniker von Saudia Williams*
    Saudia Williams mechanic
    Mécanicien de Saudia Williams
    Mecánico de Saudia Williams
    Monaco 1981

13 Jackie Stewart (GB)
    Montreal (CDN) 1992

14 Karl Wendlinger (A)
    Leyton House ILmor
    Zolder (B) 1992

15 Niki Lauda (A)
    Barcelona (E)

16 Stefan Johansson (S)
    Tyrrell Ford
    Brands Hatch (GB) 1984

17 Hans Stuck (D)
    Tabatip Shadow
    Silverstone (GB) 1978

18 Bernd Schneider (D)
    Zakspeed
    Imola (RSM) 1988

19 Gerhard Berger (A)
    Ferrari
    Estoril (P) 1988

20 Bertrand Gachot (F)
    Onyx Ford
    Hockenheim (D) 1989

21 Ayrton Senna (BR)
    Marlboro McLaren
    Le Castellet (F) 1992

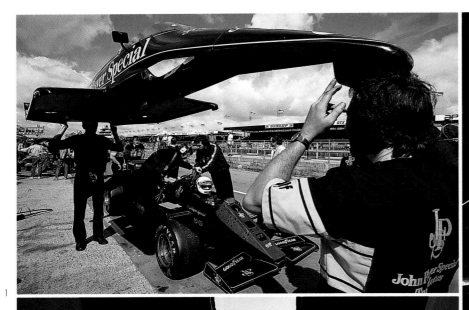

1, 2 JPS Lotus
      Silverstone (GB) 1985

3 *Weltmeister / World Champion*
   Champion du monde / Campeón mundial
   Mario Andretti (USA)
   JPS Lotus Ford
   Jarama (E) 1978

4 JPS Lotus
   Zeltweg (A) 1984
   Nach einem Ausflug ins Grüne
   After a trip into nature
   Après une excursion dans la nature
   después de una excursión a la campiña

5   Hockenheim (D) 1978

6   James Hunt (GB)
    Long Beach (USA) 1980

Photographen bei ihrer Arbeit
Photographers at work
Photographes au travail
Fotógrafos trabajando

7   Zandvoort (NL) 1971

8, 9   Hungaroring (H) 1990

SNAPSHOTS

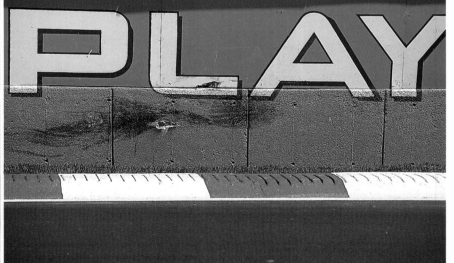

1, 2

3

4

5

6

7

8 Jacques Laffite (F)
   Imola (RSM) 1980

9 Bruno Giacomelli (I), Alfa Romeo
   Patrick Depailler (F), Alfa Romeo

   Monaco 1980

10 *Der Marlboro Mclaren von S. Johansson (S)
    nach Zusammenprall mit einem Reh /
    The Marlboro Mclaren of S. Johansson (S)
    after collision with a deer /
    La Marlboro Mclaren de S. Johansson (S)
    après une collision avec un chevreuil /
    El Marlboro Mclaren de S. Johansson (S)
    después de un choque con un ciervo*

    Zeltweg (A) 1987

11 Niki Lauda (A)
    *nach Ausfall im Training /
    after a breakdown during qualifying
    practice /
    après une panne pendant un essai /
    después de una avería durante el fogueo*

    Estoril (P) 1985

12 *Hoher Besuch in der Rial Box /
    VIP - visit in the Rial pit /
    Visite de personnes connues dans
    le stand rial /
    Visita de personajes distinguidos en
    la jaula rial*

    Paul Ricard (F) 1988

13 Pit - Walk
    Spa - Francorchamps (B) 1992

RACETRACKS

South African Grand Prix

Kyalami GP Circuit, Sandton,
72 laps
190.584 miles (306,763 km)

Spanish Grand Prix

Circuit de Catalunya,
Barcelona, 65 laps
191.750 miles (308,555 km)

Brazilian Grand Prix

Circuit Jose Carlos Pace,
Interlagos, 71 laps
190.777 miles (307,075 km)

Monaco Grand Prix

Circuit de Monaco,
Monte Carlo, 78 laps
161.304 miles (259,584 km)

European Grand Prix

Donington Park,
Castle Donington, 76 laps
189.92 miles (305,748 km)

Canadian Grand Prix

Circuit Gilles Villeneuve,
Montreal, 69 laps
189.957 miles (305,670 km)

San Marino Grand Prix

Autodromo Enzo e Dino Ferrari,
Imola, 61 laps
191.05 miles (307,440 km)

French Grand Prix

Circuit de Nevers Magny Cours,
Magny Cours, 72 laps
190.08 miles (306,000 km)

British Grand Prix

Silverstone Circuit, Silverstone, 59 laps
191.573 miles (308,334 km)

Italian Grand Prix

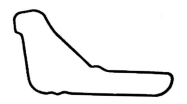

Autodromo Nazionale di Monza, Monza, 53 laps
191.012 miles (307,400 km)

German Grand Prix

Hockenheimring, Hockenheim, 45 laps
190.575 miles (306,675 km)

Portuguese Grand Prix

Autodromo do Estoril, Estoril, 71 laps
191.913 miles (308,850 km)

Hungarian Grand Prix

Hungaroring , Budapest, 77 laps
189.851 miles (305,536 km)

Japanese Grand Prix

Suzuka International Racing Course, Suzuka City, 53 laps
193.132 miles (310,792 km)

Belgian Grand Prix

Circuit de Spa - Francorchamps, Stavelot, 44 laps
190.652 miles (306,856 km)

Australian Grand Prix

Australian F1 Grand Prix Board, Adelaide, 81 laps
190.269 miles (306,180 km)

WORLD CHAMPIONS

1950	**Giuseppe Farina** (I), Alfa Romeo		1975	**Niki Lauda** (A), Ferrari
1951	**Juan-Manuel Fangio** (ARG), Alfa Romeo		1976	**James Hunt** (GB), McLaren Ford Cosworth
1952	**Alberto Ascari** (I), Ferrari		1977	**Niki Lauda** (A), Ferrari
1953	**Alberto Ascari** (I), Ferrari		1978	**Mario Andretti** (USA), Lotus Ford Cosworth
1954	**Juan-Manuel Fangio** (ARG), Maserati & Mercedes		1979	**Jody Scheckter** (ZA), Ferrari
1955	**Juan-Manuel Fangio** (ARG), Mercedes		1980	**Alan Jones** (AUS), Williams Ford Cosworth
1956	**Juan-Manuel Fangio** (ARG), Ferrari		1981	**Nelson Piquet** (BR), Brabham Ford Cosworth
1957	**Juan-Manuel Fangio** (ARG), Maserati		1982	**Keke Rosberg** (SF), Williams Ford Cosworth
1958	**Mike Hawthorn** (GB), Ferrari		1983	**Nelson Piquet** (BR), Brabham BMW
1959	**Jack Brabham** (AUS), Cooper Climax		1984	**Niki Lauda** (A), McLaren TAG Porsche
1960	**Jack Brabham** (AUS), Cooper Climax		1985	**Alain Prost** (F), McLaren TAG Porsche
1961	**Phil Hill** (USA), Ferrari		1986	**Alain Prost** (F), McLaren TAG Porsche
1962	**Graham Hill** (GB), BRM		1987	**Nelson Piquet** (BR), Williams Honda
1963	**Jim Clark** (GB), Lotus Climax		1988	**Ayrton Senna** (BR), McLaren Honda
1964	**John Surtees** (GB), Ferrari		1989	**Alain Prost** (F), McLaren Honda
1965	**Jim Clark** (GB), Lotus Climax		1990	**Ayrton Senna** (BR), McLaren Honda
1966	**Jack Brabham** (AUS), Brabham Repco		1991	**Ayrton Senna** (BR), McLaren Honda
1967	**Denis Hulme** (NZ), Brabham Repco		1992	**Nigel Mansell** (GB), Williams Renault
1968	**Graham Hill** (GB), Lotus Ford Cosworth		1993	**Alain Prost** (F), Williams Renault
1969	**Jackie Stewart** (GB), Matra Ford Cosworth			
1970	**Jochen Rindt** (A), Lotus Ford Cosworth			
1971	**Jackie Stewart** (GB), Tyrrell Ford Cosworth			
1972	**Emerson Fittipaldi** (BR), Lotus Ford Cosworth			
1973	**Jackie Stewart** (GB), Tyrrell Ford Cosworth			
1974	**Emerson Fittipaldi** (BR), McLaren Ford Cosworth			